MW00946792

HOLT McDOUGAL

Discovering FRENCH Today!

FRENCH 1A
Première partie

Jean-Paul Valette
Rebecca M. Valette

HOLT McDOUGAL

HOUGHTON MIFFLIN HARCOURT

Teacher Reviewers

Paul Giles
Forsyth Central High School, Georgia

Thierry Gustave
Lincoln School, Rhode Island

David Miller
Davis High School, Utah

Teacher Panel

Linda Davisson
Wilbur Middle School, Kansas

Korey Dugger
Austin-East Magnet High School, Tennessee

Carolyn Fletcher
Bonita High School, California

Paul Giles
Forsyth Central High School, Georgia

Carole Lapointe-Prospère
West Roxbury High School, Massachusetts

Paul J. Maher
West Seneca East Senior High School, New York

Ann Minor
St. Andrew's Episcopal School, Mississippi

Dr. Mary Schense
Manzano High School, New Mexico

Martha Schillerstrom
Glenbard East High School, Illinois

Jennifer Schoenfeld
Lawton Community Schools, Michigan

Student Reviewers

Rebecca Lange
Washington

Donald Medor
Massachusetts

Teacher Review Board

Sue Arandjelovic
Dobson High School, Arizona

Kay Dagg
Washburn Rural High School, Kansas

Olga Davis
G.H. Englesby Junior High School, Massachusetts

Tina Dietrich
Washington Junior High School, Ohio

Rosine Gardner
Newcomb Central School, New York

Bill Price
Day Junior High School, Massachusetts

T. Jeffrey Richards
Roosevelt High School, South Dakota

Margie Ricks
Dulles High School, Texas

Valerie Sacks
Britton Middle School, California

Cover photography

Front Cover ©David Noble/Travel Pictures
Back Cover Level 1a: ©David Noble/Travel Pictures; Level 1b: ©Patrice Coppee/Workbook Stock/Getty Images; Level 1: ©Travelpix Ltd/Stone/Getty Images; Level 2: ©David Sanger/The Image Bank/Getty Images; Level 3: ©Shaen Adey/Gallo Images/Getty Images

Printed in the U.S.A.

ISBN 978-0-547-87227-8

8 9 10 0868 21 20 19 18 17 16

4500592594 A B C D E F G

Bienvenue ... and welcome!

Chers amis,

Welcome to *Discovering French Today!* and congratulations on your choice of French as a foreign language! Perhaps someone in your family speaks French. Maybe you know people who are of French-speaking origin — from France or Canada or Louisiana or Haiti or western Africa — and you want to better appreciate their heritage. Or perhaps you are hoping to travel to Quebec or Martinique or Paris, and want to be able to get around easily on your own. Perhaps simply you were influenced by the fact that French is a beautiful language. Or maybe you have studied ballet and already know quite a few French expressions. Or you like to bicycle and enjoy watching the **Tour de France.** Or you love the Internet and want to explore the many exciting French sites. Or perhaps your friends have told you that French class is fun and opens doors to a whole new world. Whatever the reason or reasons, welcome and **bienvenue!**

By learning French, you will get to know and communicate with people who use French in their daily lives. These millions of French speakers or **francophones** come from a wide variety of ethnic and cultural backgrounds. As you will see, they live not only in France and other parts of Europe, but also in Africa, in North and South America, in Asia . . . in fact, on all continents.

By studying French, you will also develop a better understanding of your own language and how it works. And by exploring cultural similarities and differences, you will grow to appreciate your own culture and value the culture of others.

On the pages of this book and in the accompanying video, you will meet many young people who speak French. Listen carefully to what they say and how they express themselves. They will help you understand not only their language but also the way they live.

Bonne chance!

Jean-Paul Valette Rebecca M. Valette

Invitation au français

Unité 1

Faisons connaissance

DIGITAL FRENCH
my.hrw.com

LEÇON 2 Famille et copains

Invitation au français

Unité 2

La vie courante

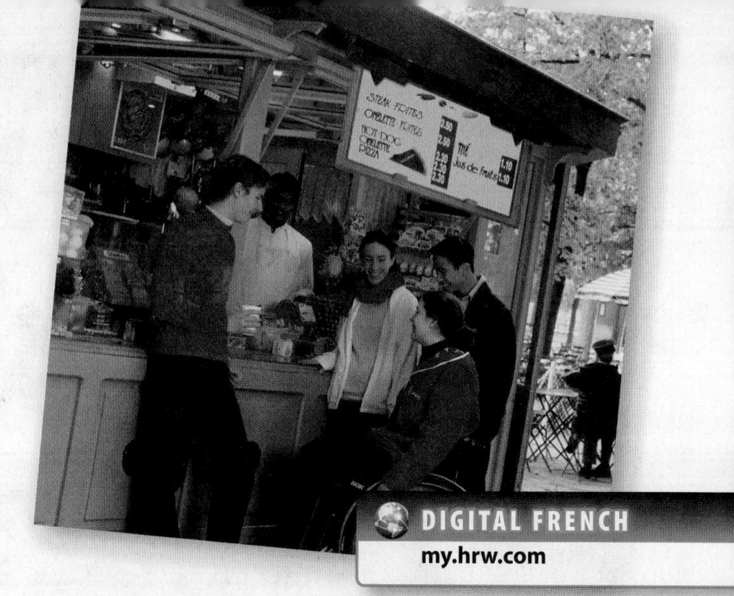

DIGITAL FRENCH
my.hrw.com

LEÇON 3 Bon appétit!

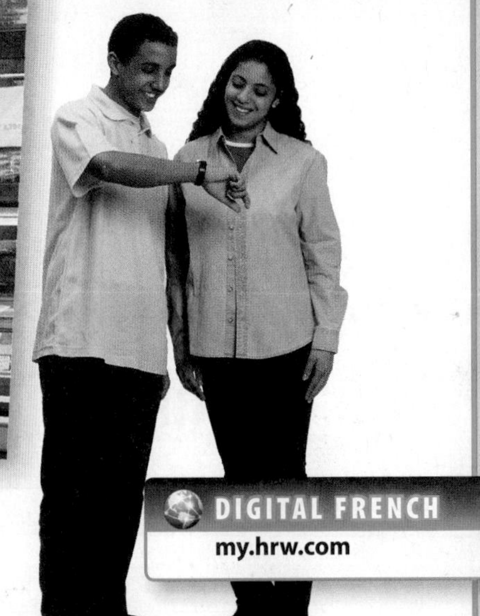

DIGITAL FRENCH
my.hrw.com

LEÇON 4 De jour en jour

Unité 3

Qu'est-ce qu'on fait?

THÈME Daily activities

Unité 4

Le monde personnel et familier

Reference Section

DIGITAL FRENCH
my.hrw.com

Pourquoi parler français?

WHY SPEAK FRENCH?

Here are ten good reasons.

1. **French is an international language.**
French is the first or second language in about fifty countries or regions in Europe, Africa, North and South America, Asia, and Oceania. It is spoken by over 100 million people around the world.

2. **French is an important diplomatic language.**
French is one of the five official languages of the United Nations and one of the two main languages of the European Union.

3. **French is the second language on the Internet.**
With French, you have immediate access to Internet sites in France and Quebec, as well as sites in Belgium, Switzerland, and French-speaking countries of Africa.

4. **France is a technologically advanced country.**
Historically, French inventors have contributed significantly to the advancement of science. Today, France is a leader in areas such as aero-space technology, high-speed transportation, automotive design, and medical research.

5. **France is a leader in the world of art and literature.**
Over the past 400 years, Paris has been an important cultural center, attracting artists and writers from around the world. France has won more Nobel Prizes in literature than any other country.

▲ un cybercafé à Paris

▲ l'Opéra National de Paris

le musée du Louvre ▶

le TGV (train à grande vitesse)
high-speed train

6. France is a prime tourist destination.
If you like to travel, it will not surprise you to learn that millions of tourists visit France every year — and speaking French makes their vacations much more meaningful and more enjoyable.

7. For many people, France evokes style and elegance.
When people think of high fashion, beauty products, perfumes, or gourmet cuisine, they think of France . . . and rightly so.

8. Knowing French will enrich your English.
In 1066, William the Conqueror, a French nobleman, invaded England and became king, bringing with him his court and his language: French. Today over one-third of all English words are derived from French. As you study French, you will increase your English vocabulary.

9. Knowing French will help you with your university studies.
University admissions officers look for candidates who have foreign language skills. In addition, research by the College Board shows that the longer students study a foreign language, the higher their math and verbal SAT scores.

10. Knowing French will be useful for your career.
Many jobs require the knowledge of another language. France and Canada are major trading partners of the United States. In addition, about 1,000 French companies have subsidiaries in this country.

l'Université Paris-Sorbonne

Et vous? *(And you?)*

Which three reasons for speaking French are most important to you? Take a class poll comparing your answers with those of your classmates. Which are the most popular reasons?

Bonjour, la France!

Connaissez-vous la France? *(Do you know France?)*

- In area, France is the second-largest country in Western Europe. It is smaller than Texas, but bigger than California.
- Geographically, France is a very diversified country, with the highest mountains in Europe (**les Alpes** and **les Pyrénées**) and an extensive coastline along the Atlantic (**l'océan Atlantique**) and the Mediterranean (**la Méditerranée**).
- France consists of many different regions which have maintained their traditions, their culture, and — in some cases — their own language. Some of the traditional provinces are Normandy and Brittany (**la Normandie** and **la Bretagne**) in the west, Alsace (**l'Alsace**) in the east, Touraine (**la Touraine**) in the center, and Provence (**la Provence**) in the south.

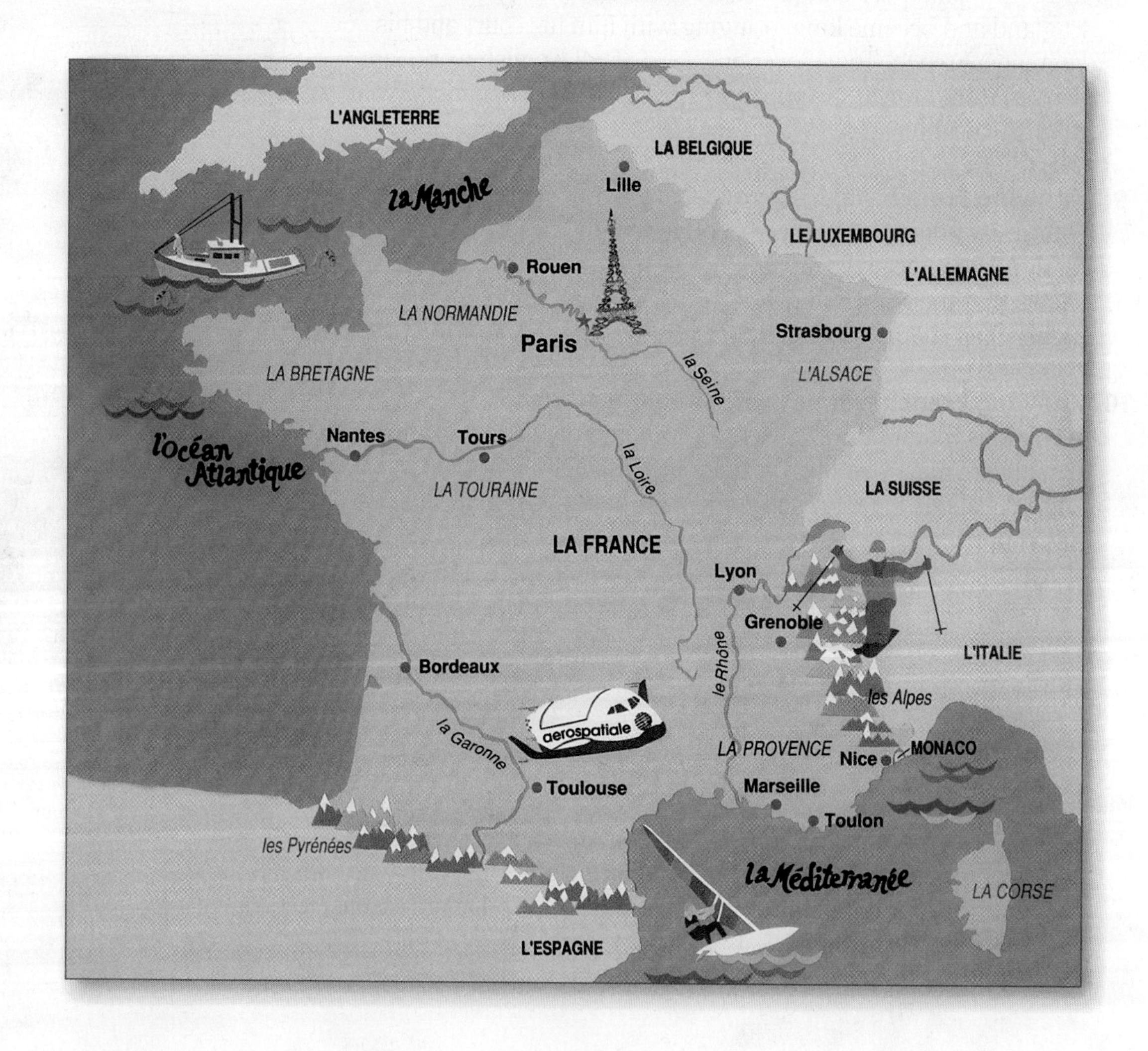

Paris: Montmartre
Paris, the capital of France, is also its economic, intellectual, and artistic center. For many people, Paris is the most beautiful city in the world.

Snowboarding in the Alps
During winter vacation, many French young people enjoy snowboarding or skiing. The most popular destinations are the Alps and the Pyrenees.

Château de Chenonceau
The long history of France is evident in its many castles and monuments. This chateau, built in the 16th century, attracts nearly one million visitors a year.

Home in Provence
The French love flowers and take pride in making their homes beautiful. This house is built in the traditional style of Provence, a region in southern France.

Bonjour, les Français!

Here are some facts about France and the French people.

LA FRANCE

Capitale: Paris

Population: 63 (soixante-trois) millions d'habitants

Drapeau: bleu, blanc, rouge

LA DRAPEAU FRANÇAIS

Devise: Liberté, Égalité, Fraternité

Monnaie: l'euro

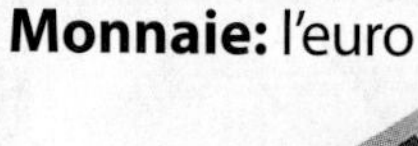

l'euro

LA MONNAIE FRANÇAISE

LES FRANÇAIS

Origine de la population: multi-ethnique

- européenne (majorité)
- nord-africaine
- africaine
- asiatique

Principales religions pratiquées:

- catholique (majorité)
- musulmane
- juive
- protestante

STRATEGY Comparing Cultures

How does France compare to the United States or to your country of origin? Make a chart like the one above. Include the capital, the population, the flag, the motto, and the currency.

These are some of the young French people you will meet in the video.

Jean-Paul âge: 14 ans

Céline âge: 15 ans

Léa âge: 15 ans

François âge: 14 ans

Isabelle âge: 14 ans

Stéphanie âge: 14 ans

Philippe âge: 15 ans

Trinh âge: 14 ans

Antoine âge: 14 ans

Bonjour, le monde francophone!

CANADA
About one-third of the population speaks French. These French speakers live mainly in the province of Quebec (**le Québec**). They are descendants of French settlers who came to Canada in the 17th and 18th centuries.

HAITI
Haïti is the first Black Republic. Its people speak Creole and French.

MARTINIQUE AND GUADELOUPE
These two Caribbean islands (**la Martinique** and **la Guadeloupe**) are part of France. Their inhabitants, primarily of African ancestry, are French citizens.

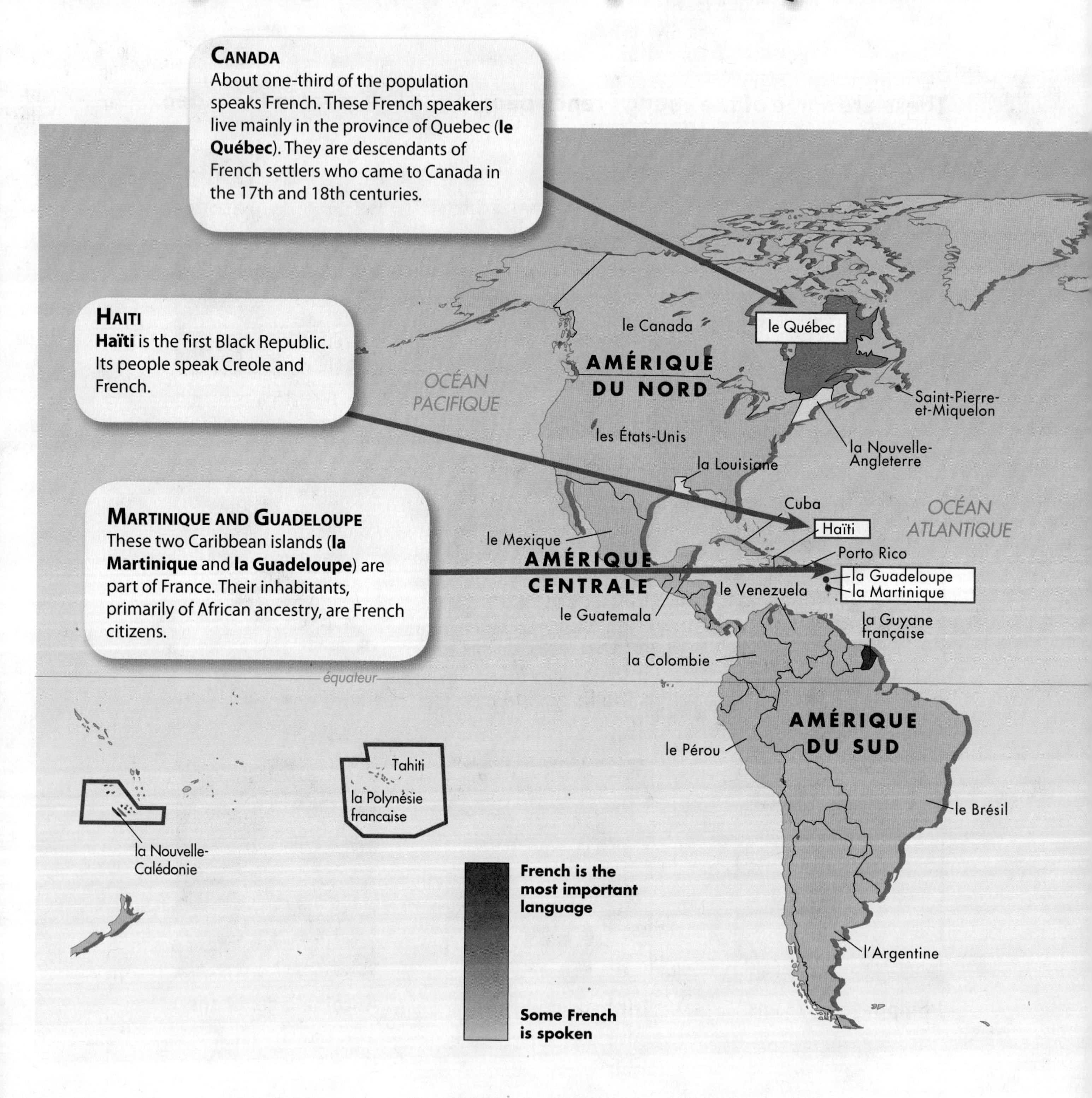

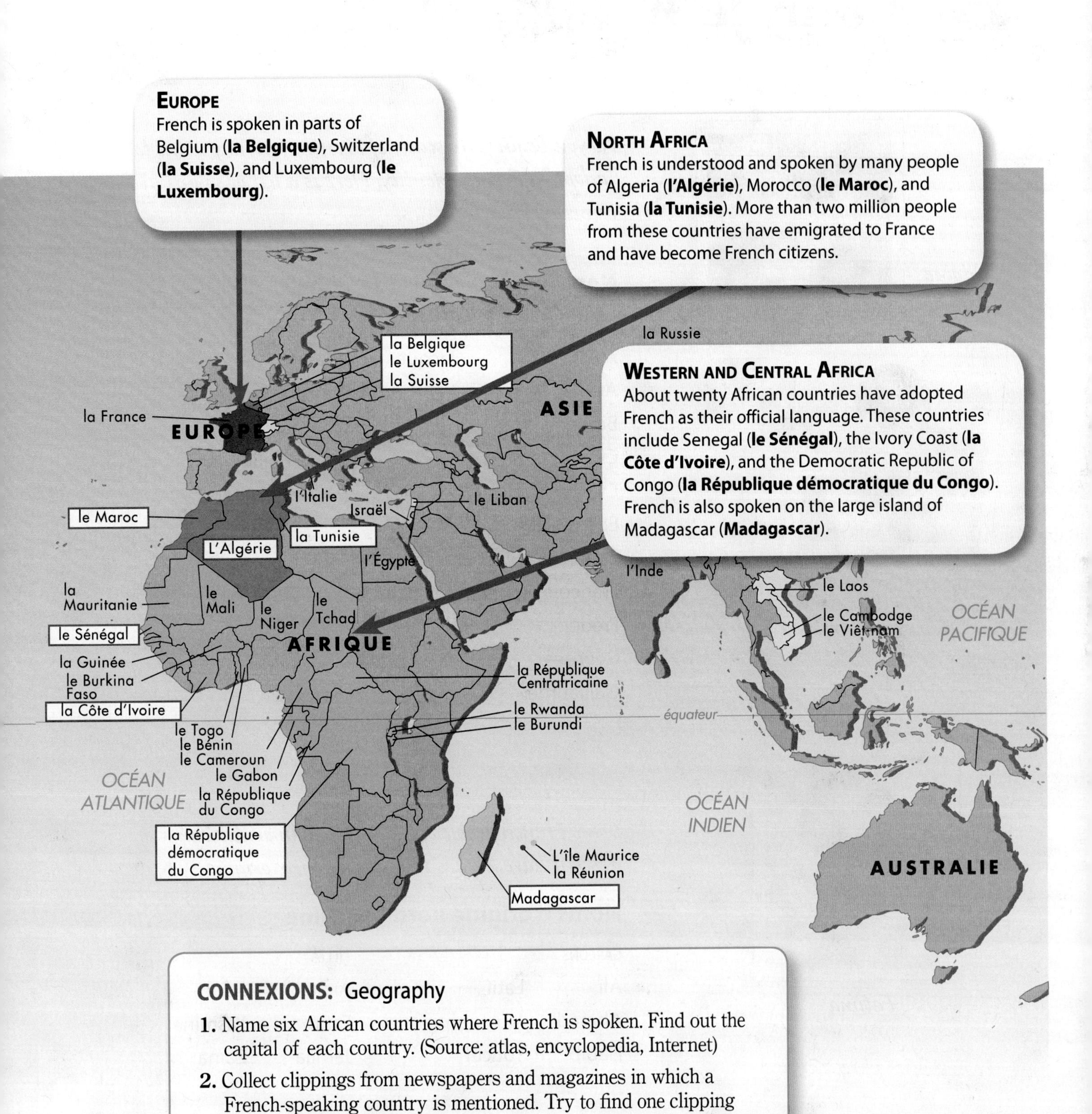

Europe

French is spoken in parts of Belgium (**la Belgique**), Switzerland (**la Suisse**), and Luxembourg (**le Luxembourg**).

North Africa

French is understood and spoken by many people of Algeria (**l'Algérie**), Morocco (**le Maroc**), and Tunisia (**la Tunisie**). More than two million people from these countries have emigrated to France and have become French citizens.

Western and Central Africa

About twenty African countries have adopted French as their official language. These countries include Senegal (**le Sénégal**), the Ivory Coast (**la Côte d'Ivoire**), and the Democratic Republic of Congo (**la République démocratique du Congo**). French is also spoken on the large island of Madagascar (**Madagascar**).

CONNEXIONS: Geography

1. Name six African countries where French is spoken. Find out the capital of each country. (Source: atlas, encyclopedia, Internet)
2. Collect clippings from newspapers and magazines in which a French-speaking country is mentioned. Try to find one clipping for each of the areas on the map.

Bonjour, je m'appelle . . .

Antoine

Jérôme

As you begin your study of French, you may want to "adopt" a French identity. Here is a list of some common French names.

Noms traditionnels (garçons):

Alain	Henri	Nicolas
André	Jacques	Olivier
Antoine	Jean	Patrick
Bernard	Jean-Louis	Paul
Christophe	Jean-Paul	Philippe
Clément	Jérôme	Pierre
Édouard	Joseph	Robert
Éric	Julien	Stéphane
François	Laurent	Thomas
Frédéric	Marc	Vincent
Georges	Mathieu	
Guillaume	Michel	

Fatima

Some French people of North African or African descent have names that reflect their origin.

Noms d'origine nord-africaine

GARÇONS		FILLES	
Ali	Latif	Aïcha	Leila
Ahmed	Mustapha	Fatima	Yasmina
Habib	Youcef	Jamila	Zaïna

Aurélie

Léa

Noms traditionnels (filles):

Anne	Florence	Michèle
Anne-Marie	Françoise	Monique
Aurélie	Hélène	Nathalie
Béatrice	Isabelle	Nicole
Caroline	Jeanne	Pauline
Cécile	Julie	Sophie
Céline	Laure	Stéphanie
Charlotte	Léa	Suzanne
Christine	Louise	Sylvie
Claire	Marie	Thérèse
Élisabeth	Marie-Christine	Véronique
Élodie	Mathilde	Virginie
Émilie	Mélanie	

Mélanie

Noms d'origine africaine

GARÇONS		FILLES	
Abdou	Kouamé	Adjoua	Latifah
Amadou	Moussa	Asta	Malika
Koffi	Ousmane	Aya	Mariama

Ousmane

Unité 1 Invitation au français

Faisons connaissance

LEÇON 1 Bonjour!

- **A VIDÉO-SCÈNE:** La rentrée
- **B VIDÉO-SCÈNE:** Tu es français?
- **C VIDÉO-SCÈNE:** Salut! Ça va?

LEÇON 2 Famille et copains

- **A VIDÉO-SCÈNE:** Copain ou copine?
- **B VIDÉO-SCÈNE:** Une coïncidence
- **C VIDÉO-SCÈNE:** Les photos d'Isabelle

THÈME ET OBJECTIFS

Getting acquainted

In this unit, you will be meeting French people.

You will learn ...

- to say hello and good-bye
- to introduce yourself and say where you are from
- to introduce friends, family, and relatives

You will also learn ...

- to count to 100
- to say how old you are and to find out someone's age

DIGITAL FRENCH my.hrw.com
ONLINE STUDENT EDITION with...

@HOMETUTOR

- Audio Resources
- Video Resources
- Interactive Flashcards
- WebQuest

PRACTICE FRENCH WITH HOLT MCDOUGAL APPS!

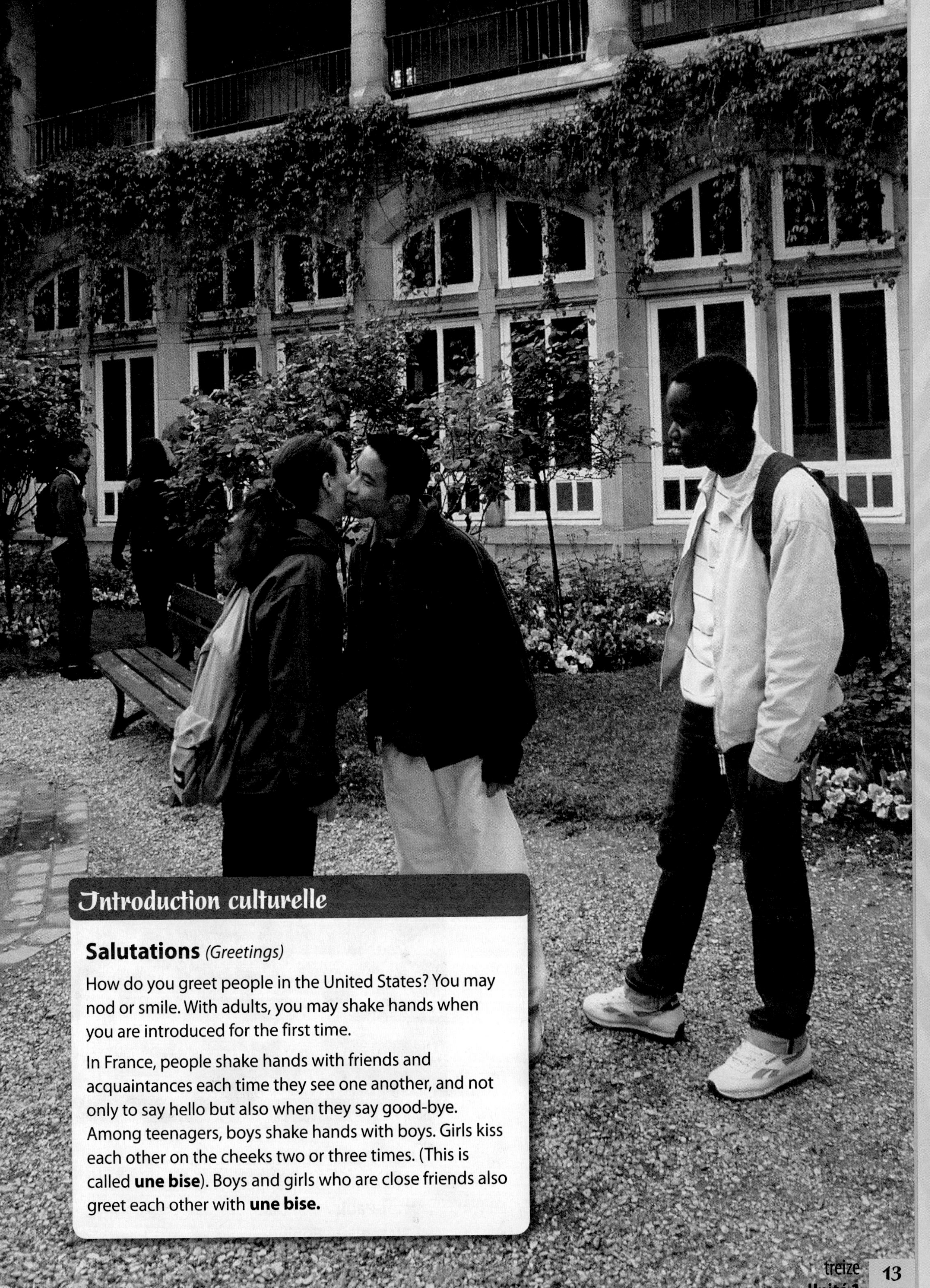

Introduction culturelle

Salutations *(Greetings)*

How do you greet people in the United States? You may nod or smile. With adults, you may shake hands when you are introduced for the first time.

In France, people shake hands with friends and acquaintances each time they see one another, and not only to say hello but also when they say good-bye. Among teenagers, boys shake hands with boys. Girls kiss each other on the cheeks two or three times. (This is called **une bise**). Boys and girls who are close friends also greet each other with **une bise.**

Leçon 1

VIDÉO-SCÈNE

DVD AUDIO

Bonjour!

A La rentrée

This is the first day of school. Students are greeting their friends and meeting new classmates.

Trinh: Bonjour! Je m'appelle Trinh.
Céline: Et moi, je m'appelle Céline.

Marc: Je m'appelle Marc. Et toi?
Isabelle: Moi, je m'appelle Isabelle.

Jean-Paul: Comment t'appelles-tu?
Nathalie: Je m'appelle Nathalie.
Jean-Paul: Bonjour.
Nathalie: Bonjour.

Pour communiquer

Bonjour!

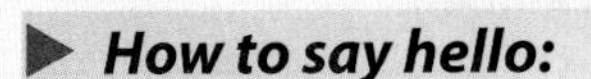

▶ How to say hello:

Bonjour!	*Hello!*	—**Bonjour,** Nathalie! —**Bonjour,** Jean-Paul!

▶ How to ask a classmate's name:

Comment t'appelles-tu? **Je m'appelle …**	*What's your name?* *My name is …*	—**Comment t'appelles-tu?** —**Je m'appelle** Céline.

Other Expressions

moi **et toi?**	*me* *and you?*	**Moi,** je m'appelle Marc. **Et toi,** comment t'appelles-tu?

NOTES Culturelles

1 La rentrée *(Back to school)*
French and American students have about the same number of days of summer vacation. In France, summer vacation usually begins at the end of June and classes resume in early September. The first day back to school in fall is called **la rentrée.**

2 Les prénoms français *(French first names)*
Many traditional French names have corresponding equivalents in English.

For boys:	For girls:
Jean *(John)*	**Marie** *(Mary)*
Pierre *(Peter)*	**Monique** *(Monica)*
Marc *(Mark)*	**Cécile** *(Cecilia)*
Philippe *(Philip)*	**Véronique** *(Veronica)*
Nicolas *(Nicholas)*	**Virginie** *(Virginia)*

Often the names **Jean** and **Marie** are combined in double names such as **Jean-Paul** and **Marie-Christine.** In recent years, names of foreign origin, like **Kevin** and **Laura,** have become quite popular.

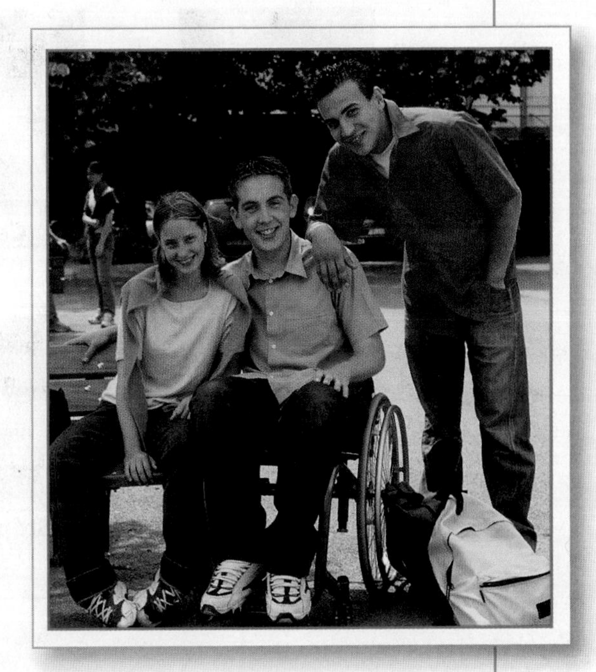

1 Bonjour!

PARLER Say hello to the student nearest to you.

▼

2 Je m'appelle ...

PARLER Introduce yourself to your classmates.

▶ Je m'appelle (Paul).

▶ Je m'appelle (Denise).

3 Et toi?

PARLER Ask a classmate his or her name.

▶ —Comment t'appelles-tu?
—Je m'appelle (Christine).

4 Bonjour, les amis! *(Hello everyone!)*

PARLER Say hello to the following students.

▶ Bonjour, Marc!

▶ Marc

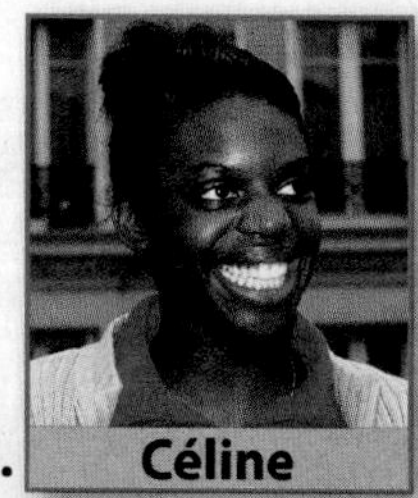

1. Céline

2. Jean-Paul

3. Isabelle

4. François

5. Stéphanie

6. Nathalie

7. Trinh

@HOMETUTOR my.hrw.com

L'alphabet

A	B	C	D	E	F	G	H	I	J	K	L	M
a	bé	cé	dé	e	effe	gé	hache	i	ji	ka	elle	emme
N	**O**	**P**	**Q**	**R**	**S**	**T**	**U**	**V**	**W**	**X**	**Y**	**Z**
enne	o	pé	ku	erre	esse	té	u	vé	double vé	ixe	i grec	zède

Prononciation

Les signes orthographiques *(Spelling marks)*

French uses accents and spelling marks that do not exist in English.
These marks are part of the spelling and cannot be left out.

In French, there are four accents that may appear on vowels.

´	**l'accent aigu** *(acute accent)*	C**é**cile, St**é**phanie
`	**l'accent grave** *(grave accent)*	Mich**è**le, Hél**è**ne
^	**l'accent circonflexe** *(circumflex)*	Jér**ô**me
¨	**le tréma** *(diaeresis)*	No**ë**l, Jo**ë**lle

There is only one spelling mark used with a consonant. It occurs under the letter "**c.**"

¸	**la cédille** *(cedilla)*	Fran**ç**ois

5 La rentrée

PARLER It is the first day of class. The following students are introducing themselves. Act out the dialogues with your classmates.

▶ Hélène et Philippe — **Je m'appelle Hélène. Et toi?**
— **Moi, je m'appelle Philippe.**

1. Stéphanie et Marc
2. Cécile et Frédéric
3. Michèle et François
4. Anaïs et Clément
5. Céline et Jérôme
6. Mélanie et Noël

Les nombres de 0 à 10

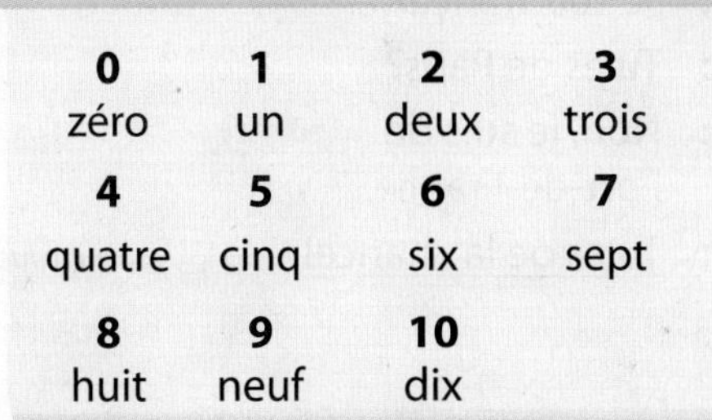

0	1	2	3
zéro	un	deux	trois
4	**5**	**6**	**7**
quatre	cinq	six	sept
8	**9**	**10**	
huit	neuf	dix	

6 Numéros de téléphone

PARLER Imagine you are visiting a family in Quebec. Give them your American phone number in French.

617-963-4028 **six, un, sept — neuf, six, trois — quatre, zéro, deux, huit**

VIDÉO-SCÈNE DVD AUDIO

B Tu es français?

It is the opening day of school and several of the students meet in the cafeteria (**la cafétéria** or **la cantine**) at lunchtime. Marc discovers that not everyone is French.

Marc: Tu es français?
Jean-Paul: Oui, je suis français.

Marc: Et toi, Patrick, tu es français aussi?
Patrick: Non! Je suis américain. Je suis de Boston.

Marc: Et toi, Stéphanie, tu es française ou américaine?
Stéphanie: Je suis française.
Marc: Tu es de Paris?
Stéphanie: Non, je suis de Fort-de-France.
Marc: Tu as de la chance! *You're lucky!*

@HOMETUTOR
my.hrw.com

Pour communiquer

Tu es de Nice?

▶ How to talk about where people are from:

Tu es de ...?	*Are you from ...?*	**—Tu es de** Nice?
Je suis de ...	*I'm from ...*	—Non, **je suis de** Paris.

▶ How to talk about one's nationality:

Tu es ...?	*Are you ...?*	—Pierre, **tu es** français?
Je suis ...	*I am ...*	—Oui, **je suis** français.

Les nationalités

	français	**française**
	anglais	**anglaise**
	**américain**	**américaine**
	**canadien**	**canadienne**

Other Expressions

oui	*yes*	Tu es français? **Oui**, je suis français.
non	*no*	Tu es canadien? **Non**, je suis américain.
et	*and*	Je suis de Paris. **Et** toi?
ou	*or*	Tu es français **ou** canadien?
aussi	*also, too*	Moi **aussi**, je suis française.

NOTE Culturelle

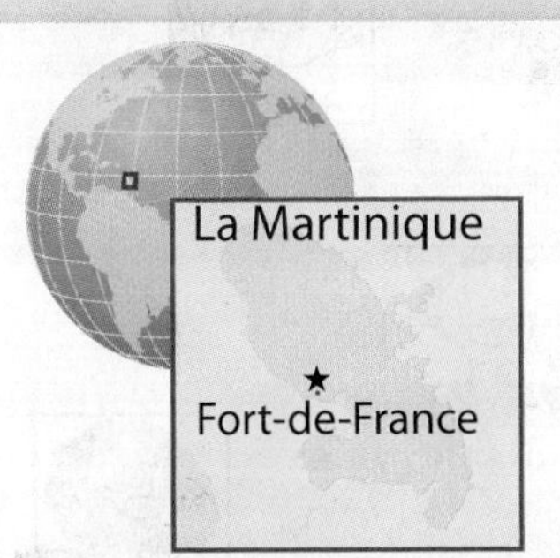

EN BREF
Capitale: Fort-de-France
Population: 400 000
Langues: créole, français

La Martinique

Martinique is a small French island located in the Caribbean, southeast of Puerto Rico. Because Martinique is part of the French national territory, its inhabitants are French citizens. Most of them are of African origin. They speak French as well as a dialect called **créole.**

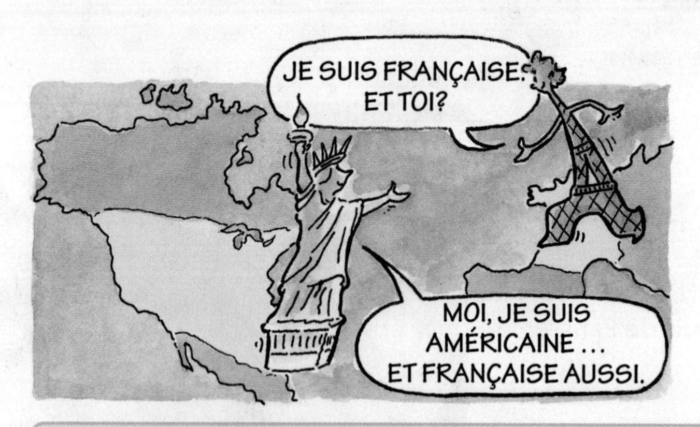

PETIT COMMENTAIRE

The Statue of Liberty **(la statue de la Liberté)** was a gift to the United States from the French people on the occasion of the 100th anniversary of American independence. The Eiffel Tower **(la tour Eiffel)** was built to celebrate the 100th anniversary of the French Revolution.

français, française

Names of nationalities may have two different forms, depending on whom they refer to:

Note In written French the feminine forms always end in **-e**.

1 Et toi?

PARLER Give your name, your nationality, and your city of origin.

▼

2 Français ou française?

PARLER You meet the following young people. Ask them if they are French. A classmate will answer you, as in the model. (Be sure to use **français** with boys and **française** with girls.)

▶ —Sophie, tu es française?
—Oui, je suis française. Je suis de Strasbourg.

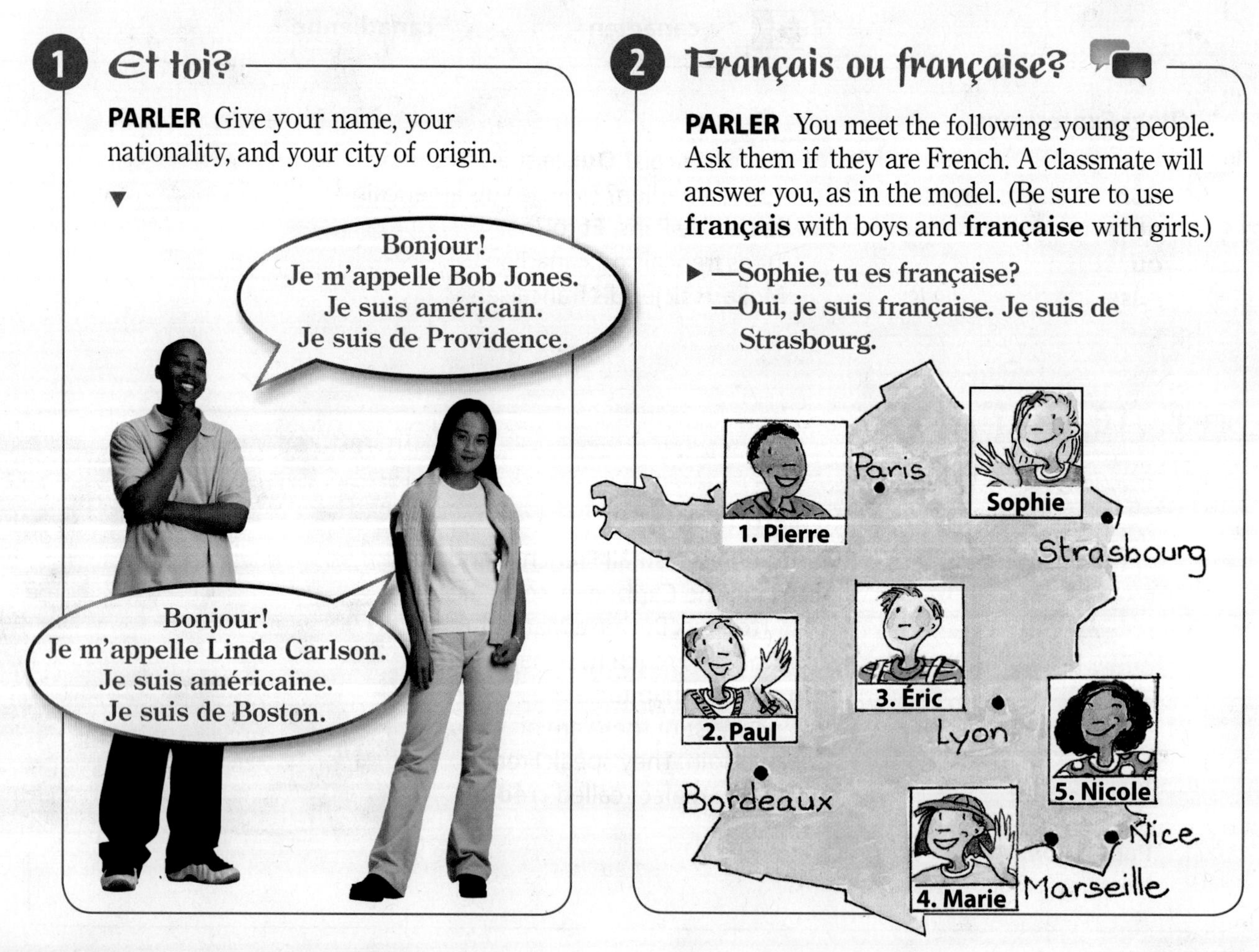

@HOMETUTOR
my.hrw.com

3 Quelle nationalité? *(Which nationality?)*

PARLER Greet the following young people and find out each one's nationality. A classmate will answer you, according to the model.

▶ **—Bonjour, Marc. Tu es canadien?**
—Oui, je suis canadien.
Je suis de Montréal.

Marc Montréal | **1. Claire** Québec | **2. Patrick** Boston

3. Denise Liverpool | **4. Donna** Memphis | **5. Paul** Cambridge

Les nombres de 10 à 20

10	11	12	13	14	15
dix	onze	douze	treize	quatorze	quinze
16	**17**	**18**	**19**	**20**	
seize	dix-sept	dix-huit	dix-neuf	vingt	

4 La fusée Ariane *(The Ariane rocket)*

PARLER Give the countdown for the liftoff of the French rocket Ariane, from 20 to 0.

Prononciation

Les lettres muettes *(Silent letters)*

In French, the last letter of a word is often not pronounced.

- Final "**e**" is always silent.
  Répétez: **Céline Philippe Stéphanie anglaise française onze douze treize quatorze quinze seize**
- Final "**s**" is almost always silent.
  Répétez: **Paris Nicolas Jacques anglais français trois**
- The letter "**h**" is always silent.
  Répétez: **Hélène Henri Thomas Nathalie Catherine Thérèse**

Paris

C Salut! Ça va?

On the way to school, François meets his friends.

François also meets his teachers.

Monsieur Masson

Madame Chollet

Mademoiselle Lacour

After class, François says good-bye to his teacher and his friends.

@HOMETUTOR
my.hrw.com

Salut!

Pour communiquer

▶ *How to greet a friend or classmate:*

Salut! *Hi!*

▶ *How to greet a teacher or another adult:*

Bonjour! *Hello!*

Bonjour, monsieur.
Bonjour, madame.
Bonjour, mademoiselle.

▶ *How to say good-bye:*

Au revoir! *Good-bye!*

Au revoir, Philippe.
Au revoir, monsieur.

→ In written French, the following abbreviations are commonly used:

M. Masson	Monsieur Masson
Mme Chollet	Madame Chollet
Mlle Lacour	Mademoiselle Lacour

→ Young people often use **Salut!** to say good-bye to each other.

NOTE *Culturelle*

Bonjour ou Salut?

French young people may greet one another with **Bonjour,** but they often prefer the less formal **Salut.** When they meet their teachers, however, they always use **Bonjour.** French young people are generally much more formal with adults than with their friends. This is especially true in their relationships with teachers, whom they treat with respect.

Have you noticed that in France adults are addressed as **monsieur, madame,** or **mademoiselle?** The last name is usually not used in greeting people.

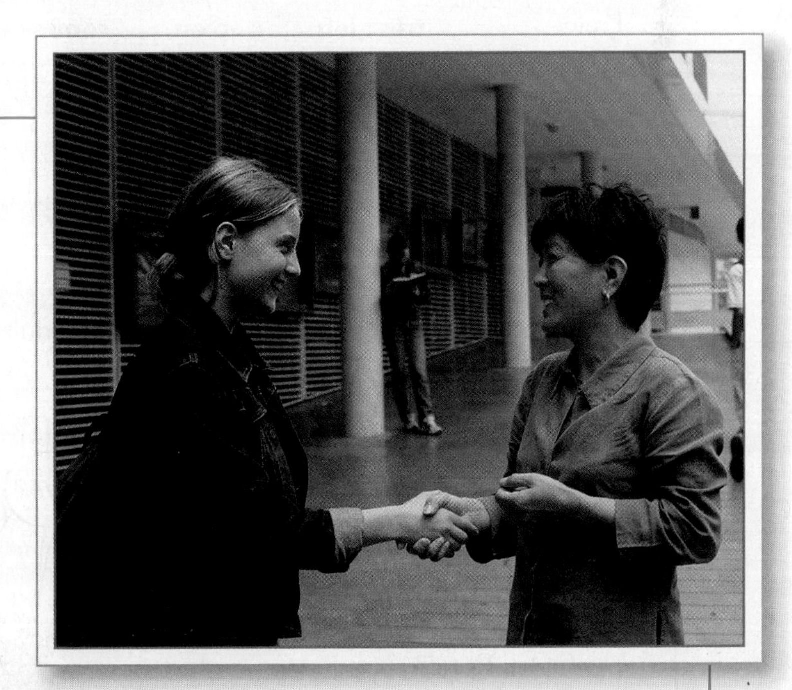

1 Bonjour ou salut?

PARLER You are enrolled in a French school. Greet your friends and teachers.

Valérie

▸ Salut, Valérie!

Mademoiselle Pinot

▸ Bonjour, mademoiselle!

1. Céline

2. Monsieur Masson

3. Nathalie

4. Marc

5. Madame Albert

6. Mademoiselle Boucher

Pour communiquer

▸ How to ask people how they feel:

—**Ça va?** *How are you? How are things going? How's everything?*
—**Ça va!** *(I'm) fine. (I'm) okay. Everything's all right.*

Ça va … **très bien** **bien** **comme ci, comme ça** **mal** **très mal**

▸ How to express one's feelings of frustration and appreciation:

Zut! *Darn!* **Zut!** Ça va mal! **Merci!** *Thanks!* Ça va, **merci.**

➔ ***Ça va?*** *(How are you?)* is an informal greeting that corresponds to the following expressions:

Comment vas-tu? (when addressing a friend)
Bonjour, Paul. Comment vas-tu?
Comment allez-vous? (when addressing an adult)
Bonjour, madame. Comment allez-vous?

2 Dialogue

PARLER Exchange greetings with your classmates and ask how they are doing.

▸ —Salut, (Thomas)! Ça va?
—Ça va! Et toi?
—Ça va bien. Merci.

@HOMETUTOR
my.hrw.com

3 Situations 

PARLER Sometimes we feel good and sometimes we don't. How would you respond in the following situations?

▶ You have the flu.
—**Ça va?**
—**Ça va mal!**

1. You just received an "A" in French.
2. You lost your wallet.
3. Your uncle gave you five dollars.
4. Your grandparents sent you a check for 100 dollars.
5. You bent the front wheel of your bicycle.
6. Your parents bought you a new video game.
7. Your little brother broke your cell phone.
8. It's your birthday.
9. You have a headache.
10. You just had an argument with your best friend.
11. Your French teacher has just canceled a quiz.

4 Ça va?

PARLER How would the following people answer the question **Ça va?**

Les nombres de 20 à 60 

20 vingt	**30** trente	**40** quarante	**50** cinquante	**60** soixante
vingt et un	trente et un	quarante et un	cinquante et un	
vingt-deux	trente-deux	quarante-deux	cinquante-deux	
vingt-trois	trente-trois	quarante-trois	cinquante-trois	
…	…	…	…	
vingt-neuf	trente-neuf	quarante-neuf	cinquante-neuf	

Note Use **et** before **un: vingt et un.**

5 Séries

PARLER Read the following number series out loud.

13 21 37 42 55 60

16 20 29 31 48 56

Prononciation

Les consonnes finales *(Final consonants)*

1 2 3
un deux trois

In French, the last consonant of a word is often not pronounced.

- Remember: Final "**s**" is usually silent.
  Répétez: **trois français anglais**
- Most other final consonants are usually silent.
  Répétez: **Richard Albert Robert salut américain canadien bien deux**

EXCEPTION: The following final consonants are usually pronounced: "**c,**" "**f,**" "**l,**" and sometimes "**r.**"
Répétez: **Éric Daniel Lebeuf Pascal Victor**

However, the ending **-er** is usually pronounced /e/.
Répétez: **Roger Olivier**

Leçon 2

VIDÉO-SCÈNE DVD AUDIO

Famille et copains

A Copain ou copine?

In French, there are certain girls' and boys' names that sound the same. Occasionally this can be confusing.

Scène 1 Philippe et Jean-Paul

Philippe is at home with his friend Jean-Paul. He seems to be expecting someone. Who could it be ... ? The doorbell rings.

Philippe: Tiens! Voilà Dominique!
Jean-Paul: Dominique? Qui est-ce? Un copain ou une copine?
Philippe: C'est une copine.

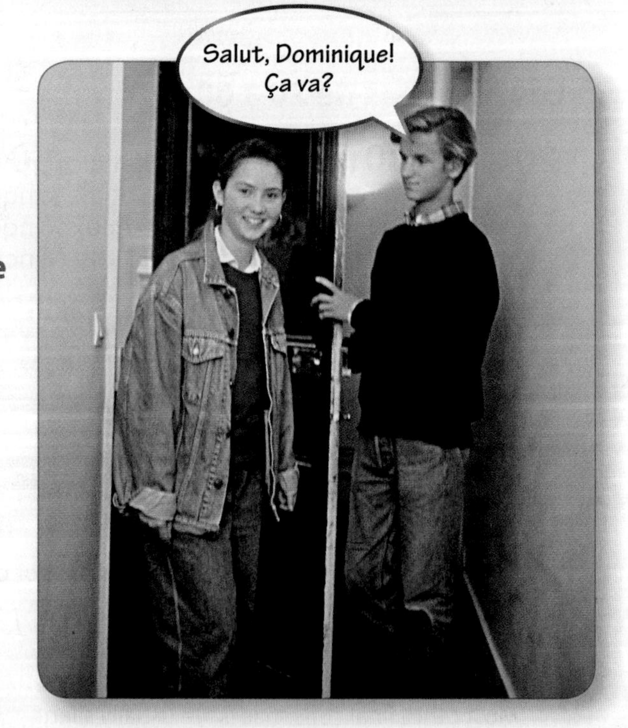

Scène 2 Philippe, Jean-Paul, Dominique

Philippe: Salut, Dominique! Ça va?
Dominique: Oui, ça va! Et toi?
Jean-Paul: *(thinking)* C'est vrai! C'est une copine!

It's true!

@HOMETUTOR
my.hrw.com

Pour communiquer

▶ How to introduce or point out someone:

Voici ...	*This is ..., Here come(s) ...*	**Voici** Jean-Paul. **Voici** Nathalie et François.
Voilà ...	*This (That) is ..., There's ...*	**Voilà** Isabelle. **Voilà** Philippe et Dominique.

▶ How to find out who someone is:

Qui est-ce?	*Who's that? Who is it?*	—**Qui est-ce?**
C'est ...	*It's ..., That's ..., He's ..., She's ...*	—**C'est** Patrick. **C'est** un copain.

▶ How to get someone's attention or to express surprise:

Tiens!	*Look! Hey!*	**Tiens,** voilà Dominique!

Les personnes

un garçon *boy*
un ami *friend (male)*
un copain *friend (male)*

un monsieur *gentleman*
un prof *teacher*

une fille *girl*
une amie *friend (female)*
une copine *friend (female)*

une dame *lady*
une prof *teacher*

NOTE Culturelle

Amis et copains

French young people, like their American counterparts, enjoy spending time with their friends. They refer to their friends as **un ami** (for a boy) and **une amie** (for a girl) or — more commonly — as **un copain** or **une copine.** Note that the words **copain, copine** can also have special meanings. When a boy talks about **une copine,** he is referring to a friend who is a girl. However, when he says **ma** (*my*) **copine,** he may be referring to his girlfriend. Similarly, a girl would call her boyfriend **mon copain.**

PETIT COMMENTAIRE

Cycling is a popular competitive sport throughout France. The most popular races are the **Tour de France** for men and the **Grande Boucle Féminine Internationale** for women. French women cyclists have won many titles.

un garçon, une fille

In French, all NOUNS are either MASCULINE or FEMININE.

Nouns referring to boys or men are almost always MASCULINE.
They are introduced by **un** *(a, an).*

Nouns referring to girls or women are almost always FEMININE.
They are introduced by **une** *(a, an).*

MASCULINE		FEMININE	
un garçon	*a boy*	**une** fille	*a girl*
un ami	*a friend (male)*	**une** amie	*a friend (female)*

1 Copain ou copine?

PARLER Say that the following people are your friends. Use **un copain** or **une copine,** as appropriate.

▶ **Élodiest une copine.**

▶ Élodie

1. Alice

2. Cécile

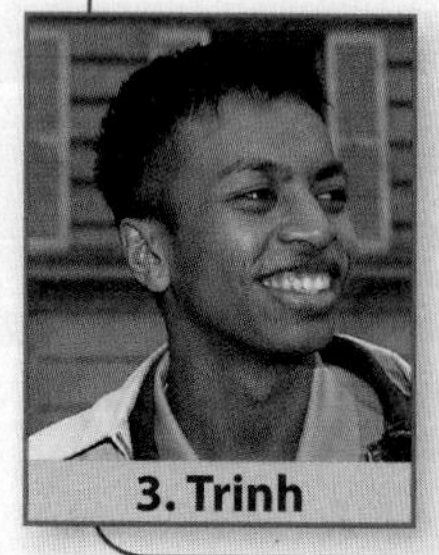
3. Trinh

4. Robert

5. Céline

2 Les amis

PARLER The same young people are visiting your school. Point them out to your classmates, using **un ami** or **une amie,** as appropriate.

▶ **—Tiens, voilà Élodie!**
—Qui est-ce?
—C'est une amie.

3 Un ou une?

PARLER Identify the people below by completing the sentences with **un** or **une.**

1. Voici … fille.
2. Voilà … garçon.
3. Voici … dame.
4. C'est … amie.
5. Nicolas est … ami.
6. Jean-Paul est … copain.
7. Cécile est … copine.
8. Voici Mlle Lacour. C'est … prof.
9. Voici M. Masson. C'est … prof.
10. Voici Mme Chollet. C'est … prof.

@HOMETUTOR my.hrw.com

À la fenêtre (At the window)

PARLER You and a friend are walking down the street and you see the following people at their windows. Identify them in short dialogues.

▸ **—Tiens, voilà un monsieur!**
—Qui est-ce?
—C'est Monsieur Mercier.

Monsieur Mercier

1. Nicole

2. Mademoiselle Lasalle

3. Éric

4. Madame Albert

5. Monsieur Lavie

6. Alain

Les nombres de 60 à 79

60 soixante		**70** soixante-dix	
61 soixante et un	66 soixante-six	71 soixante et onze	76 soixante-seize
62 soixante-deux	67 soixante-sept	72 soixante-douze	77 soixante-dix-sept
63 soixante-trois	68 soixante-huit	73 soixante-treize	78 soixante-dix-huit
64 soixante-quatre	69 soixante-neuf	74 soixante-quatorze	79 soixante-dix-neuf
65 soixante-cinq		75 soixante-quinze	

5 Numéros de téléphone

PARLER Read aloud the phone numbers of Jean-Paul's friends in Paris.

▸ **Philippe** **zéro un, quarante-deux, soixante et un, dix-neuf, soixante-quinze**

Prononciation

La liaison

Pronounce the following words:

un ami un Américain un Anglais un artiste

In general, the "**n**" of **un** is silent. However, in the above words, the "**n**" of **un** is pronounced as if it were the *first* letter of the next word. This is called LIAISON.

Liaison occurs between two words when the second one begins with a VOWEL SOUND, that is, with "**a**", "**e**", "**i**", "**o**", "**u**", and sometimes "**h**" and "**y**".

➔ Although liaison is not marked in written French, it will be indicated in your book by the symbol ‿ where appropriate.

Contrastez et répétez:

LIAISON: **un ami un Américain un Italien un artiste**

NO LIAISON: **un copain un Français un Canadien un prof**

Leçon 2

VIDÉO-SCÈNE DVD AUDIO

B Une coïncidence

Isabelle is at a party with her new Canadian friend Marc. She wants him to meet some of the other guests.

Isabelle: Tu connais la fille là-bas? *over there*
Marc: Non. Qui est-ce?
Isabelle: C'est une copine. Elle s'appelle Juliette Savard.
Marc: Elle est française?
Isabelle: Non, elle est canadienne. Elle est de Montréal.
Marc: Moi aussi!
Isabelle: Quelle coïncidence! *What a coincidence!*

Pour communiquer

▶ ***How to inquire about people:***

Tu connais ...?	*Do you know ...?*	**Tu connais** Jean-Paul?

▶ ***How to describe people and give their nationalities:***

Il est ...	*He is ...*	**Il est** canadien.
Elle est ...	*She is ...*	**Elle est** canadienne.

▶ ***How to find out another person's name:***

Comment s'appelle ...?	*What's the name of ...?*	**Comment s'appelle** le garçon? **Comment s'appelle** la fille?
Il s'appelle ...	*His name is ...*	**Il s'appelle** Marc.
Elle s'appelle ...	*Her name is ...*	**Elle s'appelle** Juliette.

NOTE Culturelle

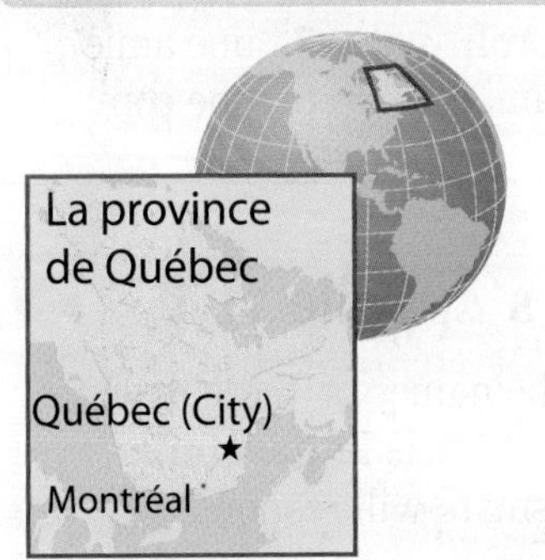

EN BREF

Capitale: *Québec (Quebec City)*
Population: 7 500 000
Langues: français, anglais

La province de Québec

The province of **Québec** is located in the eastern part of Canada. French speakers represent about 75% of its population. Most of them are descendants of French settlers who came to Canada in the 17th and 18th centuries. There are also a large number of Haitian immigrants who are of African origin.

Montréal (population 2 million) is the largest city in the province of Quebec. In population, it is the second-largest French-speaking city in the world after Paris.

PETIT COMMENTAIRE
Most French teenagers study English in school. They are generally very much interested in the United States. They love American music, American movies, and American fashions.

le garçon, la fille

The French equivalent of *the* has two basic forms: **le** and **la**.

MASCULINE		FEMININE	
le garçon	*the boy*	**la** fille	*the girl*
le copain	*the friend*	**la** copine	*the friend*

Note Both **le** and **la** become **l'** before a vowel sound.

un copain	→	le copain	une copine	→	la copine
un ami	→	**l'**ami	une amie	→	**l'**amie

1 *Qui est-ce?*

PARLER Ask who the following people are, using **le, la,** or **l'**.

▶ une prof
Qui est la prof?

1. un monsieur
2. une dame
3. une fille
4. un garçon
5. un prof
6. un ami
7. une amie
8. une copine

2 *Tu connais ...?*

PARLER Ask your classmates if they know the following people. They will answer that they do.

▶ une dame / Madame Vallée

1. un prof / Monsieur Simon
2. un garçon / Christophe
3. une fille / Charlotte
4. une dame / Mademoiselle Lenoir
5. une prof / Madame Boucher
6. un monsieur / Monsieur Duval

3 *Comment s'appelle ...?*

PARLER Ask the names of the following people, using the words **le garçon, la fille.** A classmate will respond.

▶ **—Comment s'appelle la fille?**
▼ **—Elle s'appelle Stéphanie.**

Stéphanie

1. Marc

2. Céline

3. François

4. Jean-Paul

5. Nathalie

6. Trinh

7. Isabelle

@HOMETUTOR
my.hrw.com

4 Français, anglais, canadien ou américain?

PARLER Give the nationalities of the following people.

▶ Julia Roberts?
Elle est américaine.

1. le prince Charles?
2. Céline Dion?
3. Juliette Binoche?
4. Taylor Swift?
5. Pierre Cardin?
6. Matt Damon?
7. Oprah Winfrey?
8. Brad Pitt?
9. Elton John?

Les nombres de 80 à 1000 

80 quatre-vingts
81 quatre-vingt-un
82 quatre-vingt-deux
83 quatre-vingt-trois
84 quatre-vingt-quatre
85 quatre-vingt-cinq
86 quatre-vingt-six
87 quatre-vingt-sept
88 quatre-vingt-huit
89 quatre-vingt-neuf

90 quatre-vingt-dix
91 quatre-vingt-onze
92 quatre-vingt-douze
93 quatre-vingt-treize
94 quatre-vingt-quatorze
95 quatre-vingt-quinze
96 quatre-vingt-seize
97 quatre-vingt-dix-sept
98 quatre-vingt-dix-huit
99 quatre-vingt-dix-neuf

100 cent

1000 mille

→ Note that in counting from 80 to 99, the French add numbers to the base of **quatre-vingts** *(fourscore)*:

$80 = 4 \times 20$ $90 = 4 \times 20 + 10$
$85 = 4 \times 20 + 5$ $99 = 4 \times 20 + 19$

5 Au téléphone

PARLER In France, the telephone area code **(l'indicatif)** is always a four-digit number. Your teacher will name a city **(une ville)** from the chart. Give the area code.

▶ Nice? **C'est le zéro quatre quatre-vingt-treize.**

VILLE	INDICATIF
Albi	05-63
Avignon	04-90
Dijon	03-80
Marseille	04-91
Montpellier	04-67
Nancy	03-83
Nice	04-93
Nîmes	04-66
Rennes	02-99
Saint-Tropez	04-94
Strasbourg	03-88
Vichy	04-70

Prononciation 

La voyelle nasale /ɛ̃/

In French, there are three nasal vowel sounds:

/ɛ̃/ **cinq** (5) /ɔ̃/ **onze** (11) /ɑ̃/ **trente** (30)

Practice the sound /ɛ̃/ in the following words.

→ Be sure not to pronounce an "**n**" or "**m**" after the nasal vowel.

Répétez: **"in"** **cinq quinze vingt vingt-cinq quatre-vingt-quinze**
"ain" **américain Alain copain**
"(i)en" **bien canadien tiens!**
"un" **un**
Tiens! Voilà Alain. Il est américain. Et Julien? Il est canadien.

Leçon 2

VIDÉO-SCÈNE DVD AUDIO

C Les photos d'Isabelle

Isabelle is showing her family photo album to her friend Jean-Paul.

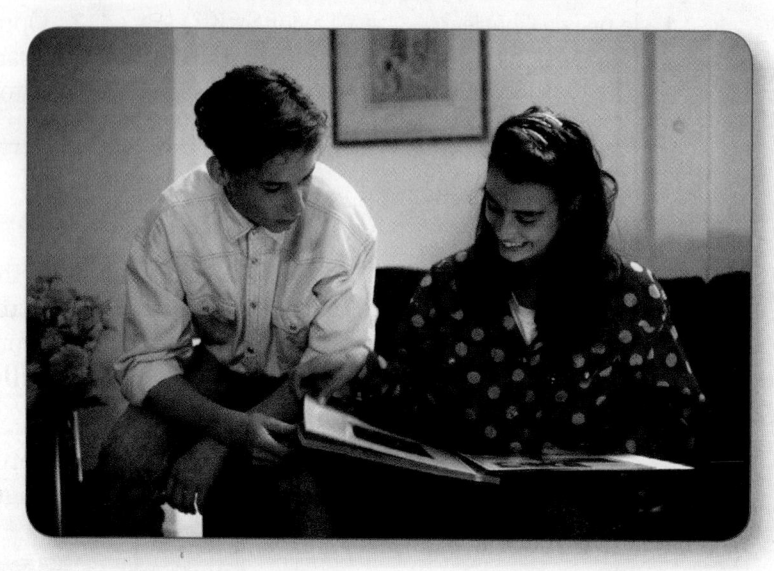

Isabelle:	Voici ma mère.	
Jean-Paul:	Et le monsieur, c'est ton père?	*the man / your*
Isabelle:	Non, c'est mon oncle Thomas.	
Jean-Paul:	Et la fille, c'est ta cousine?	*your*
Isabelle:	Oui, c'est ma cousine Béatrice. Elle a seize ans.	*She's sixteen.*
Jean-Paul:	Et le garçon, c'est ton cousin?	
Isabelle:	Non, c'est un copain.	
Jean-Paul:	Un copain ou ton copain?	
Isabelle:	Dis donc, Jean-Paul, tu es vraiment trop curieux!	*Hey there, Jean-Paul, you are really too curious!*

ma mère

mon oncle Thomas

ma cousine Béatrice

? ?

@HOMETUTOR
my.hrw.com

Pour communiquer

▶ ***How to introduce your family:***

Voici mon père. *This is my father.*

Et voici ma mère. *And this is my mother.*

La famille *(Family)*

un frère	*brother*	**une soeur**	*sister*
un cousin	*cousin*	**une cousine**	*cousin*
un père	*father*	**une mère**	*mother*
un oncle	*uncle*	**une tante**	*aunt*
un grand-père	*grandfather*	**une grand-mère**	*grandmother*

Les animaux domestiques *(Pets)*

un chat

un chien

NOTE Culturelle

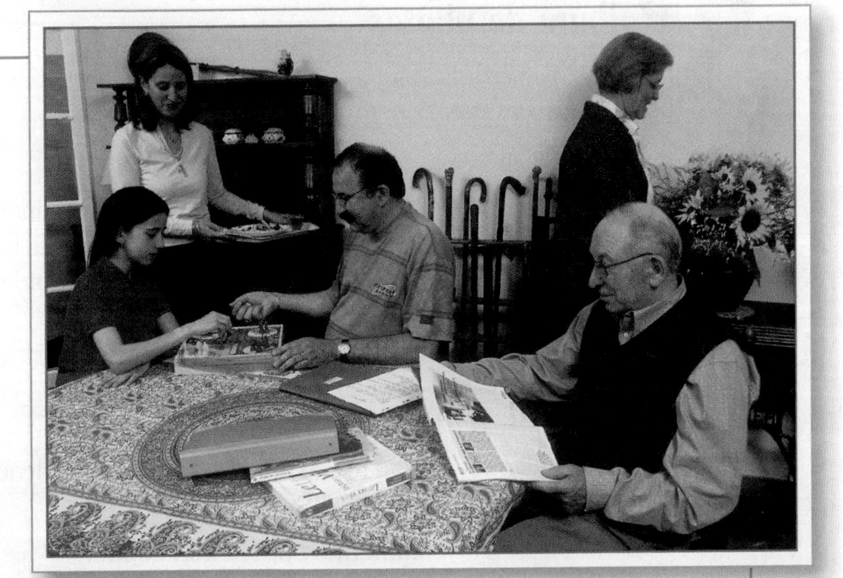

La famille française

When you and your friends talk about your families, you usually are referring to your brothers, sisters, and parents. In French, however, **la famille** refers not only to parents and children but also to grandparents, aunts, uncles, cousins, as well as a whole array of more distant relatives related by blood and marriage.

Since the various members of a family often live in the same region, French teenagers see their grandparents and cousins fairly frequently. Even when relatives do not live close by, the family finds many occasions to get together: for weekend visits, during school and summer vacations, on holidays, as well as on special occasions such as weddings and anniversaries.

PETIT COMMENTAIRE
The French people love pets, especially cats and dogs. What is important is the animal's personality and friendliness rather than its pedigree. Some common names given to animals are:
Minou, Pompon, Fifi (cats)
Titus, Milou, Azor (dogs)

mon cousin, ma cousine

The French equivalents of *my* and *your* have the following forms:

MASCULINE		FEMININE	
mon cousin	*my cousin (male)*	**ma** cousine	*my cousin (female)*
mon frère	*my brother*	**ma** soeur	*my sister*
ton cousin	*your cousin (male)*	**ta** cousine	*your cousin (female)*
ton frère	*your brother*	**ta** soeur	*your sister*

→ Note that the feminine **ma** becomes **mon** and the feminine **ta** becomes **ton** before a vowel sound. Liaison is required.

une amie → **mon** amie **ton** amie

1 L'album de photos

PARLER You are showing a friend your photo album. Identify the following people, using **mon** and **ma,** as appropriate.

▸ cousine Jacqueline **Voici ma cousine Jacqueline.**

1. frère
2. soeur
3. tante Monique
4. oncle Pierre
5. père
6. mère
7. copain Nicolas
8. ami Jérôme
9. copine Pauline
10. amie Florence
11. grand-mère Michèle
12. grand-père Robert
13. chien Toto
14. chat Minou
15. cousine Émilie
16. cousin Marc

2 Comment s'appelle ...?

PARLER Ask your classmates to name some of their friends, relatives, and pets. They can invent names if they wish.

▸ le copain **—Comment s'appelle ton copain?**
—Mon copain s'appelle Bob.

1. l'oncle
2. la tante
3. le cousin
4. la cousine
5. la copine
6. l'ami
7. le grand-père
8. la grand-mère
9. le chien
10. le chat

@HOMETUTOR my.hrw.com

Pour communiquer

▶ How to find out how old a friend is:

Quel âge as-tu?	*How old are you?*	**—Quel âge as-tu?**
J'ai … ans.	*I'm … (years old).*	**—J'ai quinze ans.**

Quel âge as-tu?

J'ai quinze ans.

▶ How to ask about how old others are:

—Quel âge a ton père?	*How old is your father?*
—Il a quarante-deux ans.	*He is 42 (years old).*
—Quel âge a ta mère?	*How old is your mother?*
—Elle a trente-neuf ans.	*She is 39 (years old).*

➔ Although *years old* may be left out in English, the word **ans** must be used in French when talking about someone's age.

Il a vingt ans. *He's twenty. (He's twenty years old.)*

3 Quel âge as-tu?

PARLER Ask your classmates how old they are.

▶ —Quel âge as-tu?
—J'ai (treize) ans.

4 Joyeux anniversaire!

(Happy birthday!)

PARLER Ask your classmates how old the following people are.

▶ —Quel âge a Stéphanie?
—Elle a quatorze ans.

Stéphanie

1. Éric

2. Mademoiselle Doucette

3. Monsieur Boucher

4. Madame Dupont

5. Monsieur Camus

6. Madame Simon

5 Curiosité

PARLER Find out the ages of your classmates' friends and relatives. If they are not sure, they can guess or invent an answer.

▶ la copine —**Quel âge a ta copine?**
—**Ma copine a (treize) ans.**

1. le père
2. la mère
3. l'oncle
4. la tante
5. le cousin
6. la cousine
7. le grand-père
8. la grand-mère

Prononciation /ã/ /ɔ̃/

Les voyelles nasales
/ã/ **et** /ɔ̃/

tante

oncle

The letters "**an**" and "**en**" usually represent the nasal vowel /ã/. Be sure not to pronounce an "**n**" after the nasal vowel.

Répétez: **ans tante français quarante trente comment Henri Laurent**

The letters "**on**" represent the nasal vowel /ɔ̃/. Be sure not to pronounce an "**n**" after the nasal vowel.

Répétez: **non bonjour oncle garçon**

Contrastez: **an—on tante—ton onze—ans**
Mon oncle François a trente ans.

À votre tour!

OBJECTIFS

Now you can . . .
- greet people and say where you are from
- introduce friends and relatives
- give your age and ask how old people are
- understand and use numbers up to 100

Digital performance space

1 Écoutez bien! 

STRATEGY Listening

Numbers As you hear each number, repeat it over and over in your head until you find the corresponding number on the card.

ÉCOUTER Loto is a French version of Bingo. You will hear a series of numbers. If the number is on Card A, raise your left hand. If it is on Card B, raise your right hand.

A

3	■	25	61	82
8	12	■	72	■
■	17	42	■	93

B

5	■	48	67	■
■	19	55	■	89
15	33	■	70	98

2 Et toi?  

ÉCOUTER ET PARLER You and Nathalie meet at a sidewalk café. Respond to her greetings and questions.

1. Salut! Ça va?
2. Comment t'appelles-tu?
3. Tu es canadien (canadienne)?
4. Quel âge as-tu?
5. Comment s'appelle ton copain (ta copine)?
6. Quel âge a ton copain (ta copine)?

3 Conversation dirigée 

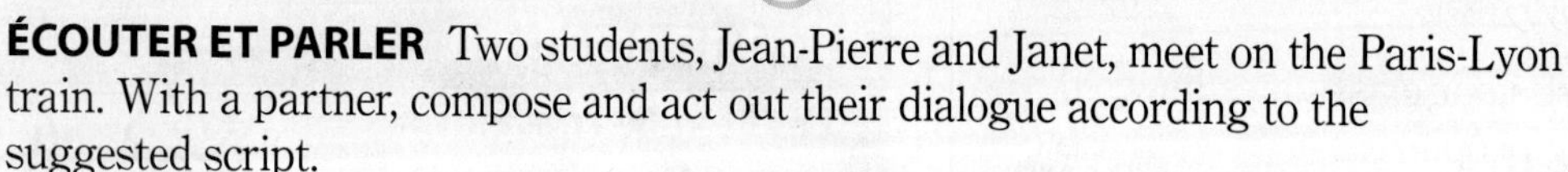

ÉCOUTER ET PARLER Two students, Jean-Pierre and Janet, meet on the Paris-Lyon train. With a partner, compose and act out their dialogue according to the suggested script.

Jean-Pierre		Janet
says hello	→ ↙	responds and asks how things are
says things are fine	→ ↙	asks him what his name is
says his name is Jean-Pierre ... asks her name	→ ↙	says her name is Janet
asks her if she is English	→ ↙	says no and responds that she is American
asks her if she is from New York	→	replies that she is from San Francisco

4 Ma famille *(My family)*

PARLER You are showing your friends pictures of your family. Introduce everyone, giving their ages. If you prefer, show your classmates a picture of your own family and give each person's age.

▶ **Voici ma soeur. Elle a douze ans.**

▶ 

1 

2 

3 

4 

5 

6 

5 En scène

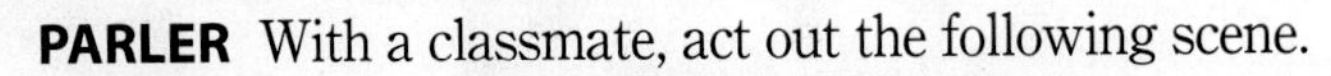

PARLER With a classmate, act out the following scene.

CHARACTERS:
You and a French guest

SITUATION:
You are in France. Your French friends have invited you to a picnic. You meet one of the guests and have a conversation.

- Greet the guest.
- Ask how things are.
- Tell the guest that you are American and ask the guest if he/she is French.
- Tell the guest how old you are and ask his/her age.
- *(The guest waves to a friend.)* Ask the guest the name of his/her friend.
- *(It is the end of the picnic.)* Say good-bye.

6 Les nombres

PARLER

1. Select any number between 0 and 15 and give the next five numbers in sequence.
2. Select a number between 1 and 9. Use that number as a starting point and count by tens to 100.

▶ deux...

douze, vingt-deux, trente-deux, etc.

Les Couleurs

rouge | orange | jaune | vert | bleu | violet | blanc | noir

Le drapeau des pays francophones

In the following countries, many people use French in their daily lives. Locate each country on the map on pages 8–9 and then describe the colors of its flag.

▶ La Belgique: **Le drapeau est noir, jaune et rouge.**

Europe

LA BELGIQUE
Population: 10 millions
Capitale: Bruxelles

LE LUXEMBOURG
Population: 0,5 million
Capitale: Luxembourg

LA SUISSE
Population: 7 millions
Capitale: Berne

Amérique

LE CANADA
Population: 33 millions
Capitale: Ottawa

HAÏTI
Population: 10 millions
Capitale: Port-au-Prince

orange jaune vert bleu violet blanc noir

Afrique

LE CAMEROUN
Population: 19 millions
Capitale: Yaoundé

LA CÔTE D'IVOIRE
Population: 20 millions
Capitale: Yamoussoukro

LE MAROC
Population: 32 millions
Capitale: Rabat

LE MALI
Population: 13 millions
Capitale: Bamako

LA RÉPUBLIQUE DÉMOCRATIQUE DU CONGO
Population: 63 millions
Capitale: Kinshasa

LE SÉNÉGAL
Population: 13 millions
Capitale: Dakar

CONNEXIONS World Geography

Increase your awareness of the francophone world. Select one of the countries mentioned and make a poster which includes the flag and a map showing the capital city. Complete the poster with pictures or other information of interest (sources: atlas, encyclopedia, Internet, travel ads, newspapers, and magazines).

Unité 2 Invitation au français

La vie courante

LEÇON 3 Bon appétit!

- **A VIDÉO-SCÈNE:** Tu as faim?
- **B VIDÉO-SCÈNE:** Au café
- **C VIDÉO-SCÈNE:** Ça fait combien?

LEÇON 4 De jour en jour

- **A VIDÉO-SCÈNE:** L'heure
- **B VIDÉO-SCÈNE:** Le jour et la date
- **C VIDÉO-SCÈNE:** Le temps

THÈME ET OBJECTIFS

Everyday life in France

In this unit, you will learn how to get along in France. In particular, you may want to know how to buy something to eat or drink.

You will learn ...

- to order snacks and beverages in a café
- to ask about prices and pay for your food/drink
- to use French money

You will also learn ...

- to tell time
- to give the date and the day of the week
- to talk about the weather

DIGITAL FRENCH my.hrw.com

ONLINE STUDENT EDITION with...

performance space

News + Networking

@HOMETUTOR

- Audio Resources
- Video Resources
- Interactive Flashcards
- WebQuest

PRACTICE FRENCH WITH HOLT MCDOUGAL APPS!

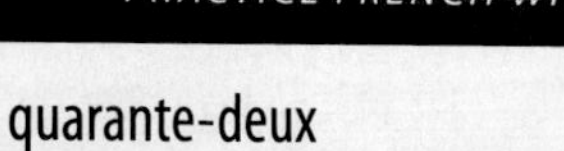

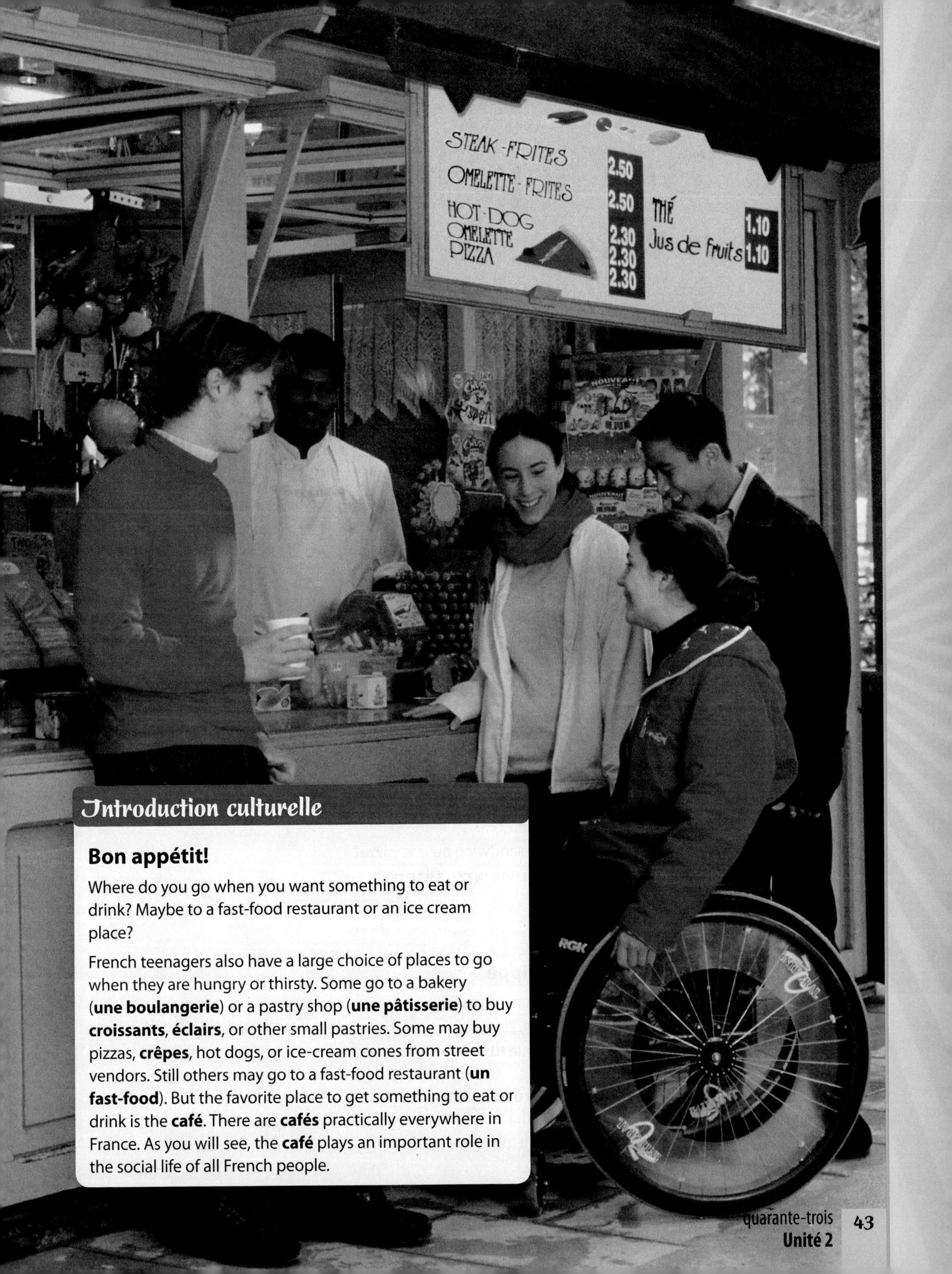

Introduction culturelle

Bon appétit!

Where do you go when you want something to eat or drink? Maybe to a fast-food restaurant or an ice cream place?

French teenagers also have a large choice of places to go when they are hungry or thirsty. Some go to a bakery (**une boulangerie**) or a pastry shop (**une pâtisserie**) to buy **croissants**, **éclairs**, or other small pastries. Some may buy pizzas, **crêpes**, hot dogs, or ice-cream cones from street vendors. Still others may go to a fast-food restaurant (**un fast-food**). But the favorite place to get something to eat or drink is the **café**. There are **cafés** practically everywhere in France. As you will see, the **café** plays an important role in the social life of all French people.

Leçon 3

VIDÉO-SCÈNE

DVD AUDIO

Bon appétit!

A Tu as faim?

Pierre, Philippe, and Nathalie are on their way home from school. They stop by a street vendor who sells sandwiches and pizza. Today it is Pierre's turn to treat his friends.

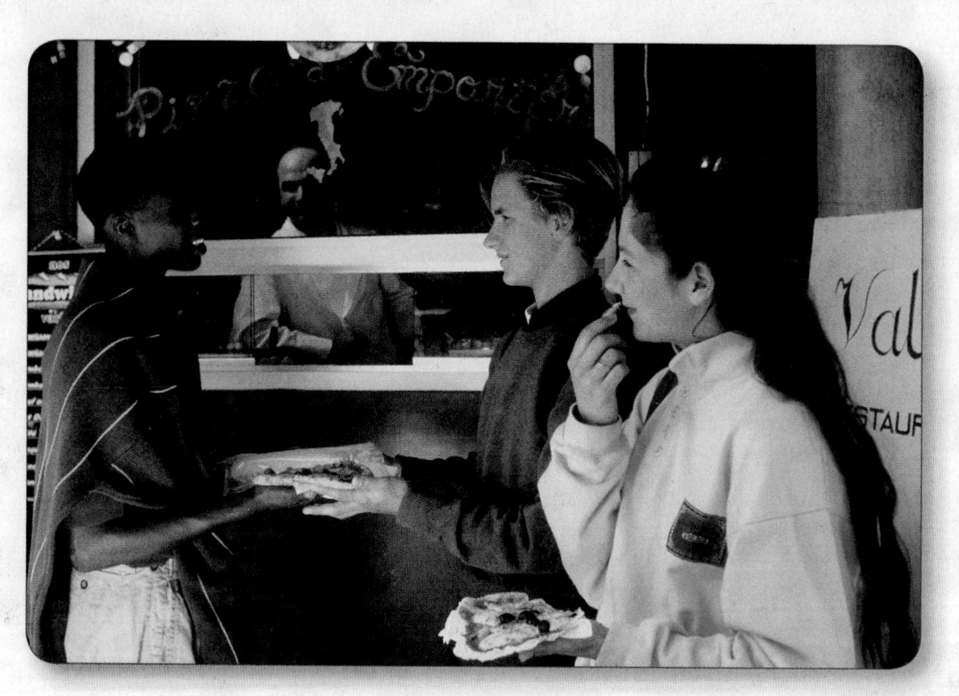

SCÈNE 1 Pierre et Nathalie

Pierre: Tu as faim?
Nathalie: Oui, j'ai faim.
Pierre: Tu veux un sandwich ou une pizza?
Nathalie: Donne-moi une pizza, s'il te plaît.
Pierre: Voilà.
Nathalie: Merci.

SCÈNE 2 Pierre et Philippe

Pierre: Et toi, Philippe, tu as faim?
Philippe: Oh là là, oui, j'ai faim.
Pierre: Qu'est-ce que tu veux? Un sandwich ou une pizza?
Philippe: Je voudrais un sandwich … euh … et donne-moi aussi une pizza. *(euh: er …)*
Pierre: C'est vrai! Tu as vraiment faim! *(vraiment: really)*

@HOMETUTOR
my.hrw.com

Pour communiquer

J'ai faim!
Tu as faim?

▶ How to say that you are hungry:

J'ai faim. — *I'm hungry.*
Tu as faim? — *Are you hungry?*

▶ How to offer a friend something:

Tu veux ... ? — *Do you want ...?*
Qu'est-ce que tu veux? — *What do you want?*

Tu veux un sandwich?
Qu'est-ce que tu veux?
Un sandwich ou une pizza?

▶ How to ask a friend for something:

Je voudrais ... — *I would like ...*
Donne-moi ... — *Give me ...*
S'il te plaît ... — *Please ...*

Je voudrais un sandwich.
Donne-moi une pizza.
S'il te plaît, François, donne-moi une pizza.

Les nourritures *(Foods)*

un croissant **un sandwich** **un steak** **un steak-frites** **un hamburger** **un hot dog**

une salade **une pizza** **une omelette** **une crêpe** **une glace**

NOTE Culturelle

Les jeunes et la nourriture

In general, French teenagers eat their main meals at home with their families. On weekends or after school, however, when they are with friends, they often stop at a fast-food restaurant or a café for something to eat.

At fast-food restaurants, French teenagers order pretty much the same types of foods as Americans: hamburgers, hot dogs, and pizza.

At a café, teenagers may order a croissant, a sandwich, or a dish of ice cream. Some favorite sandwiches are ham (**un sandwich au jambon**), Swiss cheese (**un sandwich au fromage**), or salami (**un sandwich au saucisson**). And, of course, they are made with French bread, which has a crunchy crust. Another traditional quick café meal is a small steak with French fries (**un steak-frites**).

Communication

PETIT COMMENTAIRE

In France, sandwiches are traditionally very simple: a piece of French bread with a slice of ham or cheese. However, nowadays one can buy fancier sandwiches made with different breads, such as "panini," and a variety of ingredients.

un sandwich, une pizza

You may have noted that the names of some foods are masculine and others are feminine. In French, ALL NOUNS, whether they designate people or things, are either MASCULINE or FEMININE.

MASCULINE NOUNS		FEMININE NOUNS	
un sandwich	**le** sandwich	**une** pizza	**la** pizza
un croissant	**le** croissant	**une** salade	**la** salade

1 Au choix *(Your choice)*

PARLER Offer your classmates a choice between the following items. They will decide which one they would like.

▶ **une pizza ou un sandwich?**

1. un hamburger ou un steak?
2. un hot dog ou un sandwich?
3. une salade ou une omelette?
4. un steak-frites ou une pizza?
5. une crêpe ou un croissant?
6. une glace à la vanille ou une glace au chocolat?

2 Au café

PARLER You are in a French café. Ask for the following dishes.

▶ 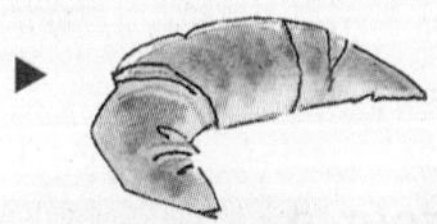

▶ **Je voudrais un croissant.**

1

2

3

4

5

6

@HOMETUTOR
my.hrw.com

3 Tu as faim? 

PARLER You have invited French friends to your home. Ask if they are hungry and offer them the following foods.

▶ **—Tu as faim?**
—Oui, j'ai faim.
—Tu veux un hamburger?
—Oui, merci.

▶ 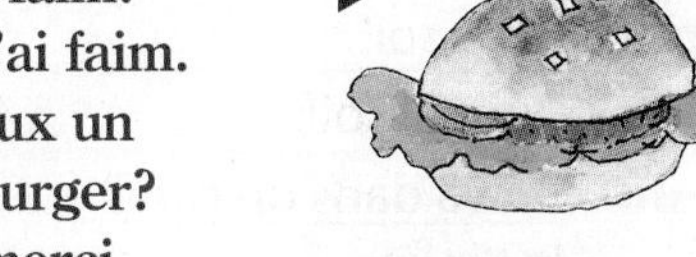

1

2

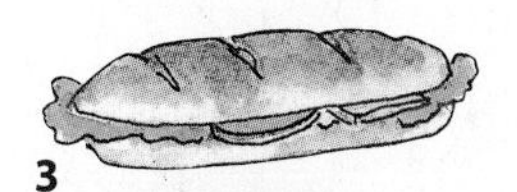
3

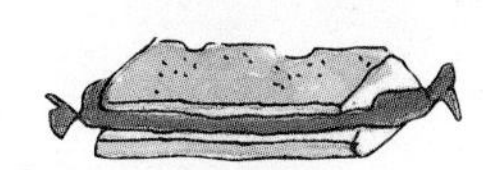
4

5

6

4 Qu'est-ce que tu veux?

PARLER Say which foods you would like to have in the following circumstances.

▶ You are very hungry.

1. You are at an Italian restaurant.
2. You are on a diet.
3. You are a vegetarian.
4. You are having breakfast.
5. You would like a dessert.
6. You want to eat something light for supper.

Prononciation

L'intonation

When you speak, your voice rises and falls. This is called INTONATION. In French, as in English, your voice goes down at the end of a statement. However, in French, your voice rises after each group of words in the middle of a sentence. (This is the opposite of English, where your voice drops a little when you pause in the middle of a sentence.)

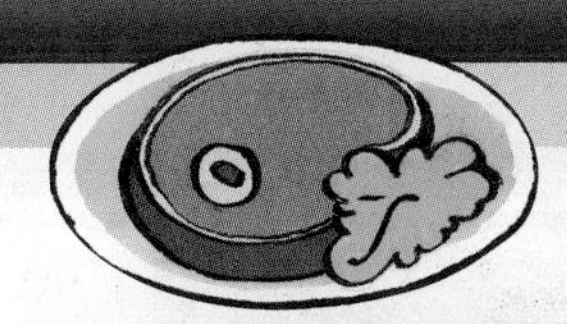

Voici un steak . . . et une salade.

Répétez: **Je voudrais une pizza.**

Je voudrais une pizza et un sandwich.

Je voudrais une pizza, un sandwich et un hamburger.

Voici un steak.

Voici un steak et une salade.

Voici un steak, une salade et une glace.

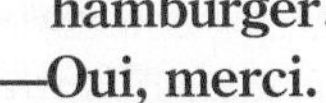

B Au café

This afternoon Trinh and Céline went shopping. They are now tired and thirsty. Trinh invites Céline to a café.

Scène 1 Trinh, Céline

Trinh: Tu as soif?
Céline: Oui, j'ai soif.
Trinh: On va dans un café? Je t'invite. — *Shall we go to a café? I'm treating (inviting).*
Céline: D'accord! — *Okay!*

Scène 2 Le garçon, Céline, Trinh

Le garçon: Vous désirez, mademoiselle?
Céline: Un jus d'orange, s'il vous plaît.
Le garçon: Et pour vous, monsieur? — *for*
Trinh: Donnez-moi une limonade,* s'il vous plaît.

Scène 3 Le garçon, Céline, Trinh

Le garçon: *(à Céline)* La limonade, c'est pour vous, mademoiselle?
Trinh: Non, c'est pour moi.
Le garçon: Ah, excusez-moi. Voici le jus d'orange, mademoiselle. — *Oh, excuse me.*
Céline: Merci.

****Une limonade** is a popular inexpensive soft drink with a slight lemon flavor.*

@HOMETUTOR
my.hrw.com

Pour communiquer

Donnez-moi une limonade, s'il vous plaît!

▶ *How to say that you are thirsty:*

J'ai soif.	*I'm thirsty.*
Tu as soif?	*Are you thirsty?*

▶ *How to order in a café:*

Vous désirez?	*May I help you?*	—**Vous désirez?**
Je voudrais ...	*I would like ...*	—**Je voudrais** un jus d'orange.

▶ *How to request something ...*

from a friend:	*from an adult:*	
S'il te plaît, donne-moi ...	**S'il vous plaît, donnez-moi ...**	*Please, give me ...*

➔ Note that French people have two ways of saying *please*. They use
s'il te plaît with friends, and
s'il vous plaît with adults.

As we will see later, young people address their friends as **tu** and adults that they do not know very well as **vous**.

Les boissons *(Beverages)*

		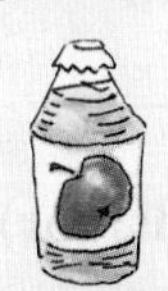						
un soda	**un jus d'orange**	**un jus de pomme**	**un jus de tomate**	**un jus de raisin***	**une limonade**	**un café**	**un thé**	**un chocolat**

NOTE Culturelle

Le café

The café is a favorite gathering place for French young people. They go there not only when they are hungry or thirsty but also to meet their friends. They can sit at a table and talk for hours over a cup of coffee or a glass of juice. French young people also enjoy mineral water and soft drinks. In a French café, a 15% service charge is included in the check. However, most people also leave some small change as an added tip.

***Jus de raisin** is a golden-colored juice made from grapes.*

PETIT COMMENTAIRE
At a café, French young people often order carbonated soft drinks. They also enjoy natural beverages, such as flavored mineral water or juice. In the larger cities, one can find inviting juice bars that offer a wide selection of freshly blended fruit drinks.

1 *Tu as soif?*

PARLER You have invited a French friend to your house. You offer a choice of beverages and your friend (played by a classmate) responds.

▶ un thé ou un chocolat?
—**Tu veux un thé ou un chocolat?**
—**Donne-moi un chocolat, s'il te plaît.**

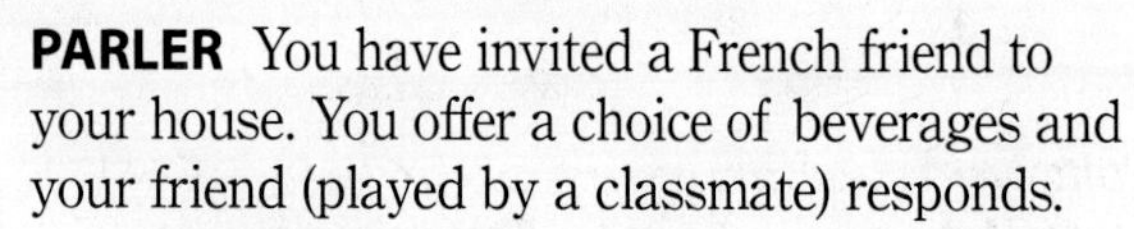

1. un thé ou un café?
2. une limonade ou un soda?
3. un jus de pomme ou un jus d'orange?
4. un jus de raisin ou un jus de tomate?

2 *Au café*

PARLER You are in a French café. Get the attention of the waiter **(Monsieur)** or the waitress **(Mademoiselle)** and place your order. Act out the dialogue with a classmate.

@HOMETUTOR
my.hrw.com

3 Que choisir? *(What to choose?)*

PARLER You are in a French café. Decide what beverage you are going to order in each of the following circumstances.

▶ You are very thirsty.
S'il vous plaît, une limonade (un jus de pomme) …

1. It is very cold outside.
2. You do not want to spend much money.
3. You like juice but are allergic to citrus fruits.
4. It is breakfast time.
5. You have a sore throat.

4 La faim et la soif *(Hungry and thirsty)*

PARLER You are having a meal in a French café. Order the food suggested in the picture. Then order something to drink with that dish. A classmate will play the part of the waiter.

Note: **Et avec ça?** means *And with that?*

Prononciation 

L'accent final

In French, the rhythm is very even and the accent always falls on the *last* syllable of a word or group of words.

Répétez: **Philippe** **Thomas** **Alice** **Sophie** **Dominique**

un café	**Je voudrais un café.**
une salade	**Donnez-moi une salade.**
un chocolat	**Donne-moi un chocolat.**

Leçon 3

VIDÉO-SCÈNE DVD AUDIO

C Ça fait combien?

At the café, Trinh and Céline have talked about many things. It is now time to go. Trinh calls the waiter so he can pay the check.

Trinh: S'il vous plaît?
Le garçon: Oui, monsieur.
Trinh: Ça fait combien?
Le garçon: Voyons, un jus d'orange, 2 euros 50, et une limonade, 1 euro 50. Ça fait 4 euros.
Trinh: 4 euros ... Très bien ... Mais, euh ... Zut! Où est mon porte-monnaie ...? Dis, Céline, prête-moi 5 euros, s'il te plaît.

euh: uh ...
Où est mon porte-monnaie ...?: Where is my wallet?
Dis: Hey

NOTE Culturelle

L'argent européen *(European money)*

In 2002, France and most of the European Union countries adopted a common currency: the euro **(l'euro).** The euro has the same value in all of these countries. It is also very convenient since you do not need to change money when you travel from one country to another.

The euro is divided into 100 cents or **centimes.** The euro currency consists of 7 different bills and 8 different coins. The euro bills are of different colors and different sizes. The largest is worth 500 euros and the smallest 5 euros.

Pour communiquer

▶ *How to ask how much something costs:*

C'est combien?	*How much is it?*	—**C'est combien?**
Ça fait combien?	*How much does that come to (make)?*	—**Ça fait combien?**
Ça fait ...	*That's ..., That comes to ...*	—**Ça fait** 10 euros.
Combien coûte ...?	*How much does ... cost?*	—**Combien coûte** le sandwich?
Il/Elle coûte ...	*It costs ...*	—**Il coûte** 5 euros.

▶ *How to ask a friend to lend you something:*

Prête-moi ...	*Lend me ..., Loan me ...*	**Prête-moi** 30 euros, s'il te plaît.

➔ Note that masculine nouns can be replaced by **il** and feminine nouns can be replaced by **elle.**

Voici **une glace.**	**Elle** coûte 2 euros.	***It*** *costs 2 euros.*
Voici **un sandwich.**	**Il** coûte 5 euros.	***It*** *costs 5 euros.*

STRATEGY Speaking

Linking words When counting in euros, be sure to use the proper liaisons and elisions.

un euro (n)	trois euros (z)	cinq euros (k)	sept euros (t)	neuf euros
deux euros (z)	quatre euros	six euros (z)	huit euros (t)	dix euros (z)

PETIT COMMENTAIRE

French people of all ages love to eat out, and French restaurants have the reputation of offering the best cuisine in the world. Of course, there are all kinds of restaurants for all kinds of budgets, ranging from the simple country inn **(l'auberge de campagne)** with its hearty regional food to the elegant three-star restaurant **(restaurant trois étoiles)** with its exquisite—and expensive—menu.

1 S'il te plaît ...

PARLER You have been shopping in Paris and discover that you did not exchange enough money. Ask a friend to loan you the following sums.

▶ 5 euros
S'il te plaît, prête-moi cinq euros.

1. 2 euros
2. 3 euros
3. 10 euros
4. 20 euros
5. 30 euros
6. 40 euros
7. 25 euros
8. 15 euros
9. 50 euros

2 Décision

PARLER Before ordering at a café, Charlotte and Fatima are checking the prices. Act out the dialogues.

▶ le chocolat

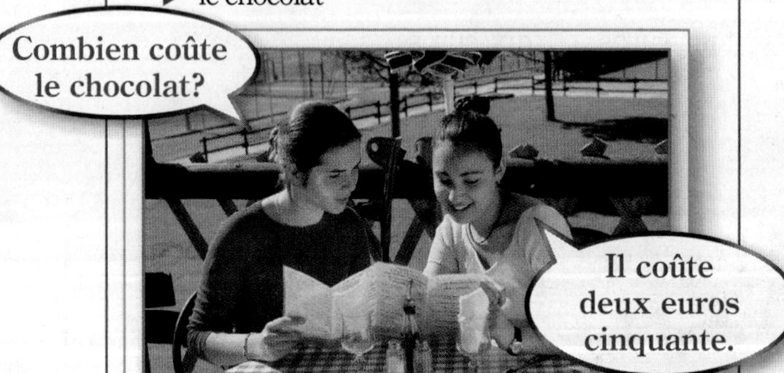

1. le thé
2. le jus d'orange
3. la salade de tomates
4. la glace à la vanille
5. le café
6. le steak-frites
7. le hot dog
8. l'omelette
9. la salade mixte
10. le jus de raisin

LE SELECT
CAFÉ RESTAURANT

BOISSONS

café	1€50
chocolat	2€50
thé	2€
limonade	2€50
jus d'orange	2€70
jus de raisin	2€70

GLACES

glace au chocolat	2€50
glace à la vanille	2€50

SANDWICHS

sandwich au jambon	3€50
sandwich au fromage	3€50

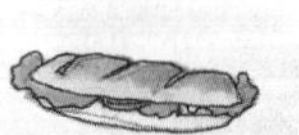

ET AUSSI . . .

steak-frites	8€
salade mixte	3€50
salade de tomates	4€
omelette	4€25
hot dog	4€
croissant	1€40
pizza	8€

3 Ça fait combien?

PARLER You have gone to Le Select with your friends and have ordered the following items. Now you are ready to leave the café, and each one wants to pay. Check the prices on the menu for Le Select, and act out the dialogue.

▶ **—Ça fait combien, s'il vous plaît?**
—Ça fait deux euros cinquante.
—Voici deux euros cinquante.
—Merci.

4 Au «Select»

PARLER You are at Le Select. Order something to eat and drink. Since you are in a hurry, ask for the check right away. Act out the dialogue with a classmate who will play the part of the waiter/waitress.

Prononciation /r/

La consonne «r»

The French consonant "**r**" is not at all like the English "**r.**" It is pronounced at the back of the throat. In fact, it is similar to the Spanish "jota" sound of José.

Répétez: **Marie Paris orange Henri**
franc très croissant fromage
bonjour pour Pierre quart
Robert Richard Renée Raoul

Marie, prête-moi trente euros.

Marie

Leçon 4

VIDÉO-SCÈNE DVD AUDIO

De jour en jour

A L'heure

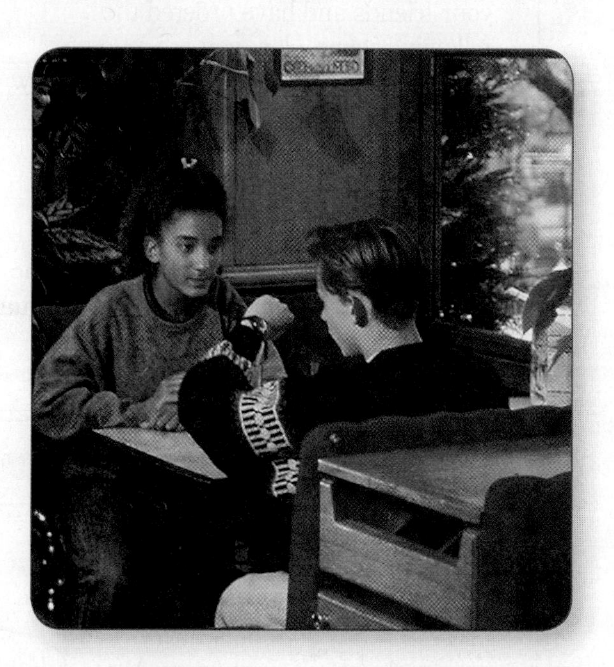

1. Un rendez-vous

Jean-Paul and Stéphanie are sitting in a café. Stéphanie seems to be in a hurry to leave.

Stéphanie:	Quelle heure est-il?	
Jean-Paul:	Il est trois heures.	
Stéphanie:	Trois heures?	
Jean-Paul:	Oui, trois heures.	
Stéphanie:	Oh là là. J'ai un rendez-vous avec David dans vingt minutes. Au revoir, Jean-Paul.	*I have a date* / *with*
Jean-Paul:	Au revoir, Stéphanie. À bientôt!	*See you soon!*

Il est huit heures!

Pour communiquer

▶ *How to talk about the time:*

Quelle heure est-il? — *What time is it?*
Il est ... — *It's ...*

					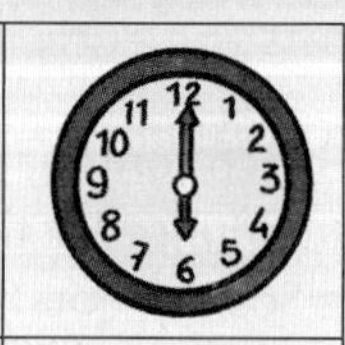
une heure	**deux heures**	**trois heures**	**quatre heures**	**cinq heures**	**six heures**

sept heures	**huit heures**	**neuf heures**	**dix heures**	**onze heures**	**midi**	**minuit**

@HOMETUTOR
my.hrw.com

1 Écoutez bien!

ÉCOUTER Listen as people talk about the time. For each dialog, indicate which of the watches below corresponds to the time you hear.

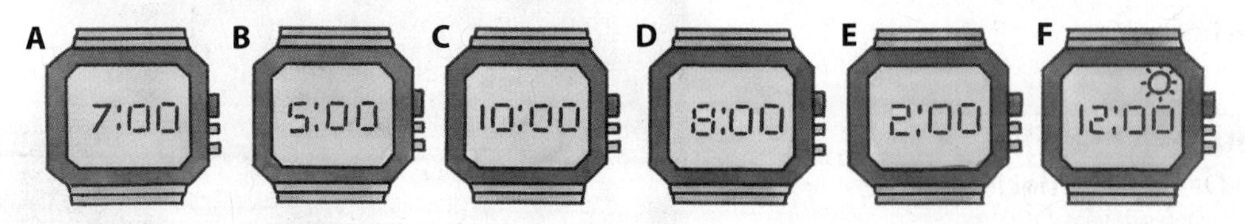

2 Quelle heure est-il?

PARLER Ask your classmates what time it is.

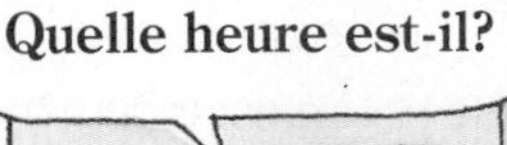

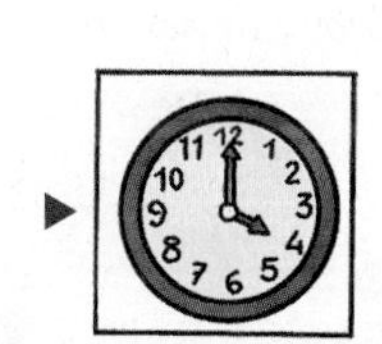

→ Although *o'clock* may be left out in English, the expression **heure(s)** must be used in French when giving the time.

It's ten. (It's ten o'clock.) **Il est dix heures.**

→ To distinguish between A.M. and P.M., the French use the following expressions:

du matin	*in the morning*	Il est dix heures **du matin.**
de l'après-midi	*in the afternoon*	Il est deux heures **de l'après-midi.**
du soir	*in the evening*	Il est huit heures **du soir.**

NOTE DE PRONONCIATION: In telling time, the NUMBER and the word **heure(s)** are linked together. Remember, in French the letter "**h**" is always silent.

une heure **deux heures** (z) **trois heures** (z) **quatre heures** **cinq heures** (k) **six heures** (z)

sept heures (t) **huit heures** (t) **neuf heures** (v) **dix heures** (z) **onze heures**

2. À quelle heure est le film?

Stéphanie and David have decided to go to a movie.

Stéphanie: Quelle heure est-il?
David: Il est trois heures et demie.
Stéphanie: Et à quelle heure est le film?
David: À quatre heures et quart.
Stéphanie: Ça va. Nous avons le temps.

That's okay. / We have time.

À quelle heure est le dîner?

Pour communiquer

▶ *How to ask at what time something is scheduled:*

À quelle heure est ...?	*At what time is ...?*
—À quelle heure est le concert?	*At what time is the concert?*
—Le concert est à huit heures.	*The concert is at eight.*

▶ *How to say that you have an appointment or a date:*

J'ai un rendez-vous à ... — *I have an appointment (a date) at ...*

J'ai un rendez-vous à deux heures.

▶ *How to indicate the minutes:*

Il est ... dix heures dix — six heures vingt-cinq — sept heures trente-cinq — deux heures cinquante-deux

▶ *How to indicate the half hour and the quarter hours:*

 **et quart**

 **et demie**

 **moins le quart**

 Il est une heure **et quart.**

 Il est deux heures **et demie.**

 Il est trois heures **moins le quart.**

@HOMETUTOR
my.hrw.com

3 L'heure

PARLER Give the times according to the clocks.

▶ **Il est une heure et quart.**

▶ 

1 

2 

3 

4 

5 

4 À quelle heure? 

PARLER Ask your classmates at what time certain activities are scheduled. They will answer according to the information below.

▶ 8h 50 le film —**À quelle heure est le film?**
—**Le film est à huit heures cinquante.**

1. 7h 15 le concert
2. 2h 30 le match de football *(soccer)*
3. 3h 45 le match de tennis
4. 5h 10 le récital
5. 7h 45 le dîner

5 Rendez-vous 

PARLER Isabelle has appointments with various classmates and teachers. Look at her notebook and act out her dialogues with Philippe.

▶ ISABELLE: **J'ai un rendez-vous avec Marc.**
PHILIPPE: **À quelle heure?**
ISABELLE: **À onze heures et demie.**

▶ 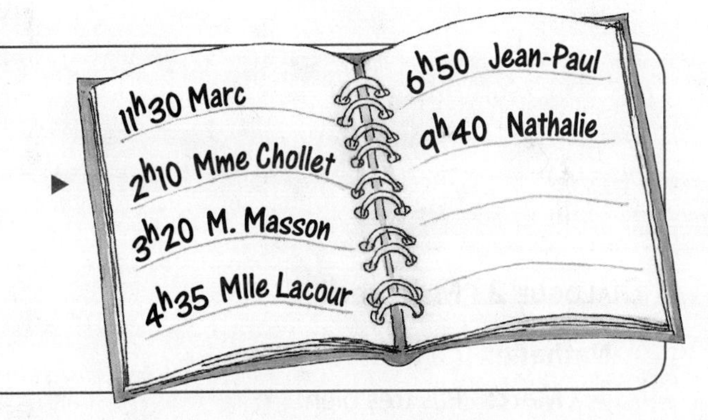

6 À la gare *(At the train station)* 

PARLER You are at the information desk of a French train station. Travelers ask you the departure times for the following trains. Answer them according to the posted schedule.

▶ le train pour Nice

▶

DÉPARTS			
NICE	6h 10	TOULON	9h 35
LYON	7h 15	COLMAR	10h 40
CANNES	7h 30	TOULOUSE	10h 45
TOURS	8h 12	MARSEILLE	10h 50
DIJON	8h 25	BORDEAUX	10h 55

Leçon 4

VIDÉO-SCÈNE DVD AUDIO

B Le jour et la date

1. Quel jour est-ce?

For many people, the days of the week are not all alike.

Dialogue 1 Vendredi

Philippe: Quel jour est-ce?
Stéphanie: C'est vendredi.
Philippe: Super! Demain, c'est samedi!

Dialogue 2 Mercredi

Nathalie: Ça va?
Marc: Pas très bien.
Nathalie: Pourquoi? *Why?*
Marc: Aujourd'hui, c'est mercredi.
Nathalie: Et alors? *So?*
Marc: Demain, c'est jeudi! Le jour de l'examen.
Nathalie: Zut! C'est vrai! *Darn! /That's right!* Au revoir, Marc.
Marc: Au revoir, Nathalie. À demain!

@HOMETUTOR
my.hrw.com

Pour communiquer

À samedi!

▶ How to talk about days of the week:

Quel jour est-ce?	*What day is it?*
Aujourd'hui, c'est mercredi.	*Today is Wednesday.*
Demain, c'est jeudi.	*Tomorrow is Thursday.*

▶ How to tell people when you will see them again:

À samedi!	*See you Saturday!*
À demain!	*See you tomorrow!*

Les jours de la semaine *(Days of the week)*

lundi	*Monday*	**vendredi**	*Friday*	**aujourd'hui**	*today*
mardi	*Tuesday*	**samedi**	*Saturday*	**demain**	*tomorrow*
mercredi	*Wednesday*	**dimanche**	*Sunday*		
jeudi	*Thursday*				

1 Questions

PARLER

1. Quel jour est-ce aujourd'hui?
2. Et demain, quel jour est-ce?

2 Un jour de retard *(One day behind)*

PARLER Georges has trouble keeping track of the date. He is always one day behind. Monique corrects him.

▶ samedi

1. lundi
2. mardi
3. jeudi
4. vendredi
5. dimanche
6. mercredi

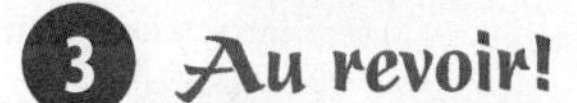

3 Au revoir!

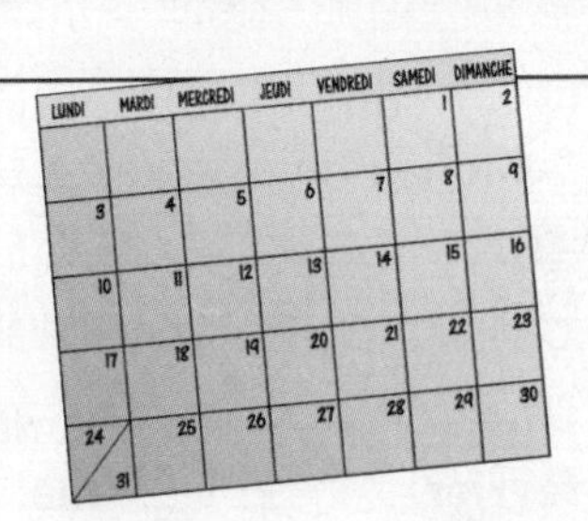

PARLER You are on the phone with the following friends. Say good-bye and tell them when you will see them.

▶ Christine/lundi
Au revoir, Christine. À lundi.

1. David/dimanche
2. Nicolas/samedi
3. Céline/mercredi
4. Julie/vendredi
5. Thomas/mardi
6. Pierre/jeudi

2. Anniversaire

François and Isabelle are on their way to Nathalie's birthday party. As they are talking, François wants to know when Isabelle's birthday is.

François: C'est quand, ton anniversaire?
Isabelle: C'est le 18 mars!
François: Le 18 mars? Pas possible! — *That's not possible!*
Isabelle: Si! Pourquoi? — *Yes, it is! Why?*
François: C'est aussi mon anniversaire.
Isabelle: Quelle coïncidence! — *What a coincidence!*

Pour communiquer

▶ *How to talk about the date:*

Quelle est la date?	*What's the date?*
C'est le 12 (douze) octobre.	*It's October 12.*
C'est le premier juin.	*It's June first.*

▶ *How to talk about birthdays:*

—C'est quand, ton anniversaire?	*When is your birthday?*
—Mon anniversaire est le 2 (deux) mars.	*My birthday is March 2.*

Les mois de l'année *(Months of the year)*

janvier	**avril**	**juillet**	**octobre**
février	**mai**	**août**	**novembre**
mars	**juin**	**septembre**	**décembre**

La date

To express a date in French, the pattern is:

le	+	NUMBER	+	MONTH
le		**11 (onze)**		**novembre**
le		**20 (vingt)**		**mai**

EXCEPTION: The first of the month is **le premier.**

→ In front of numbers, the French use **le** (and never **l'**): **le onze, le huit.**

→ Note that when dates are abbreviated in French, the day always comes first.

2/8 **le deux août** 1/11 **le premier novembre**

4 Anniversaires

PARLER Ask your classmates when their birthdays are.

5 Quelle est la date?

PARLER Ask what the date is.

▶ **—Quelle est la date?**
—C'est le douze septembre.

6 Dates importantes

PARLER Give the following dates in French.

▶ Noël *(Christmas)*: 25/12 **C'est le vingt-cinq décembre.**

1. le jour de l'An *(New Year's Day)*: 1/1
2. la fête *(holiday)* de Martin Luther King: 15/1
3. la Saint-Valentin: 14/2
4. la Saint-Patrick: 17/3
5. la fête nationale américaine: 4/7
6. la fête nationale française: 14/7
7. la fête de Christophe Colomb: 12/10

Leçon 4

VIDÉO-SCÈNE DVD AUDIO

C Le temps

It is nine o'clock Sunday morning. Cécile and her brother Philippe have planned a picnic for the whole family. Cécile is asking about the weather.

Cécile: Quel temps fait-il?
Philippe: Il fait mauvais!
Cécile: Il fait mauvais?
Philippe: Oui, il fait mauvais! Regarde! Il pleut! — *Look!*
Cécile: Zut, zut et zut!
Philippe: !!!???
Cécile: Et le pique-nique? — *picnic*
Philippe: Le pique-nique? Ah oui, le pique-nique! … Écoute, ça n'a pas d'importance. — *Listen, it doesn't matter. (It's not important.)*
Cécile: Pourquoi? — *Why?*
Philippe: Pourquoi? Parce que Papa va nous inviter au restaurant. — *Because Dad is going to take us out (invite us) to a restaurant.*
Cécile: Super!

@HOMETUTOR
my.hrw.com

Pour communiquer

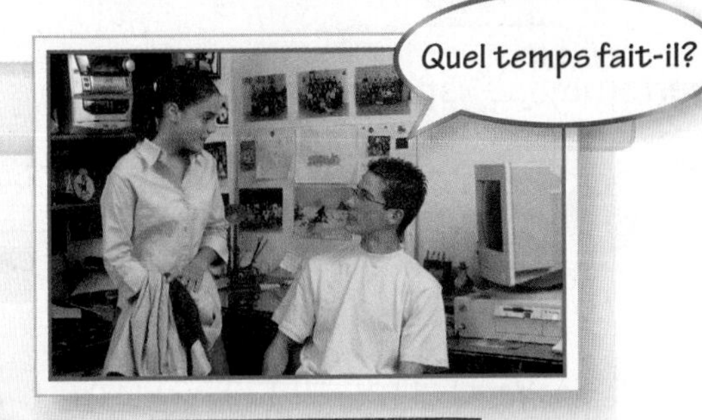

▶ *How to talk about the weather:*

Quel temps fait-il? *How's the weather?*

Il fait beau.

Il fait bon.

Il fait chaud.

Il fait frais.

Il fait froid.

Il fait mauvais.

Il pleut.

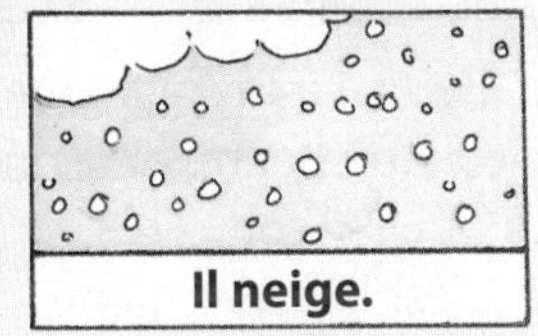
Il neige.

Les saisons *(Seasons)*

le printemps	*spring*	**au printemps**	*in (the) spring*
l'été	*summer*	**en été**	*in (the) summer*
l'automne	*fall, autumn*	**en automne**	*in (the) fall*
l'hiver	*winter*	**en hiver**	*in (the) winter*

1 Ta région

PARLER Say what the weather is like in your part of the country.

▶ en juillet

1. en août
2. en septembre
3. en novembre
4. en janvier
5. en mars
6. en mai

2 Les quatre saisons

PARLER Describe what the weather is like in each of the four seasons in the following cities.

▶ à Miami

1. à Chicago
2. à San Francisco
3. à Denver
4. à Boston
5. à Seattle
6. à Dallas

À votre tour!

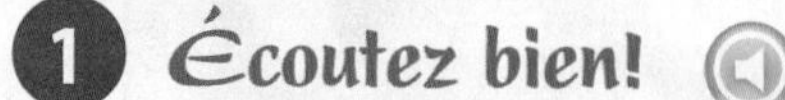

OBJECTIFS

Now you can . . .
- order snacks and beverages in a café
- ask about prices and pay for your food/drink
- tell time and give the date
- talk about the weather

1 Écoutez bien!

ÉCOUTER Isabelle is in a café talking to Jean-Paul. You will hear Isabelle asking questions. For each of Isabelle's questions, select Jean-Paul's response from the suggested answers.

a. Deux euros cinquante.
b. Quatre heures et demie.
c. Oui, j'ai soif.
d. C'est le 3 novembre.
e. Oui, j'ai faim.
f. Il fait beau.

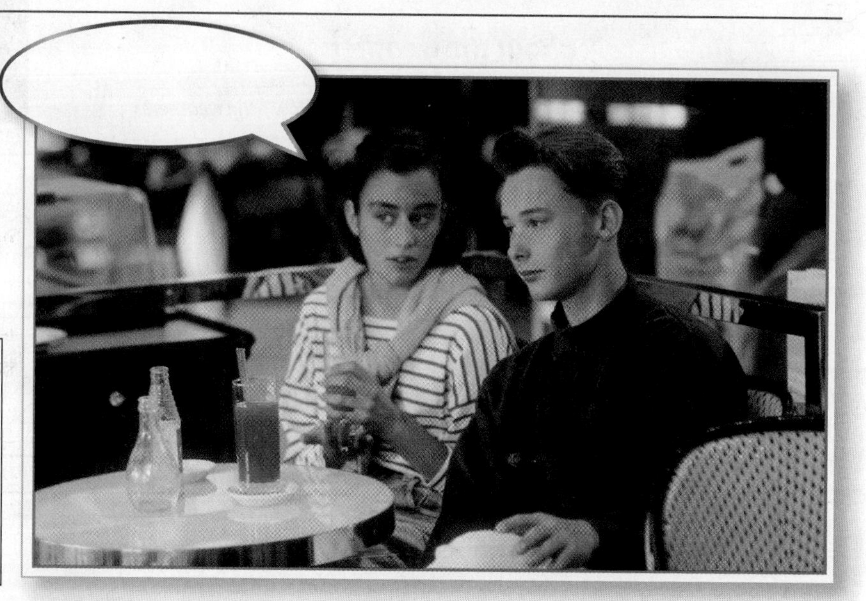

2 Quelle heure est-il?

PARLER Give the times indicated on the following clocks.

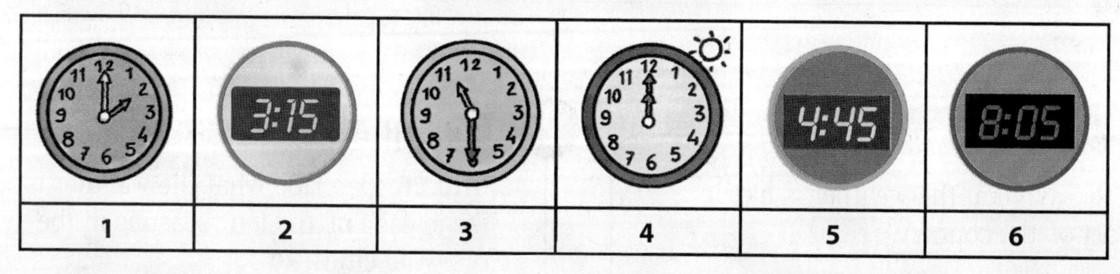

1	2	3	4	5	6

3 Conversation dirigée

ÉCOUTER ET PARLER Stéphanie is in a café called Le Select. The waiter is taking her order. With a partner, compose and act out a dialogue according to the script suggested below.

le garçon		Stéphanie
greets client and asks if he may help her	→ ↙	says that she would like a croissant and asks how much an orange juice costs
answers 2 euros	→ ↙	asks for an orange juice... calls the waiter and asks how much she owes
says 4 euros cinquante	→ ↙	gives waiter 5 euros (Voici...)
says thank you		

4 Au café 

PARLER You are in a French café. Call the waiter/waitress and order the following items. A classmate will play the part of the waiter/waitress.

▶ **—Monsieur (Mademoiselle), s'il vous plaît!**
—Vous désirez?
—Un croissant, s'il vous plaît!
(Donnez-moi un croissant, s'il vous plaît!)
(Je voudrais un croissant, s'il vous plaît!)

5 En scène 

STRATEGY Speaking

Sounding French If you want French people to understand you, the most important thing is to speak with an even rhythm and to stress the last syllable in each group of words. (Try speaking English this way: people will think you have a French accent!)

PARLER With two other classmates, act out the following scene.

CHARACTERS:

You, a French friend, and the waiter in the café

SITUATION:

A French friend has been showing you around Paris. You invite your friend to a café and discover too late that you have not changed enough money. Your friend will respond to your questions.

- Ask your friend if he/she is thirsty.
- Ask if he/she wants a soft drink.
- Ask if he/she is hungry.
- Ask if he/she wants a sandwich.
- When the waiter comes, your friend orders and you ask for a croissant and a cup of hot chocolate.
- Ask the waiter how much everything is.
- Ask your friend to please lend you 20 euros.

6 La date, la saison et le temps

PARLER Look at the calendar days. For each one, give the day and the date, the season, and the weather.

▶ **C'est mardi, le dix avril.**
C'est le printemps.
Il pleut.

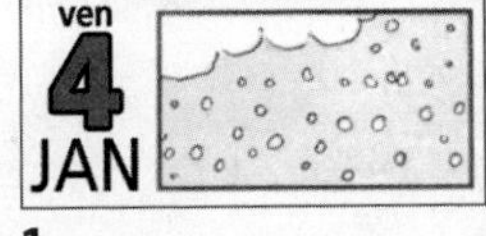

1

2

3

4

5

LESSON REVIEW
my.hrw.com

Les parties du corps

(Parts of the body)

Un jeu: Jacques a dit

The French sometimes play a game called **Jacques a dit** *(Jim said)*. The rules are the same as the English game of *Simon Says*. Everyone stands up to play.

The game leader says: **Jacques a dit: Les mains sur la tête!** placing her hands on her head. The other players also place their hands on their heads.

Then the game leader may say: **Les mains sur le dos!** placing her hands on her back. This time, however, the other players should not move, because the game leader did not first say **Jacques a dit**. Any player that did move must sit down, but may continue playing.

The game continues until only one player is left standing.

Additional readings @ my.hrw.com
FRENCH InterActive Reader

Une chanson: Alouette

ALOUETTE *(The Lark)* is a popular folk song of French-Canadian origin. As the song leader names the various parts of the bird's anatomy, he points to his own body. The chorus repeats the refrain with enthusiasm.

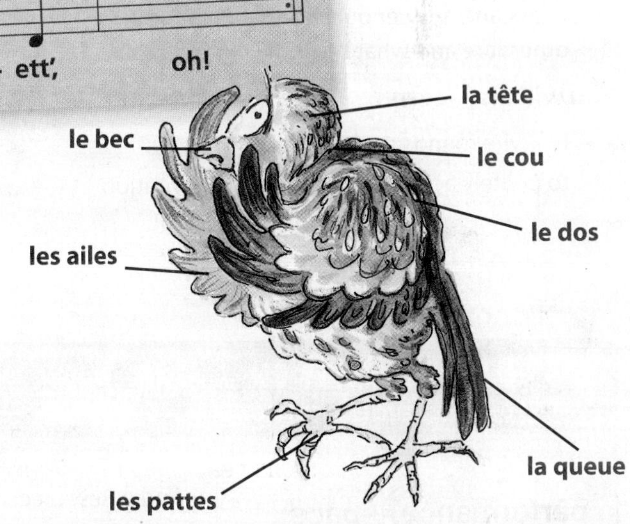

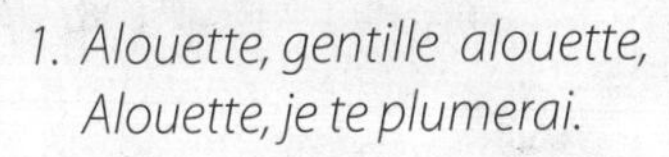

1. *Alouette, gentille alouette,*
   Alouette, je te plumerai.

   Je te plumerai la tête,
   Je te plumerai la tête.

   Et la tête—et la tête
   Alouette—Alouette
   Oh oh oh oh

2. *Alouette, gentille alouette*
   Alouette, je te plumerai.

   Je te plumerai le bec,
   Je te plumerai le bec.

   Et le bec—et le bec
   Et la tête—et la tête
   Alouette—Alouette
   Oh oh oh oh

3. *Je te plumerai le cou ...*
4. *Je te plumerai les ailes ...*
5. *Je te plumerai le dos ...*
6. *Je te plumerai les pattes ...*
7. *Je te plumerai la queue ...*

Communautés: French song

As a class project, you might want to memorize *Alouette* and perform it at a senior center or teach the song to a local grade school class.

Unité 3

Qu'est-ce qu'on fait?

LEÇON 5 **LE FRANÇAIS PRATIQUE:** Mes activités

LEÇON 6 Une invitation

LEÇON 7 Une boum

LEÇON 8 Un concert de musique africaine

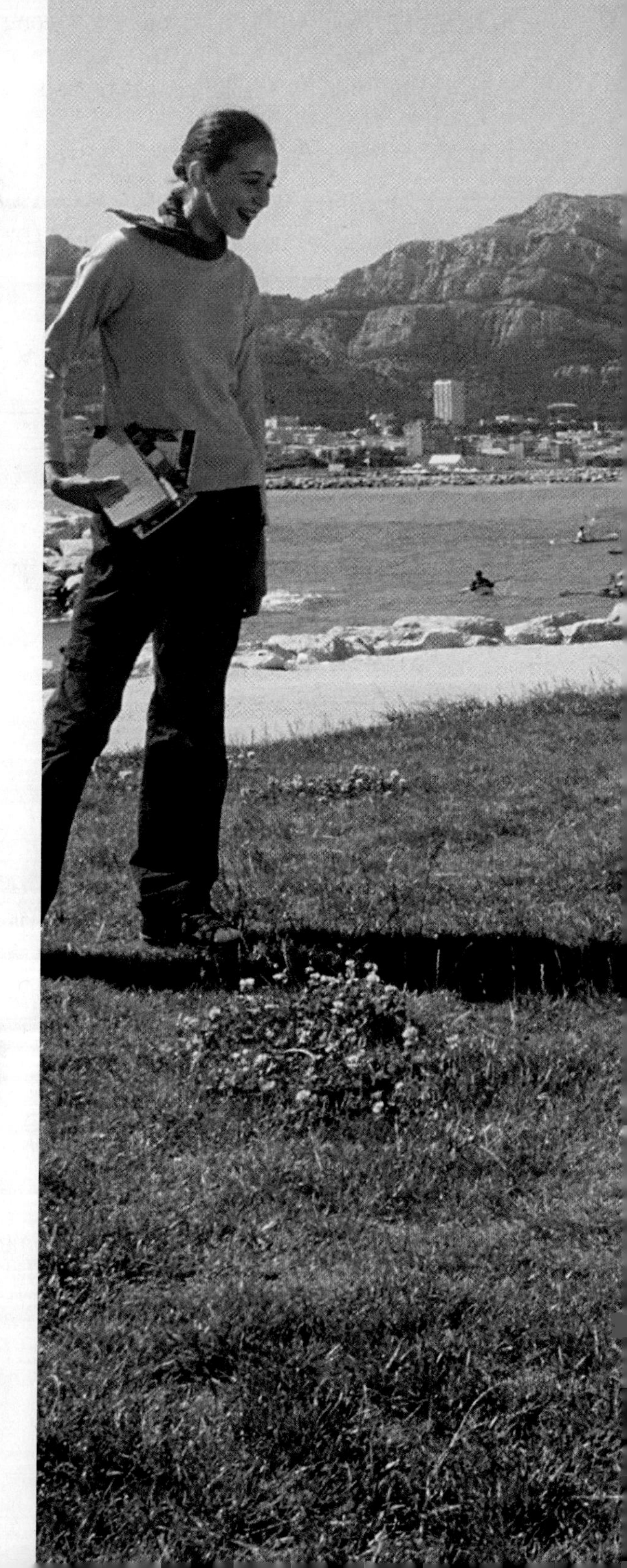

THÈME ET OBJECTIFS

Daily activities

In this unit, you will be talking about the things you do every day, such as working and studying, as well as watching TV or playing sports.

You will learn ...

- to describe some of your daily activities
- to say what you like and do not like to do
- to ask and answer questions about where others are and what they are doing

You will also learn ...

- to invite friends to do things with you
- to politely accept or turn down an invitation

Leçon 5

LE FRANÇAIS PRATIQUE

DVD AUDIO

Mes activités

Accent sur ... Les activités de la semaine

French teenagers spend a great deal of time on their studies since they and their families consider it important to do well in school. They have a longer class day than American students and are given more homework.

However, French teenagers do not study all the time. They also enjoy listening to music, watching TV, and playing computer games. Many participate in various sports activities, but to a lesser extent than American students. On weekends, they like to go out with their friends to shop or see a movie. They also go to parties and love dancing.

Sandrine est à la maison.
Elle écoute de la musique.
Sandrine: J'aime le rock anglais.

Marc, Élodie et David sont au stade. Ils jouent au foot.
Marc: Nous jouons au foot.
Élodie: Nous jouons aussi au basket.
David: Nous aimons les sports.

@HOMETUTOR
my.hrw.com

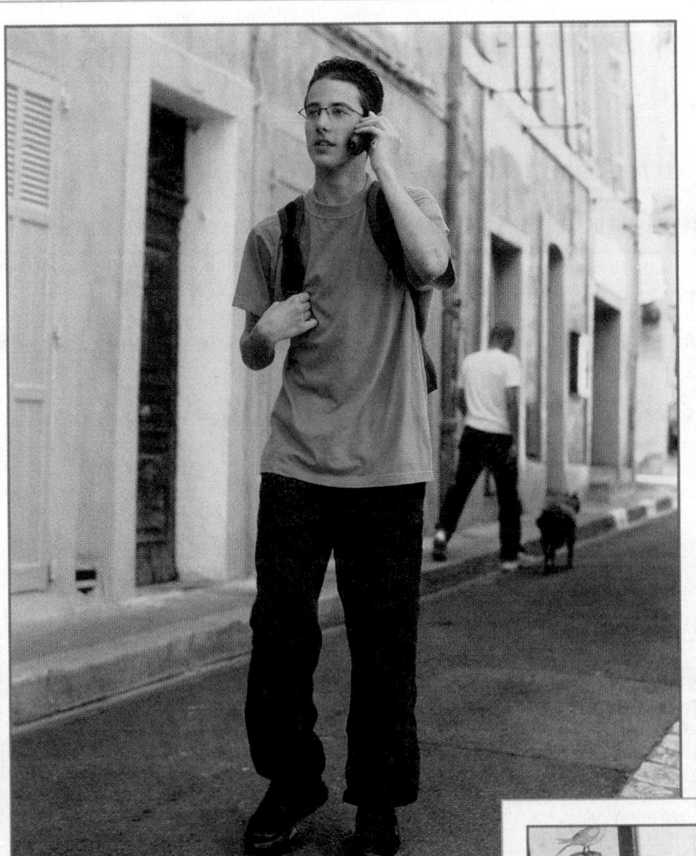

Olivier est en ville. Il téléphone.

Olivier: J'aime téléphoner.
Je téléphone à une copine.

Zaïna joue aux jeux vidéo.

Zaïna: J'aime jouer aux jeux vidéo.
J'aime aussi regarder la télé.

A VOCABULAIRE Préférences 

▶ How to talk about what you like and don't like to do:

Est-ce que tu aimes ...?	*Do you like ...?*	**Est-ce que tu aimes** parler *(to speak)* français?
J'aime ...	*I like ...*	Oui, **j'aime** parler français.
Je n'aime pas ...	*I don't like ...*	Non, **je n'aime pas** parler français.
Je préfère ...	*I prefer ...*	**Je préfère** parler anglais.

téléphoner
to phone

parler français
to talk, speak French

parler anglais
to speak English

parler espagnol
to speak Spanish

manger
to eat

chanter
to sing

danser
to dance

nager
to swim

1 Et toi?

PARLER/ÉCRIRE Indicate what you like to do in the following situations by completing each sentence with two of the suggested activities.

1. En classe, j'aime ... mais je préfère ...
   étudier • écouter le professeur • parler avec *(with)* **un copain • parler avec une copine**
2. En été, j'aime ... mais je préfère ...
   travailler • nager • voyager • jouer au volley *(volleyball)*

@HOMETUTOR
my.hrw.com

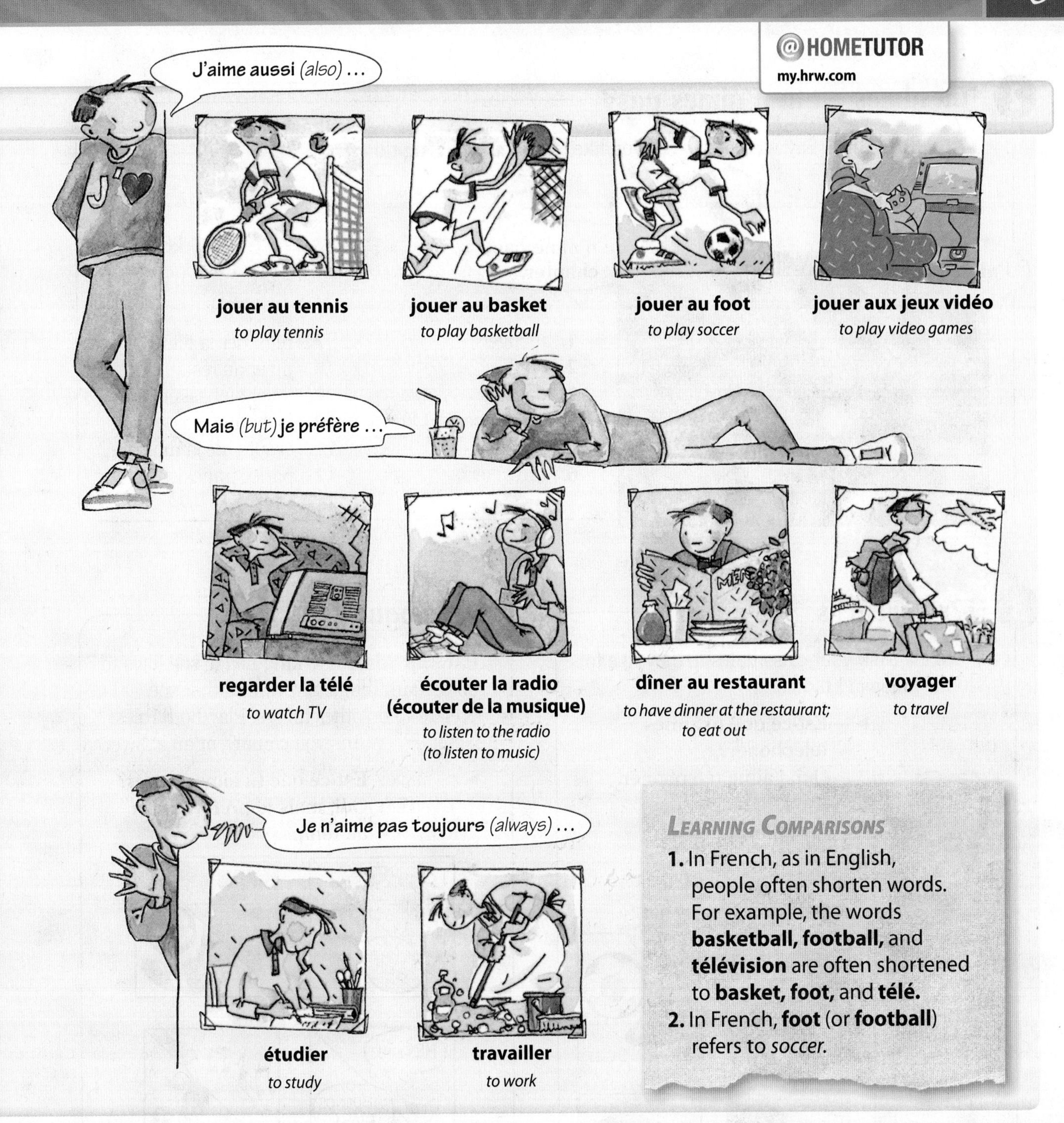

jouer au tennis
to play tennis

jouer au basket
to play basketball

jouer au foot
to play soccer

jouer aux jeux vidéo
to play video games

regarder la télé
to watch TV

écouter la radio (écouter de la musique)
to listen to the radio (to listen to music)

dîner au restaurant
to have dinner at the restaurant; to eat out

voyager
to travel

étudier
to study

travailler
to work

Learning Comparisons

1. In French, as in English, people often shorten words. For example, the words **basketball, football,** and **télévision** are often shortened to **basket, foot,** and **télé.**
2. In French, **foot** (or **football**) refers to *soccer.*

3. Avec mes *(my)* copains, j'aime ... mais je préfère ...
   chanter • manger • écouter de la musique • jouer au basket
4. Avec ma famille, j'aime ... mais je préfère ...
   voyager • regarder la télé • jouer aux jeux vidéo • dîner au restaurant
5. À la maison *(At home)*, j'aime ... mais je préfère ...
   étudier • téléphoner • manger • écouter de la musique

2 Tu aimes ou tu n'aimes pas?

PARLER/ÉCRIRE Say whether or not you like to do the following things.

▶ chanter?

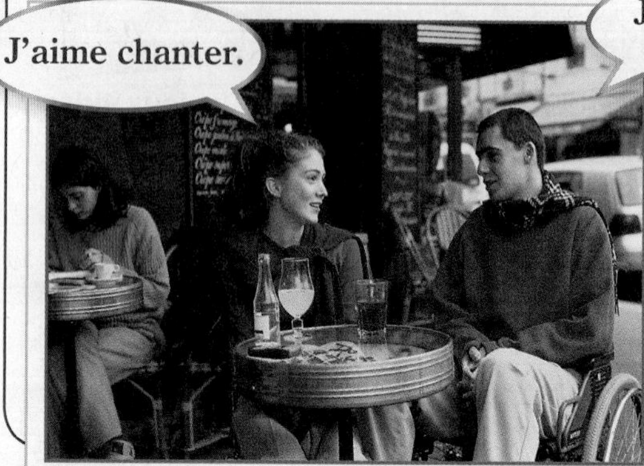

1. manger?
2. étudier?
3. danser?
4. téléphoner?
5. voyager?
6. travailler?
7. regarder la télé?
8. dîner au restaurant?
9. jouer au basket?
10. jouer aux jeux vidéo?
11. écouter de la musique?
12. parler français?

3 Préférences 

PARLER Ask your classmates if they like to do the following things.

▶ **—Est-ce que tu aimes téléphoner?**
—Oui, j'aime téléphoner. (Non, je n'aime pas téléphoner.)

1

2

3

4

5

6

7

8

9

4 Dialogue 

PARLER Marc is asking Léa if she likes to do certain things. She replies that she prefers to do other things. Play both roles. Note: "??" means you can invent an answer.

▶ MARC: **Est-ce que tu aimes nager?**
LÉA: **Oui, mais je préfère jouer au tennis.**

▶ 

1

2

3

4

5

@HOMETUTOR
my.hrw.com

B VOCABULAIRE Souhaits *(Wishes)*

▶ ***How to talk about what you want, would like, and do not want to do:***

Je veux ...	*I want ...*	**Je veux** parler français.
Je voudrais ...	*I would like ...*	**Je voudrais** voyager en France.
Je ne veux pas ...	*I don't want ...*	**Je ne veux pas** étudier aujourd'hui.

5 Ce soir *(Tonight)*

PARLER/ÉCRIRE Say whether or not you want to do the following things tonight.

▶ étudier?
Oui, je veux étudier.
(Non, je ne veux pas étudier.)

1. parler français?
2. travailler?
3. jouer aux jeux vidéo?
4. chanter?
5. danser?
6. regarder la télé?
7. écouter de la musique?
8. dîner avec une copine?
9. manger une pizza?
10. téléphoner à mon cousin?

6 Week-end

PARLER/ÉCRIRE Léa and her friends are discussing their weekend plans. What do they say they would like to do?

▶ **LÉA: Je voudrais jouer au tennis.**

▶ Léa

1. Jérôme

2. Monique

3. Jean-Louis

4. Caroline

5. Patrick

7 Trois souhaits *(Three wishes)*

ÉCRIRE Read the list of suggested activities and select the three that you would like to do most.

parler français	voyager avec ma cousine
parler espagnol	voyager en France
parler avec *(with)* Oprah Winfrey	chanter comme *(like)* Britney Spears
dîner avec le Président	jouer au tennis comme Venus Williams
dîner avec Matt Damon	jouer au basket comme Shaquille O'Neal

▶ **Je voudrais parler espagnol.**
Je voudrais chanter comme Britney Spears.
Je voudrais voyager en France.

Est-ce que tu veux jouer au tennis?

C VOCABULAIRE Invitations

▶ How to invite a friend:

Est-ce que tu veux ...?	*Do you want to ...?*	**Est-ce que tu veux** jouer au tennis?
Est-ce que tu peux ...?	*Can you ...?*	**Est-ce que tu peux** parler à mon copain?
avec moi/toi	*with me/you*	Est-ce que tu veux dîner **avec moi?**

▶ How to accept an invitation:

Oui, bien sûr ...	*Yes, of course ...*	
Oui, merci ...	*Yes, thanks ...*	
Oui, d'accord ...	*Yes, all right, okay ...*	
je veux bien.	*I'd love to.*	**Oui, bien sûr, je veux bien.**
je veux bien ...	*I'd love to ...*	**Oui, merci, je veux bien** dîner avec toi.

▶ How to turn down an invitation:

Je regrette, mais je ne peux pas ...	*I'm sorry, but I can't ...*	**Je regrette, mais je ne peux pas** dîner avec toi.
Je dois ...	*I have to, I must ...*	**Je dois** étudier.

8 Oui, d'accord 

PARLER Invite the following French students (played by your classmates) to do things with you. They will accept.

▶ Monique / dîner

1. Thomas / parler français
2. Simon / étudier
3. Céline / jouer au tennis
4. Anne / manger une pizza
5. Jean-Claude / chanter
6. Caroline / danser

9 Conversation 

PARLER Ask your classmates if they want to do the following things. They will answer that they cannot and explain why.

▶ jouer au basket? (étudier)
— **Est-ce que tu veux jouer au basket?**
— **Non, je ne peux pas. Je dois étudier.**

1. jouer aux jeux vidéo? (travailler)
2. jouer au ping-pong? (téléphoner à ma cousine)
3. étudier avec moi? (étudier avec ma copine)
4. dîner avec moi? (dîner avec ma famille)
5. nager? (jouer au foot à deux heures)

NOTE *Culturelle*

Le téléphone

French teenagers, like their American counterparts, love to talk with their friends on the phone. At home, they can use the family phone, but now more and more young people also have a cell phone which is called **un téléphone portable** or simply un **portable** for short. (**Portable** comes from the French verb **porter**, which means *to carry.*)

Europeans have been ahead of Americans in the use of mobile phones. In France, for instance, over half of the people own a cell phone. This proportion is higher with teenagers and college students. Text messaging is also popular. In France, it is illegal to make cell phone calls while driving a car. Moreover, students are not allowed to bring cell phones to class. It is also considered impolite to use them in restaurants, cinemas, and concert halls.

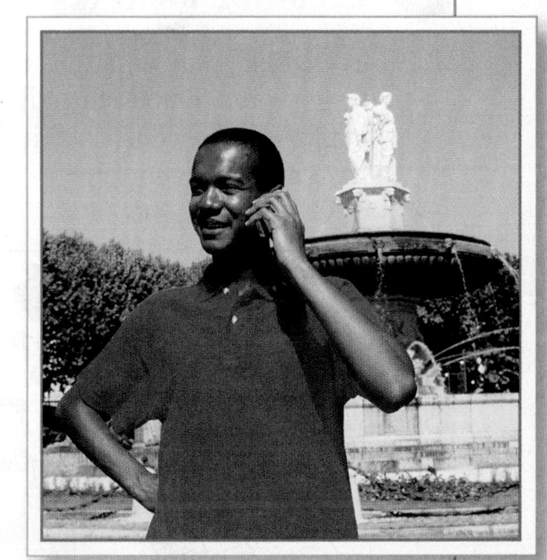

COMPARAISONS *Culturelles*

Compare the French and American attitudes toward the use of cell phones.

How do you feel about people using cell phones in the following circumstances? Indicate whether you think it is appropriate or not by saying: **C'est acceptable.** or **Ce n'est pas acceptable.**

- au café
- au cinéma
- au restaurant
- pendant (*during*) la classe de français
- pendant un concert de rock
- en conduisant (*while driving*)

L'étiquette téléphonique

- to introduce yourself when phoning a friend, you say:

  Allô … Ici Thomas. Bonjour. Ça va?
- if your friend is not home and if a parent answers, you say:

  Allô … Ici Thomas Rémi. Bonjour, monsieur (madame).

  Est-ce que je pourrais *(May I)* parler à Mélanie?
- if you would like to leave a message, you ask:

  Est-ce que je peux *(Can I)* laisser un message?
- before hanging up, you say:

  Merci, monsieur (madame). Au revoir.

10 Allô!

PARLER Céline is phoning Trinh to ask him if he wants to go to a movie. Trinh's mother says that he is not home. Céline asks her to take a message. Act out the conversation between Céline and Trinh's mother.

À votre tour!

OBJECTIFS

Now you can . . .
- talk about activities you like and do not like
- extend and accept invitations
- give an excuse when you cannot accept

Digital performance space

1 Écoutez bien!

ÉCOUTER You will hear French young people telling you what they like to do. Listen carefully to each activity. If it is illustrated in the picture on the left, mark A. If it is illustrated in the picture on the right, mark B.

A

B

	A	B
1.		
2.		
3.		
4.		
5.		
6.		

2 Communication

ÉCOUTER You have invited a French friend to spend the weekend at your house. Ask your friend ...

- if he/she likes to watch TV
- if he/she wants to play video games
- if he/she likes to listen to the radio
- if he/she wants to eat a pizza

A classmate will play the role of your French friend and answer your questions.

3 Conversation dirigée

PARLER Trinh is phoning Céline. Write out their conversation according to the directions. You may want to act out the dialogue with a classmate.

Trinh		Céline
asks Céline how she is	→ ←	answers that she is fine
asks her if she wants to eat out	→ ←	asks at what time
says at 8 o'clock	→ ←	says that she is sorry but that she has to study
says it is too bad **(Dommage!)**		

4 Créa-dialogue 

Est-ce que tu veux jouer au tennis avec moi?

Non, je ne peux pas. Je dois travailler.

PARLER Ask your classmates if they want to do the following things with you. They will answer that they cannot and will give one of the excuses below.

▶ jouer au tennis

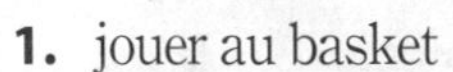

1. jouer au basket
2. manger une pizza
3. regarder la télé
4. jouer au ping-pong
5. dîner au restaurant
6. jouer aux jeux vidéo

EXCUSES:

téléphoner à une copine
étudier
travailler
parler avec ma mère
dîner avec ma cousine
chanter avec la chorale *(choir)*

5 Expression personnelle

PARLER/ÉCRIRE What we like to do often depends on the circumstances. Complete the sentences below saying what you like and don't like to do in the following situations.

▶ En hiver ...

En hiver, j'aime regarder la télé.
J'aime aussi jouer au basket.
Je n'aime pas nager.

1. En été ...
2. En automne ...
3. Le samedi *(On Saturdays)*...
4. Le dimanche ...
5. Le soir *(In the evening)*...
6. En classe ...
7. Avec mes *(my)* amis ...
8. Avec ma famille ...

6 Correspondance 

ÉCRIRE This summer you are going to spend two weeks in France. Your e-mail correspondent Vincent has written asking what you like and don't like to do on vacation **(en vacances).** Respond with a short e-mail, answering his questions.

STRATEGY Writing

1. Make a list of activities you like and do not like. Use only vocabulary that you know.

2. Write your e-mail. *Cher Vincent,*
   En vacances, j'aime ...
3. Read over your letter to be sure you have used the right verb forms.

Une invitation

DVD AUDIO

It is Wednesday afternoon. Antoine is looking for his friends but cannot find anyone. Finally he sees Céline at the Café Le Bercy and asks her where everyone is.

Antoine:	Où est Léa?	*Where*
Céline:	Elle est à la maison.	*at home*
Antoine:	Et Mathieu? Il est là?	*here*
Céline:	Non, il n'est pas là.	
Antoine:	Où est-il?	
Céline:	Il est en ville avec une copine.	*in town*
Antoine:	Et Julie et Stéphanie? Est-ce qu'elles sont ici?	*here*
Céline:	Non, elles sont au restaurant.	
Antoine:	Alors, qui est là?	*So*
Céline:	Moi, je suis ici.	
Antoine:	C'est vrai, tu es ici! Eh bien, puisque tu es là, je t'invite au cinéma. D'accord?	*true / since* *I'll invite you to the movies.*
Céline:	Super! Antoine, tu es un vrai copain!	*real*

Compréhension

Indicate where the following people are by selecting the appropriate completions.

1. Léa est …
2. Mathieu est …
3. Julie et Stéphanie sont …
4. Antoine et Céline sont …

en ville
au café
à la maison
au restaurant

NOTE *Culturelle*

Le mercredi après-midi

French middle school students do not usually have classes on Wednesday afternoons. Some young people use this free time to go out with their friends or to catch up on their homework. For other students, Wednesday afternoon is also the time for music and dance lessons as well as sports activities. Many students play soccer with their school team or with their local sports club. Other popular activities include tennis, skateboarding, and in-line skating.

COMPARAISONS *Culturelles*

- How does the school week in France compare to the school week in the United States?
- Do you see any differences in the ways French and American teenagers spend their free time? Explain.
- Do American and French teenagers like the same sports? Explain.

A Le verbe *être* et les pronoms sujets

Être *(to be)* is the most frequently used verb in French. Note the forms of **être** in the chart below.

	être	to be	
SINGULAR	je **suis**	*I am*	Je **suis** américain.
	tu **es**	*you are*	Tu **es** canadienne.
	il/elle **est**	*he/she is*	Il **est** anglais.
PLURAL	nous **sommes**	*we are*	Nous **sommes** à Paris.
	vous **êtes**	*you are*	Vous **êtes** à Dallas.
	ils/elles **sont**	*they are*	Ils **sont** à Genève.

→ Note the liaison in the **vous** form:

Vous êtes français?

→ Note the expression **être d'accord** (*to agree*):

—Tu **es d'accord** avec moi? *Do you agree with me?*

—Oui, je **suis d'accord!** *Yes, I agree!*

LEARNING ABOUT LANGUAGE

- The words **je** (*I*), **tu** (*you*), **il** (*he*), **elle** (*she*), etc. are called SUBJECT PRONOUNS.
  - SINGULAR pronouns refer to one person (or object).
  - PLURAL pronouns refer to two or more people (or objects).
- The verb **être** *(to be)* is IRREGULAR because its forms do not follow a predictable pattern.
- A chart showing the subject pronouns and their corresponding verb forms is called a CONJUGATION.

TU OR VOUS?

When talking to ONE person, the French have two ways of saying *you*:

- **tu** ("familiar *you*") is used to talk to someone your own age (or younger) or to a member of your family
- **vous** ("formal *you*") is used when talking to anyone else

When talking to TWO or more people, the French use **vous.**

RAPPEL

You should use ...

- **vous** to address your teacher
- **tu** to address a classmate

@HOMETUTOR
my.hrw.com

ILS OR ELLES?

The French have two ways of saying *they:*

- **ils** refers to two or more males or to a mixed group of males and females
- **elles** refers to two or more females

1 En France

PARLER/ÉCRIRE The following students are on vacation in France. Which cities are they in?

▶ Sophie … à Nice. **Sophie est à Nice.**

1. Antoine … à Tours.
2. Nous … à Toulouse.
3. Vous … à Marseille.
4. Je … à Strasbourg.
5. Julie et Marie … à Lille.
6. Éric et Vincent … à Lyon.
7. Ma cousine … à Paris.
8. Tu … à Bordeaux.

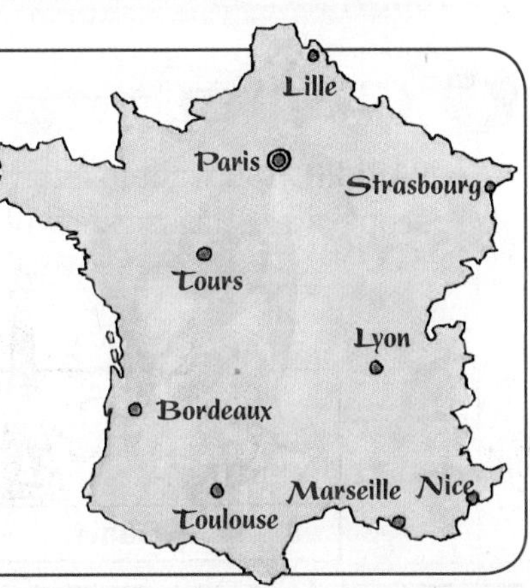

VOCABULAIRE Où?

Où est Cécile? *Where is Cécile?*

Elle est …

ici *(here)*	**là** *(here, there)*	**là-bas** *(over there)*
à Paris *(in Paris)*	**à** Boston	**à** Québec
en classe *(in class)*	**en ville** *(in town)*	
en vacances *(on vacation)*	**en** France *(in France)*	
au café *(at the café)*	**au restaurant**	**au cinéma** *(at the movies)*
à la maison *(at home)*		

2 À Tours

PARLER/ÉCRIRE You are spending your summer vacation in Tours at the home of your friend Léa. Ask the following people questions using **Tu es** or **Vous êtes** as appropriate.

▶ *(the mailman)* … français? **Vous êtes français?**

1. *(Léa's mother)* … de Tours?
2. *(Léa's best friend)* … française?
3. *(Léa's brother)* … en vacances?
4. *(a lady in the park)* … française?
5. *(Léa's cousin)* … de Paris?
6. *(a little girl)* … avec ta mère?
7. *(Léa's teacher)* … strict?
8. *(a tourist)* … américain?

3 Où sont-ils?

PARLER Corinne is wondering if some of the people she knows are in certain places. Tell her she is right, using **il, elle, ils,** or **elles** in your answers.

▶ Ta cousine est à Chicago? **Oui, elle est à Chicago.**

1. Stéphanie est à Lyon?
2. Monsieur Thomas est à San Francisco?
3. Léa et Céline sont à la maison?
4. Cécile et Charlotte sont au café?
5. Ta soeur est en ville?
6. Ton cousin est en vacances?
7. Claire, Alice et Éric sont au cinéma?
8. Monsieur et Madame Joli sont à Montréal?

4 Où?

PARLER You want to know where certain people are. A classmate will answer you.

▶ —**Où est Céline?**
—**Elle est à New York.**

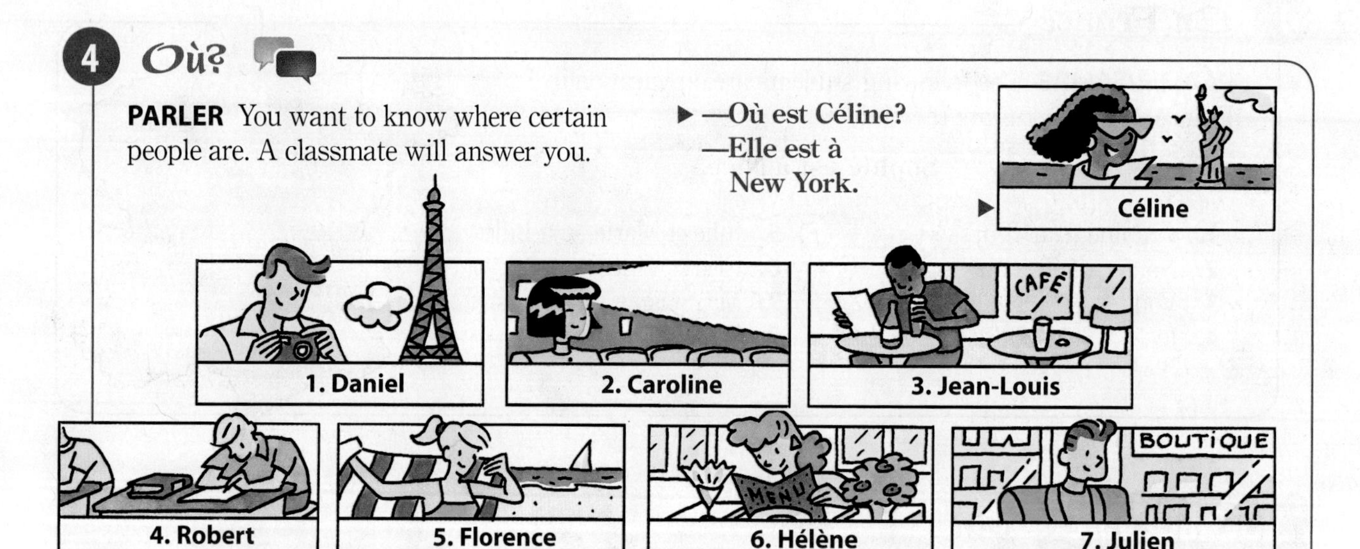

B Les questions à réponse affirmative ou négative

The sentences on the left are statements. The sentences on the right are questions. These questions are called YES / NO QUESTIONS because they can be answered by *yes* or *no*. Note how the French questions begin with **est-ce que.**

STATEMENTS	YES/NO QUESTIONS	
Stéphanie est ici.	**Est-ce que** Stéphanie est ici?	*Is Stéphanie here?*
Tu es français.	**Est-ce que** tu es français?	*Are you French?*
Paul et Marc sont au café.	**Est-ce qu'**ils sont au café?	*Are they at the café?*
Tu veux jouer au foot.	**Est-ce que** tu veux jouer au foot?	*Do you want to play soccer?*

Yes/no questions can be formed according to the pattern:

est-ce que + STATEMENT?	**Est-ce que** Pierre est ici?
est-ce qu' (+ VOWEL SOUND)	**Est-ce qu'**il est en ville?

@HOMETUTOR
my.hrw.com

→ In yes/no questions, the voice goes up at the end of the sentence.

Est-ce que Paul et Florence sont au café?

→ In casual conversation, yes/no questions can be formed without **est-ce que** simply by letting your voice rise at the end of the sentence.

Tu es français? Cécile est en ville?

Observation When you expect someone to agree with you, another way to form a yes/no question is to add the tag **n'est-ce pas** at the end of the sentence.

Tu es américain, **n'est-ce pas?**	*You are American,* ***aren't you?***
Tu aimes parler français, **n'est-ce pas?**	*You like to speak French,* ***don't you?***
Vous êtes d'accord, **n'est-ce pas?**	*You agree,* ***don't you?***

5 Nationalités

PARLER/ÉCRIRE You are attending an international music camp. Ask about other people's nationalities.

▶ Marc/canadien? **Est-ce que Marc est canadien?**

1. Jim / américain?
2. Luisa / mexicaine?
3. Paul et Philippe / français?
4. tu / canadien?
5. vous / anglais?
6. Anne / française?
7. Ellen et Carol / américaines?

VOCABULAIRE Expressions pour la conversation

How to answer a yes/no question:

Oui!	*Yes!*	**Peut-être ...**	*Maybe...*	**Non!**	*No!*
Mais oui!	*Sure!*			**Mais non!**	*Of course not!*
Bien sûr!	*Of course!*				

6 Conversation 

PARLER Ask your classmates the following questions. They will answer, using an expression from **Expressions pour la conversation.**

▶ Ton cousin est français?

1. Ta mère est à la maison?
2. Ta cousine est en France?
3. Ton copain est en classe?
4. Tu veux manger une pizza avec moi?
5. Tu veux jouer aux jeux vidéo avec moi?

ne pas être d'accord
je ne suis pas d'accord.
je suis d'accord

C La négation

Compare the affirmative and negative sentences below:

AFFIRMATIVE	NEGATIVE	
Je **suis** américain.	Je **ne suis pas** français.	***I'm not** French.*
Nous **sommes** en classe.	Nous **ne sommes pas** en vacances.	*We **are not** on vacation.*
Claire **est** là-bas.	Elle **n'est pas** ici.	*She **is not** here.*
Tu **es** d'accord avec moi.	Tu **n'es pas** d'accord avec Marc.	*You **do not** agree with Marc.*

Negative sentences are formed as follows:

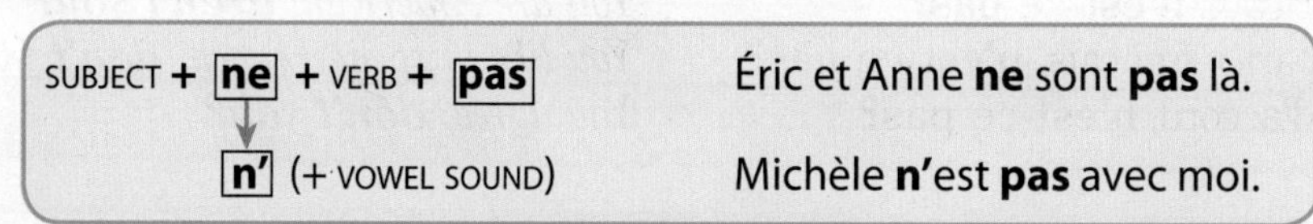

7 Non!

PARLER Answer the following questions negatively.

▶ **—Est-ce que tu es français (française)?**
— Non, je ne suis pas français (française).

1. Est-ce que tu es canadien (canadienne)?
2. Est-ce que tu es à Québec?
3. Est-ce que tu es à la maison?
4. Est-ce que tu es au café?
5. Est-ce que tu es en vacances?
6. Est-ce que tu es au cinéma?

8 D'accord

PARLER It is raining. François suggests to his friends that they go to the movies. Say who agrees and who does not, using the expression **être d'accord.**

▶ Philippe

▶ Hélène

1. ☺ nous
2. ☺ je
3. ☹ tu
4. ☹ vous
5. ☺ Patrick et Marc
6. ☹ Claire et Stéphanie
7. ☺ ma copine
8. ☹ mon frère

@HOMETUTOR
my.hrw.com

VOCABULAIRE Mots utiles *(Useful words)*

à	*at*	Je suis **à** la maison **à** dix heures.
	in	Nous sommes **à** Paris.
de	*from*	Vous êtes **de** San Francisco.
	of	Voici une photo **de** Paris.
et	*and*	Anne **et** Sophie sont en vacances.
ou	*or*	Qui est-ce? Juliette **ou** Sophie?
avec	*with*	Philippe est **avec** Pauline.
pour	*for*	Je veux travailler **pour** Monsieur Martin.
mais	*but*	Je ne suis pas français, **mais** j'aime parler français.

➔ **De** becomes **d'** before a vowel sound:
Patrick est **de** Lyon. François est **d'**Annecy.

9 Le mot juste *(The right word)*

PARLER/ÉCRIRE Complete each sentence with the word in parentheses that fits logically.

1. Monsieur Moreau est en France. Aujourd'hui, il est … Lyon. (à/de)
2. Martine est canadienne. Elle est … Montréal. (de/et)
3. Florence n'est pas ici. Elle est … Jean-Claude. (et/avec)
4. Léa … Paul sont en ville. (avec/et)
5. Jean-Pierre n'est pas à la maison. Il est au café … au cinéma. (ou/et)
6. J'aime jouer au tennis … je ne veux pas jouer avec toi. (ou/mais)
7. Je travaille … mon père. (pour/à)

10 Être ou ne pas être

PARLER/ÉCRIRE We cannot be in different places at the same time. Express this according to the model.

▶ Aline est en ville. (ici)
Aline n'est pas ici.

1. Frédéric est là-bas. (à la maison)
2. Nous sommes en classe. (au restaurant)
3. Tu es à Nice. (à Tours)
4. Vous êtes au café. (au cinéma)
5. Jean est avec Sylvie. (avec Julie)
6. Juliette et Sophie sont avec Éric. (avec Marc)

Prononciation  /a/

La voyelle /a/

The letter "**a**" alone always represents the sound /a/ as in the English word *ah*. It never has the sound of "*a*" as in English words like *class*, *date*, or *cinema*.

Répétez: **chat ça va à la là-bas avec ami voilà**
classe café salade dame date Madame Canada
Anne est au Canada avec Madame Laval.

chat

À votre tour!

OBJECTIFS

Now you can . . .
- say where people are
- ask and answer simple yes/no questions

1 Allô

PARLER Jacques is phoning some friends. Match his questions on the left with his friends' answers on the right.

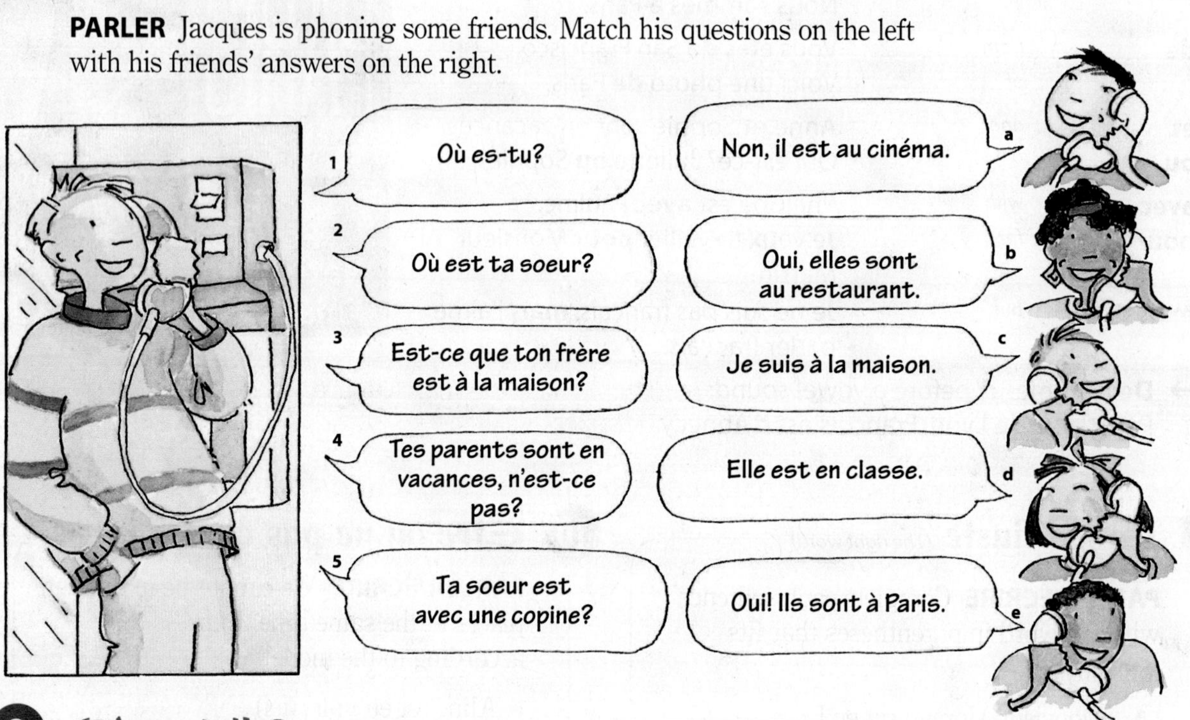

2 Où sont-ils?

LIRE Read what the following people are saying and decide where they are.

▶ Anne et Éric sont au café.

▶ Anne et Éric — 1. nous — 2. les touristes

3. vous — 4. tu — 5. Valérie

3 Créa-dialogue 

PARLER You are working for a student magazine in France. Your assignment is to interview tourists who are visiting Paris. Ask them where they are from. (Make sure to address the people appropriately as **tu** or **vous.**) Remember: The symbol "??" means you may invent your own responses.

	Nationalité	Villes *(Cities)*
▶	anglaise	Londres? *(London)* Liverpool

▶ **—Bonjour. Vous êtes anglaise?**
—Oui, je suis anglaise.
—Est-ce que vous êtes de Londres?
—Mais non, je ne suis pas de Londres. Je suis de Liverpool.

	Nationalité	Villes
1	américaine	New York? Washington
2	canadien	Québec? Montréal
3	française	Paris? Nice
4	mexicain	Mexico? Puebla
5	??	?? ??
6	??	?? ??

4 Composition: Personnellement 

ÉCRIRE On a separate piece of paper, or on a computer, write where you are and where you are not at each of the following times. Use only words you know.

▶ à 9 heures du matin

- à 4 heures
- à 7 heures du soir
- samedi
- dimanche
- en juillet

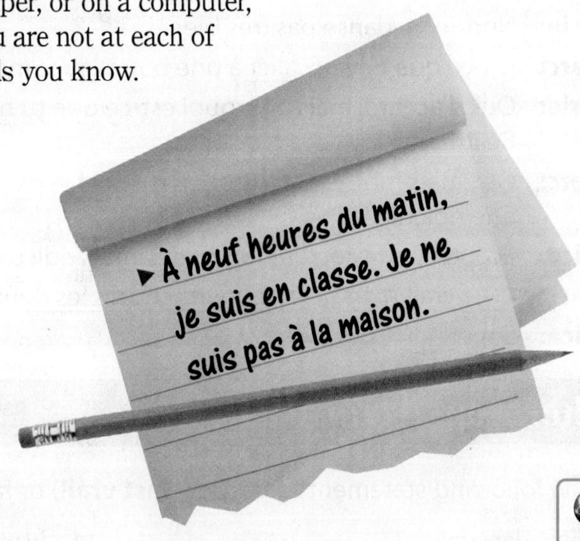

LESSON REVIEW
my.hrw.com

Leçon 7

Conversation et Culture

Une boum

AUDIO

Jean-Marc has been invited to a party. He is trying to decide whether to bring Béatrice or Valérie.

Jean-Marc:	Dis, Béatrice, tu aimes danser?	*Hey*
Béatrice:	Oui, j'adore danser. Je danse très, très bien.	*very well*
Jean-Marc:	Et toi, Valérie, tu danses bien?	
Valérie:	Non, je ne danse pas très bien.	
Jean-Marc:	Est-ce que tu veux aller à une boum avec moi samedi?	*to go*
Valérie:	Oui, d'accord, mais pourquoi est-ce que tu n'invites pas Béatrice? Elle adore danser …	*why*
Jean-Marc:	Oui, mais moi, je ne sais pas danser et je ne veux pas être ridicule …	*don't know how* / *ridiculous*
Béatrice:	Écoute. Entre copains, on n'est jamais ridicule.	*Among / one is never*
Jean-Marc:	C'est vrai! Alors, je vous invite toutes les deux!	*Then / invite both of you*
Béatrice:	Super!	

Compréhension: Vrai ou faux?

Say whether the following statements are true **(C'est vrai!)** or false **(C'est faux!).**

1. Béatrice aime danser.
2. Elle danse bien.
3. Valérie danse très bien.
4. Jean-Marc adore danser.
5. Jean-Marc ne veut pas être ridicule.
6. Jean-Marc invite Béatrice et Valérie.

@HOMETUTOR
my.hrw.com

NOTE Culturelle

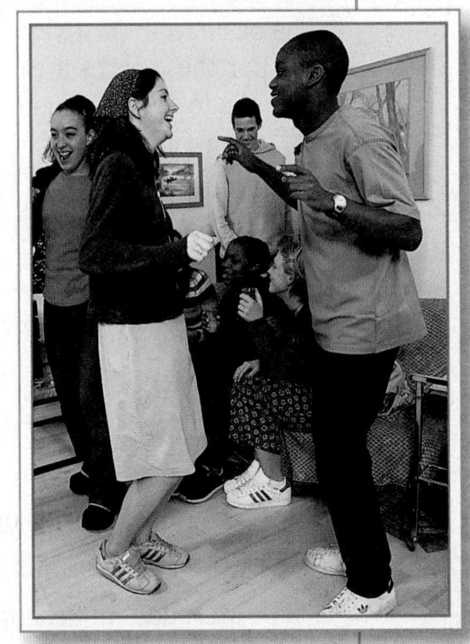

Une boum

On weekends, French teenagers like to go to parties that are organized at a friend's home. These informal parties have different names according to the age group of the participants. For students at a **collège** (middle school), a party is sometimes known as **une boum** or **une fête**. For older students at a **lycée** (high school), it is called **une soirée**.

At a **boum**, parents are usually around to help out and set up a buffet which often features items contributed by the guests. Pizza and chips are very popular. There may also be homemade sandwiches or Chinese food. Preferred beverages are sodas and mineral waters.

Most of the young people like to dance and listen to their favorite music. Some may get drawn into the latest video games. Others simply enjoy getting together to talk about the week's events. For everyone, it is a way to spend a relaxing evening with friends.

COMPARAISONS Culturelles

How do French parties compare to parties that you and your friends organize? Explain.

A Les verbes en *-er:* le singulier

The basic form of a verb is called the infinitive. Many French infinitives end in **-er.** Most of these verbs are conjugated like **parler** *(to speak)* and **habiter** *(to live)*. Note the forms of the present tense of these verbs in the singular. Pay attention to their endings.

INFINITIVE	parler	habiter	ENDINGS
STEM	**parl-**	**habit-**	
PRESENT TENSE (SINGULAR)	Je **parle** français. Tu **parles** anglais. Il/Elle **parle** espagnol.	J' **habite** à Paris. Tu **habites** à Boston. Il/Elle **habite** à Madrid.	**-e** **-es** **-e**

The present tense forms of **-er** verbs consist of two parts:

STEM + ENDING

- The STEM does not change. It is the infinitive minus **-er:**

  parler **parl-** **habiter** **habit-**

- The ENDINGS change with the subject:

  je → **-e** **tu** → **-es** **il/elle** → **-e**

→ The above endings are silent.
→ **Je** becomes **j'** before a vowel sound.
je parle **j'**habite

LEARNING ABOUT LANGUAGE

Verbs conjugated like **parler** and **habiter** follow a *predictable pattern.*

They are called REGULAR VERBS.

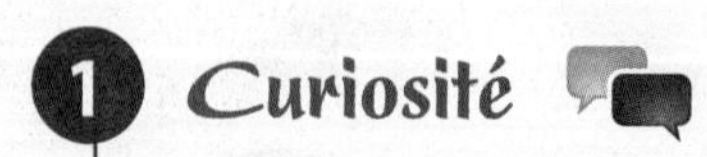

1 Curiosité

PARLER At the party, Olivier wants to learn more about Isabelle. She answers his questions affirmatively. Play both roles.

▶ parler anglais?

1. parler espagnol?
2. habiter à Paris?
3. danser bien?
4. jouer aux jeux vidéo?
5. jouer au basket?
6. chanter?
7. téléphoner à ton copain?
8. travailler en été?

@HOMETUTOR
my.hrw.com

VOCABULAIRE Les verbes en *-er*

▶ *Verbs you already know:*

chanter	*to sing*	**nager**	*to swim*
danser	*to dance*	**parler**	*to speak, talk*
dîner	*to have dinner*	**regarder**	*to watch, look at*
écouter	*to listen (to)*	**téléphoner (à)**	*to phone, call*
étudier	*to study*	**travailler**	*to work*
jouer	*to play*	**voyager**	*to travel*
manger	*to eat*		

▶ *New verbs:*

aimer	*to like*	Tu **aimes** Paris?
habiter (à)	*to live (in + city)*	Philippe **habite** à Toulouse?
inviter	*to invite*	J'**invite** un copain.
organiser	*to organize*	Sophie **organise** une **boum**/ une **soirée**/une **fête** *(party)*.
visiter	*to visit (places)*	Céline **visite** Québec.

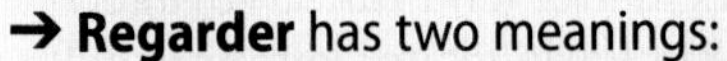
➔ **Regarder** has two meanings:

to look (at) — Paul **regarde** Cécile.
to watch — Cécile **regarde** la télé.

➔ Note the construction **téléphoner à:**

Céline **téléphone**	**à**	Marc.
Céline calls	…	*Marc.*

➔ Note the constructions with **regarder** *(to look at)* and **écouter** *(to listen to)*:

Philippe **regarde**	…	Alice.
Philippe looks	*at*	*Alice.*

Alice **écoute**	…	le professeur.
Alice listens	*to*	*the teacher.*

2 Quelle activité?

PARLER/ÉCRIRE Describe what the following people are doing by completing the sentences with one of the verbs below. Be logical.

écouter · travailler · voyager · inviter · chanter · parler · manger · regarder · habiter

1. Je … un sandwich. Tu … une pizza.
2. Tu … anglais. Je … français.
3. Éric … la radio. Claire … un CD.
4. Jean-Paul … la télé. Tu … un match de tennis.
5. M. Simon … en *(by)* bus. Mme Dupont … en train.
6. Nicolas … Marie à la boum. Tu … Alain.
7. Mlle Thomas … dans *(in)* un hôpital. Je … dans un supermarché *(supermarket)*.
8. La chorale *(choir)* … bien. Est-ce que tu … bien?
9. Tu … en France. Aya … en Afrique.

3 Les voisins *(The neighbors)*

PARLER/ÉCRIRE Simon is explaining what his neighbors are doing. Describe each person's activity.

▶ —**Madame Dumas téléphone.**

4 Où sont-ils?

PARLER You want to know where the following people are. A classmate tells you and says what they are doing.

▶ Jacques? (en classe/étudier)

1. Pauline? (au restaurant/dîner)
2. Véronique? (à la maison/téléphoner)
3. Mme Dupont? (en ville/travailler)
4. M. Lemaire? (en France/voyager)
5. Léa? (à Paris/visiter la tour Eiffel)
6. André? (au stade/jouer au foot)
7. Alice? (à l'Olympic Club/nager)

B Les verbes en *-er:* le pluriel

Note the plural forms of **parler** and **habiter**, paying attention to the endings.

INFINITIVE	parler	habiter	ENDINGS
STEM	**parl-**	**habit-**	
PRESENT TENSE (PLURAL)	Nous **parlons** français. Vous **parlez** anglais. Ils/Elles **parlent** espagnol.	Nous **habitons** à Québec. Vous **habitez** à Chicago. Ils/Elles **habitent** à Caracas.	**-ons** **-ez** **-ent**

→ In the present tense, the plural endings of **-er** verbs are:
nous → **-ons** vous → **-ez** ils / elles → **-ent**

→ The **-ent** ending is silent.

→ Note the liaison when the verb begins with a vowel sound:
Nous étudions. Vous invitez Thomas. Ils habitent en France. Elles aiment Paris.

Observation When the infinitive of the verb ends in **-ger**, the **nous** form ends in **-geons**.
nager: nous na**geons** **manger:** nous man**geons** **voyager:** nous voya**geons**

@HOMETUTOR
my.hrw.com

5 Qui?

PARLER/ÉCRIRE Élodie is speaking to or about her friends. Complete her sentences with **tu, elle, vous,** or **ils**.

▶ ... étudient à Toulouse.
Ils étudient à Toulouse.

1. ... habitez à Tours.
2. ... joue aux jeux vidéo.
3. ... étudiez à Bordeaux.
4. ... aiment danser.
5. ... organisent une boum.
6. ... parlez espagnol.
7. ... téléphone à Jean-Pierre.
8. ... invites un copain.
9. ... dîne avec Cécile.
10. ... invitent Monique.

6 À la boum

PARLER At a party, Olivier is talking to two Canadian students, Monique and her friend. Monique answers yes to his questions.

▶ parler français?

Vous parlez français, n'est-ce pas?

Oui, nous parlons français.

1. parler anglais?
2. habiter à Québec?
3. étudier à Montréal?
4. voyager en France?
5. voyager en train?
6. visiter Paris?
7. aimer Paris?
8. aimer la France?

7 En colonie de vacances *(At summer camp)*

PARLER/ÉCRIRE Describe the activities of the following campers by completing the sentences.

▶ À cinq heures, Alice et Marc ... **À cinq heures, Alice et Marc jouent au foot.**

▶       

1. À neuf heures, nous ...
2. À quatre heures, vous ...
3. À huit heures, Véronique et Pierre ...
4. À sept heures, nous ...
5. À trois heures, Thomas et François ...
6. À six heures, vous ...

8 Un voyage à Paris

PARLER/ÉCRIRE A group of American students is visiting Paris. During their stay, they do all of the following things:

voyager en bus	téléphoner à un copain	inviter une copine
visiter la tour Eiffel	dîner au restaurant	parler français

Describe the trips of the following people.

▶ Jim **Il voyage en bus, il visite la tour Eiffel ...**

1. Linda
2. Paul et Louise
3. nous
4. vous
5. Jen et Sarah

C Le présent des verbes en *-er:* forme affirmative et forme négative

Compare the affirmative and negative forms of **parler**.

AFFIRMATIVE		NEGATIVE	
je	**parle**	je	**ne parle pas**
tu	**parles**	tu	**ne parles pas**
il/elle	**parle**	il/elle	**ne parle pas**
nous	**parlons**	nous	**ne parlons pas**
vous	**parlez**	vous	**ne parlez pas**
ils/elles	**parlent**	ils/elles	**ne parlent pas**

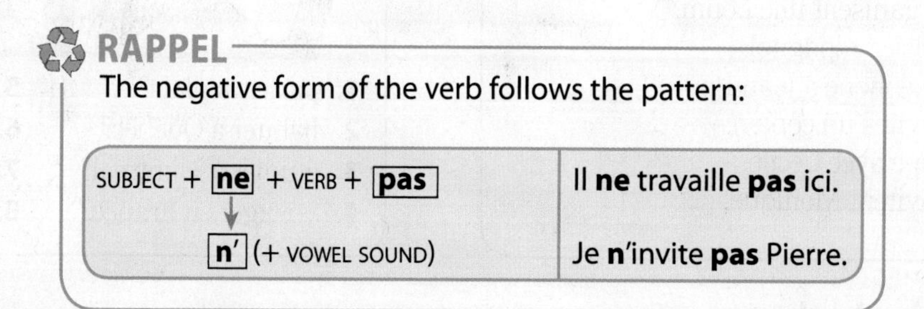

Il ne travaille pas.

Ils n'écoutent pas.

Elle ne chante pas bien.

LANGUAGE COMPARISONS

English has several verb forms for expressing actions in the present.
In French there is only one form. Compare:

Je **joue** au tennis. { ***I play*** *tennis.* / ***I do play*** *tennis.* / ***I am playing*** *tennis.* }

Je **ne joue pas** au tennis. { ***I do not play*** *tennis.* (***I don't play*** *tennis.*) / ***I am not playing*** *tennis.* (***I'm not playing*** *tennis.*) }

9 Non!

PARLER One cannot do everything. From the following list of activities, select at least three that you do *not* do.

▶ **Je ne joue pas au bridge.**

parler espagnol
parler italien
danser le tango
jouer au hockey
jouer au water-polo
jouer au bridge
étudier à Paris
habiter à Québec
étudier le japonais
nager en hiver
dîner avec le prof
travailler dans un restaurant

10 Écoutez bien!

STRATEGY Listening

Negative sentences To know if a sentence is negative, listen for the word **pas** immediately after the verb.

ÉCOUTER You will hear French young people tell you what they do and do not do. Listen carefully to what they each say and determine if they do the following activities.

▶ Marc: jouer au foot?
Non. Marc ne joue pas au foot.

1. Sophie: parler espagnol?
2. Vincent: habiter à Tours?
3. Mélanie: dîner à la maison?
4. Nicolas: téléphoner à un copain?
5. Julie: manger une pizza?
6. Jean: étudier l'anglais?
7. Marie: écouter un CD?

11 Un jeu: Week-end!

PARLER/ÉCRIRE On weekends, people like to do different things. For each person, pick an activity and say what that person does. Select another activity and say what that person does not do.

▶ Antoine et Isabelle
Antoine et Isabelle dansent.
Ils ne regardent pas la télé.

1. je
2. tu
3. ma cousine
4. nous
5. Nicolas et Élodie
6. Madame Jolivet
7. vous
8. le professeur

VOCABULAIRE Mots utiles

bien	*well*	Je joue **bien** au tennis.
très bien	*very well*	Je ne chante pas **très bien.**
mal	*badly, poorly*	Tu joues **mal** au volley.
beaucoup	*a lot, much, very much*	Paul aime **beaucoup** voyager.
un peu	*a little, a little bit*	Nous parlons **un peu** français.
souvent	*often*	Thomas joue **souvent** aux jeux vidéo.
toujours	*always*	Charlotte travaille **toujours** en été.
aussi	*also, too*	Je téléphone à Marc. Je téléphone **aussi** à Véronique.
maintenant	*now*	J'étudie **maintenant.**
rarement	*rarely, seldom*	Vous voyagez **rarement.**

→ In French, the above expressions *never* come *between* the subject and the verb. They usually come *after* the verb. Compare their positions in French and English.

Nous parlons **toujours** français. — *We **always** speak French.*
Tu joues **bien** au tennis. — *You play tennis **well**.*

12 Expression personnelle

PARLER/ÉCRIRE Complete the following sentences with one of the suggested expressions.

bien mal très bien toujours souvent rarement un peu beaucoup

1. Je chante ...
2. Je nage ...
3. Je regarde ... la télé.
4. Je mange ...
5. Je voyage ... en bus.
6. Le prof parle ... français.
7. Mes copains surfent ... sur l'Internet.
8. Mon ami joue ... aux jeux vidéo.
9. Les Yankees jouent ... au baseball.

VOCABULAIRE Expressions pour la conversation

How to express approval or regret:

Super!	*Terrific!*	Tu parles français? **Super!**
Dommage!	*Too bad!*	Tu ne joues pas au tennis? **Dommage!**

13 Conversation 

PARLER Ask your classmates if they do the following things. Then express approval or regret.

▶ parler français?

1. parler espagnol?
2. jouer au basket?
3. chanter bien?
4. voyager beaucoup?
5. dîner souvent au restaurant?
6. inviter souvent ton copain?

@HOMETUTOR
my.hrw.com

D La construction: verbe + infinitif

Note the use of the infinitive in the following French sentences.

J'aime **parler** français. — *I like **to speak** French. I like **speaking** French.*
Ils n'aiment pas **danser.** — *They don't like **to dance.** They don't like **dancing.***

To express what they like and don't like to do, the French use these constructions:

SUBJECT + PRESENT TENSE of **aimer** + INFINITIVE ...			SUBJECT + **n'** + PRESENT TENSE of **aimer** + **pas** + INFINITIVE ...		
Nous	**aimons**	**voyager.**	Nous	**n'aimons pas**	**voyager.**

Note that in this construction, the verb **aimer** may be affirmative or negative:

AFFIRMATIVE: Jacques **aime** voyager. NEGATIVE: Philippe **n'aime pas** voyager.

→ The infinitive is also used after the following expressions:

Je préfère ...	*I prefer ...*	**Je préfère travailler.**
Je voudrais ...	*I would like ...*	**Je voudrais voyager.**
Je (ne) veux (pas) ...	*I (don't) want ...*	**Je veux jouer** au foot.
Est-ce que tu veux ...	*Do you want ...*	**Est-ce que tu veux danser?**
Je (ne) peux (pas) ...	*I can (I can't) ...*	**Je ne peux pas dîner** avec toi.
Je dois ...	*I have to ...*	**Je dois étudier.**

14 Dialogue

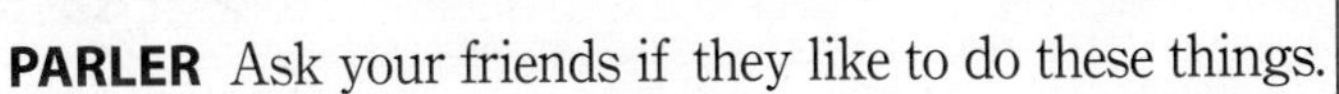

PARLER Ask your friends if they like to do these things.

▸ nager?

—**Est-ce que tu aimes nager?**
—**Oui, j'aime nager. (Non, je n'aime pas nager.)**

1. étudier?
2. voyager?
3. chanter?
4. téléphoner?
5. manger?
6. danser?
7. jouer au foot?
8. jouer au basket?
9. travailler en été?

15 Une excellente raison *(An excellent reason)*

PARLER/ÉCRIRE The following people are doing certain things. Say that they like these activities.

▸ Thomas joue au tennis. **Il aime jouer au tennis.**

1. Alice chante.
2. Pierre voyage.
3. Céline joue au foot.
4. Tu téléphones.
5. Nous travaillons.
6. Julie et Paul dansent.
7. Nous jouons au frisbee.
8. Éric et Lise nagent.
9. Vous surfez sur l'Internet.
10. Léa organise la boum.

Prononciation

Les voyelles /i/ **et** /u/

/u/ **où?** /i/ **ici!**

Be sure to pronounce the French **"i"** as in **Mimi.**

Répétez:

/i/ **ici Philippe il Mimi Sylvie visite**

Alice visite Paris avec Sylvie.

/u/ **où nous vous écoute joue toujours**

Vous jouez au foot avec nous?

OBJECTIFS

Now you can . . .
- describe what you and other people are doing and not doing
- talk about what you and other people like and don't like to do

Digital performance space

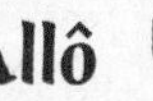

1 Allô

PARLER Sophie is phoning some friends. Match her questions on the left with her friends' answers on the right.

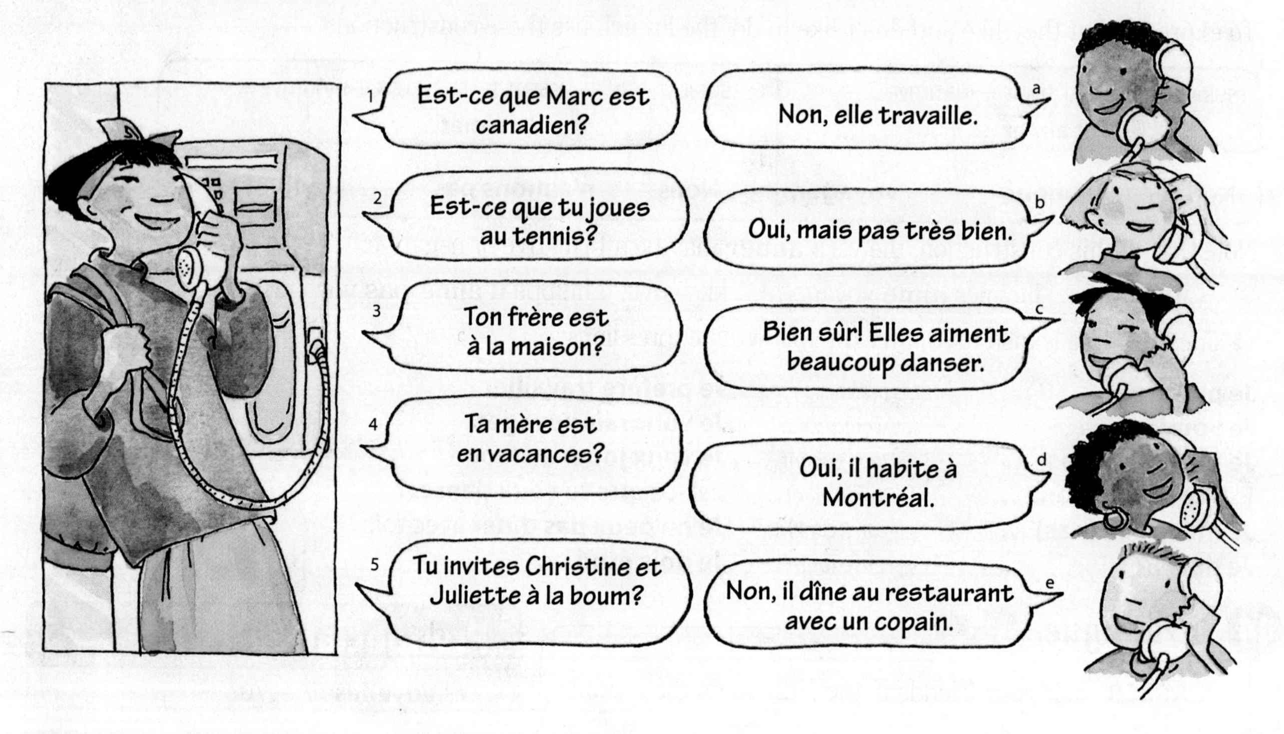

2 Créa-dialogue

PARLER Find out how frequently your classmates do the following activities. They will respond using one of the expressions on the scale.

NON	OUI
	rarement → un peu → souvent → beaucoup

▶
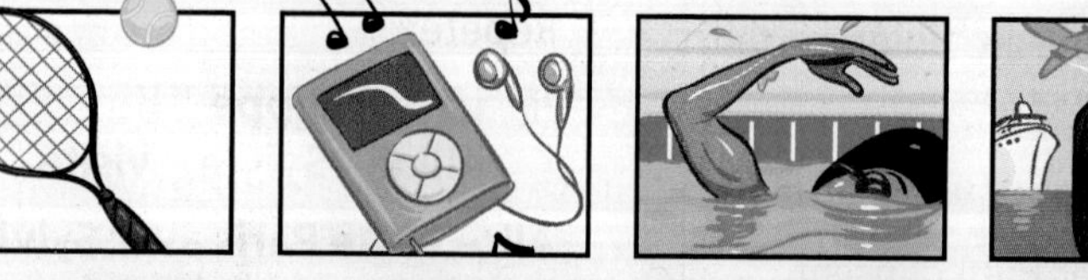

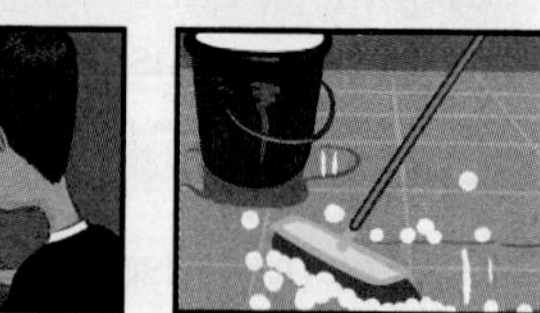

▶ —Robert, est-ce que tu joues au tennis?
—Non, je ne joue pas au tennis.
—Est-ce que tu écoutes de la musique?
—Oui, j'écoute souvent de la musique.

3 Qu'est-ce qu'ils font?

(What do they do?)

PARLER/ÉCRIRE Look at what the following students have put in their lockers and say what they like to do.

4 Message illustré

ÉCRIRE Marc wrote about certain activities, using pictures. On a separate sheet, write out his description replacing these pictures with the missing words.

Après *After* **mes** *my* **Parfois** *Sometimes*

5 Point de vue personnel

ÉCRIRE Write a short composition in which you describe some of the activities you do and don't do in different situations: at home, in class, on vacation, with your friends, and with your family. If appropriate, you may indicate how frequently you engage in certain activities..

STRATEGY Writing

- First list the activities you want to mention, using infinitives.
- Write out your paragraph describing your activities and those that you do not do.
- Check your composition to be sure all verb forms are correct.

	☺	☹
• à la maison	• ______	• ______
• en classe	• ______	• ______
• en vacances	• ______	• ______
• avec mes copains	• ______	• ______
• avec ma famille	• ______	• ______

Leçon 8

Conversation et Culture

Un concert de musique africaine

DVD AUDIO

Nicolas is at a café with his new friend Fatou. He is interviewing her for an article in his school newspaper.

Nicolas: Bonjour, Fatou. Ça va?
Fatou: Oui, ça va.
Nicolas: Tu es sénégalaise, n'est-ce pas? — *from Senegal*
Fatou: Oui, je suis sénégalaise.
Nicolas: Où est-ce que tu habites?
Fatou: Je suis de Dakar, mais maintenant j'habite à Paris avec ma famille.
Nicolas: Est-ce que tu aimes Paris?
Fatou: J'adore Paris.
Nicolas: Qu'est-ce que tu fais le week-end?
Fatou: Ça dépend. En général, je regarde la télé ou je sors avec mes copains. Dis, Nicolas! Est-ce que je peux te poser une question? — *That / go out*; *ask you*
Nicolas: Oui, bien sûr!
Fatou: Qu'est-ce que tu fais ce week-end? — *this*
Nicolas: Euh, … je ne sais pas. — *I don't know*
Fatou: Est-ce que tu veux aller avec nous à un concert de Youssou N'Dour, le musicien sénégalais?
Nicolas: Oui, bien sûr! Où? Quand? Et à quelle heure? — *Where? / When?*

Compréhension

1. Est-ce que Fatou est française?
2. Où est-ce qu'elle habite maintenant?
3. Qu'est-ce que *(What)* Fatou aime faire *(to do)* le week-end?
4. Qui est-ce qu'elle invite au concert de musique africaine?

NOTE *Culturelle*

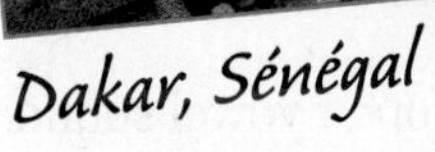
Dakar, Sénégal

EN BREF: Le Sénégal

Capitale: Dakar
Population: 14 000 000
Langue officielle: français

A former French colony, Senegal became an independent republic in 1960. Its population is divided into about a dozen ethnic groups, each with its own language, the most important being **wolof** and **pulaar.**

Des jeunes Sénégalais

Youssou N'Dour

Youssou N'Dour is an internationally known musician from Senegal who combines traditional African music with pop, rock, and jazz. He sings in French and English, as well as in three Senegalese dialects. His lyrics promote African unity and human dignity. In many of his songs, he also plays the **tama**, a traditional Senegalese drum covered with reptile skins.

CONNEXIONS Senegal and African Music

- As a class project, make a display board on Senegal, using information and pictures from travel brochures or from the Internet.
- Obtain a CD of Youssou N'Dour or of music from another French-African country and play your favorite selection for the class.

A Les questions d'information

The questions below ask for specific information and are called INFORMATION QUESTIONS. The INTERROGATIVE EXPRESSIONS in heavy print indicate what kind of information is requested.

—**Où** est-ce que tu habites?	***Where*** *do you live?*
—J'habite **à Nice.**	*I live* ***in Nice.***
—**À quelle heure** est-ce que vous dînez?	***At what time*** *do you eat dinner?*
—Nous dînons **à sept heures.**	*We eat* ***at seven.***

→ In French, information questions may be formed according to the pattern:

INTERROGATIVE EXPRESSION	+ **est-ce que**	+ SUBJECT	+ VERB ... ?
À quelle heure	**est-ce que**	vous	travaillez?

→ **Est-ce que** becomes **est-ce qu'** before a vowel sound.

Quand **est-ce qu'**Alice et Roger dînent?

→ In information questions, your voice rises on the interrogative expression and then falls until the last syllable.

Quand est-ce que tu travailles?

À quelle heure est-ce que vous dînez?

Observation In casual conversation, French speakers frequently form information questions by placing the interrogative expression at the end of the sentence. The voice rises on the interrogative expression.

Vous habitez **où?**

Vous dînez **à quelle heure?**

VOCABULAIRE Expressions interrogatives

où	*where?*	**Où** est-ce que vous travaillez?
quand?	*when?*	**Quand** est-ce que ton copain organise une boum?
à quelle heure?	*at what time?*	**À quelle heure** est-ce que tu regardes la télé?
comment?	*how?*	**Comment** est-ce que tu chantes? Bien ou mal?
pourquoi?	*why?*	—**Pourquoi** est-ce que tu étudies le français?
parce que	*because*	—**Parce que** je veux voyager en France.

→ **Parce que** becomes **parce qu'** before a vowel sound.

Juliette invite Olivier **parce qu'**il danse bien.

@HOMETUTOR
my.hrw.com

1 Écoutez bien!

STRATEGY Listening

Understanding questions Pay attention to the interrogative expression. It tells what type of information is asked for.

ÉCOUTER The questions that you will hear can be logically answered by only one of the following options. Listen carefully to each question and select the logical answer.

a. à sept heures
b. à Paris
c. en octobre
d. assez bien

2 Curiosité 

PARLER At a party in Paris, Nicolas meets Béatrice, a Canadian student. He wants to know more about her. Play both roles.

▶ où / habiter? (à Québec)

NICOLAS: **Où est-ce que tu habites?**
BÉATRICE: **J'habite à Québec.**

1. où/étudier? (à Montréal)
2. où/travailler? (dans *[in]* une pharmacie)
3. quand/parler français? (toujours)
4. quand/parler anglais? (souvent)
5. comment/jouer au tennis? (bien)
6. comment/danser? (très bien)
7. pourquoi/être en France? (parce que j'aime voyager)
8. pourquoi/être à Paris? (parce que j'étudie ici)

VOCABULAIRE Expressions pour la conversation

How to express surprise or mild doubt:

Ah bon?	*Oh? Really?*	—Stéphanie organise une soirée. —**Ah bon?** Quand?

 Au téléphone 

PARLER Jacques calls Élodie to tell her about his plans.

▶ organiser une soirée (quand? samedi)

1. organiser un pique-nique (quand? dimanche)
2. dîner avec Pauline (quand? lundi)
3. dîner avec Caroline (où? au restaurant Belcour)
4. regarder «Batman» (à quelle heure? à 9 heures)
5. inviter Brigitte (où? à un concert)
6. parler espagnol (comment? assez bien)
7. étudier l'italien (pourquoi? je veux voyager en Italie)

 Questions personnelles PARLER/ÉCRIRE

1. Où est-ce que tu habites? *(name of your city)*
2. Où est-ce que tu étudies? *(name of your school)*
3. À quelle heure est-ce que tu dînes?
4. À quelle heure est-ce que tu regardes la télé?
5. Quand est-ce que tu nages? (en été? en hiver?)
6. Quand est-ce que tu joues au volley? (en mai? en juillet?)
7. Comment est-ce que tu chantes? (bien? très bien? mal?)
8. Comment est-ce que tu nages?

B Les expressions interrogatives avec *qui*

To ask about PEOPLE, French speakers use the following interrogative expressions:

qui?	*who(m)?*	**Qui** est-ce que tu invites au concert?
à qui?	*to who(m)?*	**À qui** est-ce que tu téléphones?
de qui?	*about who(m)?*	**De qui** est-ce que vous parlez?
avec qui?	*with who(m)?*	**Avec qui** est-ce que Pierre étudie?
pour qui?	*for who(m)?*	**Pour qui** est-ce que Laure organise la boum?

To ask *who is doing something,* French speakers use the construction:

qui + VERB ... ?

Qui habite ici?	***Who** lives here?*
Qui organise la boum?	***Who** is organizing the party?*

5 *Curiosité*

PARLER Anne is telling Élodie what certain people are doing. Élodie asks for more details. Play both roles.

▶ Alice dîne. (avec qui? avec une copine)

1. Jean-Pierre téléphone. (à qui? à Sylvie)
2. Frédéric étudie. (avec qui? avec un copain)
3. Madame Masson parle. (à qui? à Madame Bonnot)
4. Monsieur Lambert travaille. (avec qui? avec Monsieur Dumont)
5. Juliette danse. (avec qui? avec Georges)
6. François parle à Michèle. (de qui? de toi)

6 *Un sondage* (A poll)

PARLER Take a survey to find out how your classmates spend their free time. Ask who does the following things.

▶ écouter la radio
Qui écoute la radio?

1. voyager souvent
2. aimer chanter
3. nager
4. aimer danser
5. regarder la télé
6. jouer au tennis
7. parler italien
8. travailler
9. regarder les clips *(music videos)*
10. jouer aux jeux vidéo
11. étudier beaucoup
12. visiter souvent New York

7 Questions 

PARLER/ÉCRIRE For each illustration, prepare a short dialogue with a classmate using the suggested cues.

où?

à la maison

▶ **—Où est-ce que tu dînes?**
—Je dîne à la maison.

1. à quelle heure?

à 8 heures

2. quand?

en septembre

3. comment?

très bien

4. avec qui?

avec Denise

5. à qui?

à mon cousin

6. de qui?

de toi

7. pour qui?

pour M. Lambert

C Qu'est-ce que?

Note the use of the interrogative expression **qu'est-ce que** *(what)* in the questions below.

Qu'est-ce que tu regardes?	Je regarde un match de tennis.
Qu'est-ce qu'Alice mange?	Elle mange une pizza.

To ask *what people are doing,* the French use the following construction:

qu'est-ce que + SUBJECT + VERB + ...?	**Qu'est-ce que** tu regardes?
↓ **qu'est-ce qu'** (+ VOWEL SOUND)	**Qu'est-ce qu'**elle mange?

8 À la FNAC

PARLER People in Column A are at the FNAC, a store that sells books and recordings. Use a verb from Column B to ask what they are listening to or looking at. A classmate will answer you, using an item from Column C.

A	B	C
tu	écouter?	un livre de photos
vous	regarder?	un poster
Alice		un CD de rock
Éric		un CD de jazz
Antoine et Claire		un CD de Youssou N'Dour

Qu'est-ce qu'Éric écoute?

Il écoute un CD de Youssou N'Dour.

D Le verbe *faire*

Faire *(to do, make)* is an IRREGULAR verb. It is used in many French expressions. Note the forms of **faire** in the present tense.

	faire *(to do, make)*	
je	**fais**	Je **fais** un sandwich.
tu	**fais**	Qu'est-ce que tu **fais** maintenant?
il/elle	**fait**	Qu'est-ce que ton copain **fait** samedi?
nous	**faisons**	Nous **faisons** une pizza.
vous	**faites**	Qu'est-ce que vous **faites** ici?
ils/elles	**font**	Qu'est-ce qu'elles **font** pour la boum?

VOCABULAIRE Expressions avec *faire*

faire un match	*to play a game (match)*	Mes cousins **font un match** de tennis.
faire une promenade	*to go for a walk*	Caroline **fait une promenade** avec Olivier.
faire un voyage	*to take a trip*	Ma copine **fait un voyage** en France.
faire attention	*to pay attention*	Je **fais attention** quand le prof parle.

9 La boum de Léa

PARLER/ÉCRIRE Léa's friends are helping her prepare food for a party. Use the verb **faire** to say what everyone is doing.

▶ Je … une crêpe.

1. Nous … une salade.
2. Tu … une salade de fruits.
3. Vous … une tarte *(pie)*.
4. Cécile et Marina … un gâteau *(cake)*.
5. Christine … une pizza.
6. Marc … un sandwich.
7. Patrick et Thomas … une omelette.
8. Pierre et Karine … une quiche.

10 Qu'est-ce qu'ils font?

PARLER/LIRE Read the descriptions below and say what the people are doing. Use the verb **faire** and an expression from the list.

un voyage
une promenade
une pizza
un match
attention

▶ Madame Dumont est en Chine.
Elle fait un voyage.

1. Léa travaille dans *(in)* un restaurant.
2. Nous sommes en ville.
3. Céline et Jean-Paul jouent au tennis.
4. Je suis dans la cuisine *(kitchen)*.
5. Marc est dans le train Paris-Nice.
6. Vous jouez au volley.
7. Je suis dans le parc.
8. Monsieur Lambert visite Tokyo.
9. Nous écoutons le prof.

@HOMETUTOR
my.hrw.com

E L'interrogation avec inversion

LEARNING ABOUT LANGUAGE

In conversational French, questions are usually formed with **est-ce que.** However, when the subject of the sentence is a pronoun, French speakers often use inversion, that is, they invert or reverse the order of the subject pronoun and the verb.

REGULAR ORDER: **Vous parlez** français. (SUBJECT VERB) INVERSION: **Parlez-vous** anglais? (VERB SUBJECT)

The pairs of questions below ask the same thing. Compare the position of the subject pronouns.

Est-ce que **tu** parles anglais?	Parles-**tu** anglais?	*Do you speak English?*
Est-ce que **vous** habitez ici?	Habitez-**vous** ici?	*Do you live here?*
Où est-ce que **nous** dînons?	Où dînons-**nous**?	*Where are we having dinner?*
Où est-ce qu'**il** est?	Où est-**il**?	*Where is he?*

Inverted questions are formed according to the patterns:

YES/NO QUESTION	VERB / SUBJECT PRONOUN	...?	
	Voyagez-vous	souvent?	
INFORMATION QUESTION	INTERROGATIVE EXPRESSION + VERB / SUBJECT PRONOUN		...?
	Avec qui	**travaillez-vous**	demain?

→ In inversion, the verb and the subject pronoun are connected by a hyphen.

Observation In inversion, liaison is required before **il/elle** and **ils/elles.** If a verb in the singular ends on a vowel, the letter **"t"** is inserted after the verb so that liaison can occur:

Où travaille-**t**-il? Où travaille-**t**-elle? Avec qui dîne-**t**-il? Avec qui dîne-**t**-elle?

11 Conversation

PARLER Ask your classmates a few questions, using inversion.

▶ où / habiter? —**Où habites-tu?**
—**J'habite à (Boston).**

1. à quelle heure / dîner?
2. à quelle heure / regarder la télé?
3. avec qui / parler français?
4. à qui / téléphoner souvent?
5. comment / nager?
6. avec qui / étudier?
7. où / jouer aux jeux vidéo?
8. comment / chanter?

Prononciation  /y/

La voyelle /y/

Super!

The vowel sound /y/ — represented by the letter "**u**" — does not exist in English.

To say **super**, first say the French word **si.** Then round your lips as if to whistle and say **si** with rounded lips: /sy/. Now say **si-per.** Then round your lips as you say the first syllable: **super!**

Répétez: /y/ **super tu étudie bien sûr**
Lucie Luc
Tu étudies avec Lucie.

À votre tour!

OBJECTIFS

Now you can . . .
- ask and answer information questions
- ask about what people are doing

1 Allô!

PARLER Fatou is phoning some friends. Match her questions on the left with her friends' answers on the right.

2 Les questions

LIRE/PARLER The following people are answering questions. Read what they say and figure out what questions they were asked.

▶ **Comment est-ce que tu chantes?**

3 Créa-dialogue  

PARLER Ask your classmates what they do on different days of the week. Carry out conversations similar to the model. Note: "??" means you can invent your own answers.

▶ **—Qu'est-ce que tu fais lundi?**
—Je joue au tennis.
—Ah bon? À quelle heure est-ce que tu joues?
—À deux heures.
—Et avec qui?
—Avec Anne-Marie.

	lundi	mardi	mercredi	jeudi	vendredi	samedi	dimanche
ACTIVITÉ						??	??
À QUELLE HEURE?	2 heures	6 heures	??	??	??	??	??
AVEC QUI?	avec Anne-Marie	avec un copain	??	??	??	??	??

4 Faisons connaissance! *(Let's get acquainted!)* 

PARLER/ÉCRIRE Get better acquainted with a classmate. Ask five or six questions in French. Then write a summary of your conversation and give it to the friend you have interviewed.

▶ **Mon ami(e) s'appelle ...**
Il/elle habite ...

You might ask questions like:

- Where does he/she live?
- Does he/she speak French at home? With whom?
- Does he/she watch TV? When? What programs **(quelles émissions)**?
- Does he/she play video games? When? With whom?
- Does he/she play soccer (or another sport)? Where? When?
- Does he/she like to swim? When? Where?
- What does he/she like to do on weekends? When? Where? With whom?

5 Curiosité 

ÉCRIRE Imagine that a French friend has just made the following statements. For each one, write down three or four related questions you could ask him or her. ▼

Tests de contrôle

By taking the following tests, you can check your progress in French and also prepare for the unit test. Write your answers on a separate sheet of paper.

Review...
- the uses and forms of **-er** verbs: pp. 94, 95, 96, and 98

1 The right activity

Complete each of the following sentences by filling in the blank with the appropriate form of one of the verbs in the box. Be logical in your choice of verbs.

chanter	manger	écouter	habiter
jouer	parler	regarder	travailler

1. Jean-Paul — une pizza.
2. Vous — aux jeux vidéo.
3. Isabelle — un CD de rock.
4. Monsieur Mercier — pour une banque *(bank)*.
5. Mon cousin — à Chicago.
6. Ils — dans une chorale *(choir)*.
7. Nous — une comédie à la télé.
8. Est-ce que tu — français ou anglais?

Review...
- **être** and **faire**: pp. 84 and 110

2 Être and faire

For each item, fill in the first blank with the appropriate form of **être** and the second blank with the appropriate form of **faire**.

1. Je — en classe. Je — attention.
2. Léa — dans la cuisine *(kitchen)*. Elle — un sandwich.
3. Nous — en ville. Nous — une promenade.
4. Les touristes — en France. Ils — un voyage.
5. Vous — au stade *(stadium)*. Vous — un match de foot.

Review...
- negative sentences: pp. 88 and 98

3 Non!

Rewrite the following sentences in the negative, replacing the underlined words with the words in parentheses.

▶ Thomas parle <u>français</u>. **(anglais)** **Thomas ne parle pas anglais.**

1. Léa est <u>française</u>. **(américaine)**
2. Nous jouons <u>au foot</u>. **(au basket)**
3. Vous dînez <u>au restaurant</u>. **(à la maison)**
4. Tu invites <u>Céline</u>. **(Isabelle)**
5. Ils habitent <u>à Québec</u>. **(à Montréal)**

4 The right question

Write out the questions that correspond to the answers below. Make sure to begin your sentences with the question words that correspond to the underlined information. Use **tu** in your questions.

> **Review...**
> - information questions: pp. 106 and 108

▶ J'habite à Paris. **Où est-ce que tu habites?**

1. Je téléphone à Marc.
2. Je dîne à sept heures.
3. Je mange une pizza.
4. Je voyage en juillet.
5. J'écoute un CD.
6. Je joue très bien au foot.

5 The right choice

Choose the word or expression in parentheses which logically completes each of the following sentences.

> **Review...**
> - vocabulary: pp. 77, 78, 85, 89, 95, 100, 106

1. François habite — France. **(à, au, en)**
2. Isabelle est au café — Céline. **(et, avec, pour)**
3. Nicolas parle français, — il ne parle pas espagnol. **(pourquoi, mal, mais)**
4. Pierre écoute — musique. **(à, les, de la)**
5. Je n'habite pas ici. J'habite —. **(où, aussi, là-bas)**
6. Tu ne chantes pas bien. Tu chantes —. **(mal, souvent, beaucoup)**
7. Philippe aime beaucoup jouer au foot. Il joue —. **(pour, mais non, souvent)**
8. Je ne peux pas dîner avec toi. Je — étudier pour l'examen. **(dois, veux, n'aime pas)**
9. J'étudie l'espagnol — je voudrais visiter Madrid. **(où, comment, parce que)**
10. Qui est-ce? Jérôme — Patrick? **(pour, ou, aussi)**

6 Composition: Les vacances

Digital performance space

Write a short paragraph of five or six sentences saying what you and your friends do and don't do during summer vacation. Use only vocabulary and expressions that you know in French.

STRATEGY Writing

	oui	non
a Make a list of activities that you do and a second list of things that you don't do. Use infinitives.	• *nager*	•
	•	•
b Organize your ideas and write your paragraph, using **je** or **nous**.	•	•
c Check each sentence to be sure that the verb endings agree with the subject.	•	•
	•	•

Vocabulaire

POUR COMMUNIQUER

Talking about likes and preferences

Est-ce que tu aimes	**parler anglais?**	*Do you like*	*to speak English?*
J'aime		*I like*	
Je n'aime pas		*I don't like*	
Je préfère	**parler français.**	*I prefer*	*to speak French.*
Je veux		*I want*	
Je voudrais		*I would like*	
Je ne veux pas		*I don't want*	

Inviting a friend

Est-ce que tu veux [jouer au tennis]?	*Do you want to [play tennis]?*
Est-ce que tu peux [jouer au foot] avec moi?	*Can you [play soccer] with me?*

Accepting or declining an invitation

Oui, bien sûr.	*Yes, of course.*	**Je regrette, mais je ne peux pas.**	*I'm sorry, but I can't.*
Oui, merci.	*Yes, thanks.*	**Je dois [travailler].**	*I have to, I must [work].*
Oui, d'accord.	*Yes, all right, okay.*		
Oui, je veux bien.	*Yes, I'd love to.*		

Expressing approval, regret, or surprise

Super!	*Terrific!*
Dommage!	*Too bad!*
Ah bon?	*Oh? Really?*

Answering a yes/no question

Oui!	*Yes!*	**Non!**	*No!*
Mais oui!	*Sure!*	**Mais non!**	*Of course not!*
Bien sûr!	*Of course!*	**Peut-être ...**	*Maybe ...*

Asking for information

où?	*where?*	**qu'est-ce que ...?**	*what?*
quand?	*when?*	**qui?**	*who, whom?*
à quelle heure?	*at what time?*	**à qui?**	*to who(m)?*
comment?	*how?*	**de qui?**	*about who(m)?*
pourquoi?	*why?*	**avec qui?**	*with who(m)?*
parce que ...	*because*	**pour qui?**	*for who(m)?*

Saying where people are

Pierre est ...

ici	*here*	**à la maison**	*at home*	**en classe**	*in class*
là	*here, there*	**au café**	*at the café*	**en France**	*in France*
là-bas	*over there*	**au cinéma**	*at the movies*	**en vacances**	*on vacation*
à [Paris]	*in [Paris]*	**au restaurant**	*at the restaurant*	**en ville**	*in town*

Saying how well, how often, and when

bien	*well*	**beaucoup**	*a lot, much, very much*	**maintenant**	*now*
très bien	*very well*	**un peu**	*a little, a little bit*	**souvent**	*often*
mal	*badly, poorly*	**rarement**	*rarely, seldom*	**toujours**	*always*

MOTS ET EXPRESSIONS

Verbes réguliers en *-er*

aimer	*to like*
chanter	*to sing*
danser	*to dance*
dîner	*to have dinner*
dîner au restaurant	*to eat out*
écouter de la musique	*to listen to music*
écouter la radio	*to listen to the radio*
étudier	*to study*
habiter (à Paris)	*to live (in Paris)*
inviter	*to invite*
jouer au basket	*to play basketball*
jouer au foot	*to play soccer*
jouer au tennis	*to play tennis*
jouer aux jeux vidéo	*to play video games*
manger	*to eat*
nager	*to swim*
organiser une boum	*to organize a party*
parler anglais	*to speak English*
parler espagnol	*to speak Spanish*
parler français	*to speak French*
regarder	*to watch, to look at*
regarder la télé	*to watch TV*
téléphoner (à Céline)	*to phone (Céline)*
travailler	*to work*
visiter (Paris)	*to visit (Paris)*
voyager	*to travel*

Verbes irréguliers

être	*to be*
être d'accord	*to agree*
faire	*to do, make*
faire un match	*to play a game (match)*
faire une promenade	*to go for a walk*
faire un voyage	*to take a trip*
faire attention	*to pay attention*

Mots utiles

à	*at, in*
aussi	*also*
avec	*with*
de	*from, of*
et	*and*
mais	*but*
ou	*or*
pour	*for*

Ce week-end, à la télé

Le week-end, les jeunes Français regardent souvent la télé. Ils aiment regarder les films et le sport. Ils regardent aussi les jeux et les séries américaines et françaises. Les principales chaînes° sont TF1, France 2, France 3, France 5, Arte, M6 et Canal Plus. Aujourd'hui, les français ont accès à un large choix de chaînes publiques et privées. Voici un exemple des programmes que tu peux regarder le samedi et dimanche soir.

chaînes *channels*

Note In French TV listings, times are expressed using a 24-hour clock. In this system, 8 p.m. is 20.00 **(vingt heures)**, 9 p.m. is 21.00 **(vingt et une heures)**, 10 p.m. is 22 heures **(vingt-deux heures)**, etc.

	Samedi	Dimanche
TV1	20.50 Film **Intouchables** d'O. Nakache et E. Toledano avec François Cluzet et Omar Sy 23.10 Magazine de l'information – **Focus Élection**	20.50 Film **Casino royale** de Martin Campbell, avec Daniel Craig 23.30 Actualité – Revue de la semaine
Télé2	20.50 Télé-Réalité **En vacances** 22.50 Magazine littéraire **À livre ouvert** – Invité : Marc Lévy	20.50 Variétés **Fans de musique**, avec Renan Luce et Vanessa Paradis 23.00 Série – **Urgences**
Canal3	20.50 Série policière **Julie Lescault**, d'A. Lecaye 22.00 Magazine/Variété – **Mieux vaut en rire**	20.50 Film **Le Discours d'un roi**, de Tom Hooper, avec Colin Firth et Geoffrey Rush 22.00 Magazine – **George VI, l'histoire derrière le film**
TLTP	20.30 Film d'animation **L'Âge de Glace**, de Chris Wadge et Carlos Saldanha 22:30 Dessin animé, **Scooby-Doo**	20.30 Film **Les Aventures de Tintin : Le Secret de La Licorne**, de Steven Spielberg et Peter Jackson 23:00 Dessin animé, **Barbapapa**
MaxiSPORT	20.50 Football **OM – PSG** 23.00 Championnat d'Angleterre	20.40 Magazine **Une semaine de Sport** 22.30 Tennis - Résumé

Additional readings @ **my.hrw.com**
FRENCH InterActive Reader

COMPARAISONS *Culturelles*

The TV schedule on the opposite page presents a sample of programs which are broadcast after the evening news on some French channels. As in the United States, French viewers also have access to numerous cable and satellite channels. Research some French television stations online. What similarities and differences do you see between French and American prime time TV?

- number of major channels
- starting times of the shows
- variety of programming
- importance of movies in programming

Samedi sport

Compréhension

1. À quelle heure est le match de foot samedi? Sur quelle chaîne?
2. Comment s'appelle le programme de variétés sur Télé 2? Qui sont les invités?
3. Quels films passent sur TLTP? Pour qui sont ces programmes? Quels sont les titres de ces films en anglais?
4. Comment s'appelle le film sur TV1 samedi soir? Qui sont les acteurs?

Et vous?

Vous êtes en France et vous aimez les films. Quel film est-ce que vous aimeriez *(would like)* regarder à la télé ce week-end? Sur quelle chaîne? À quelle heure? Est-ce que c'est un film français ou américain?

L'INTERNET, c'est cool!

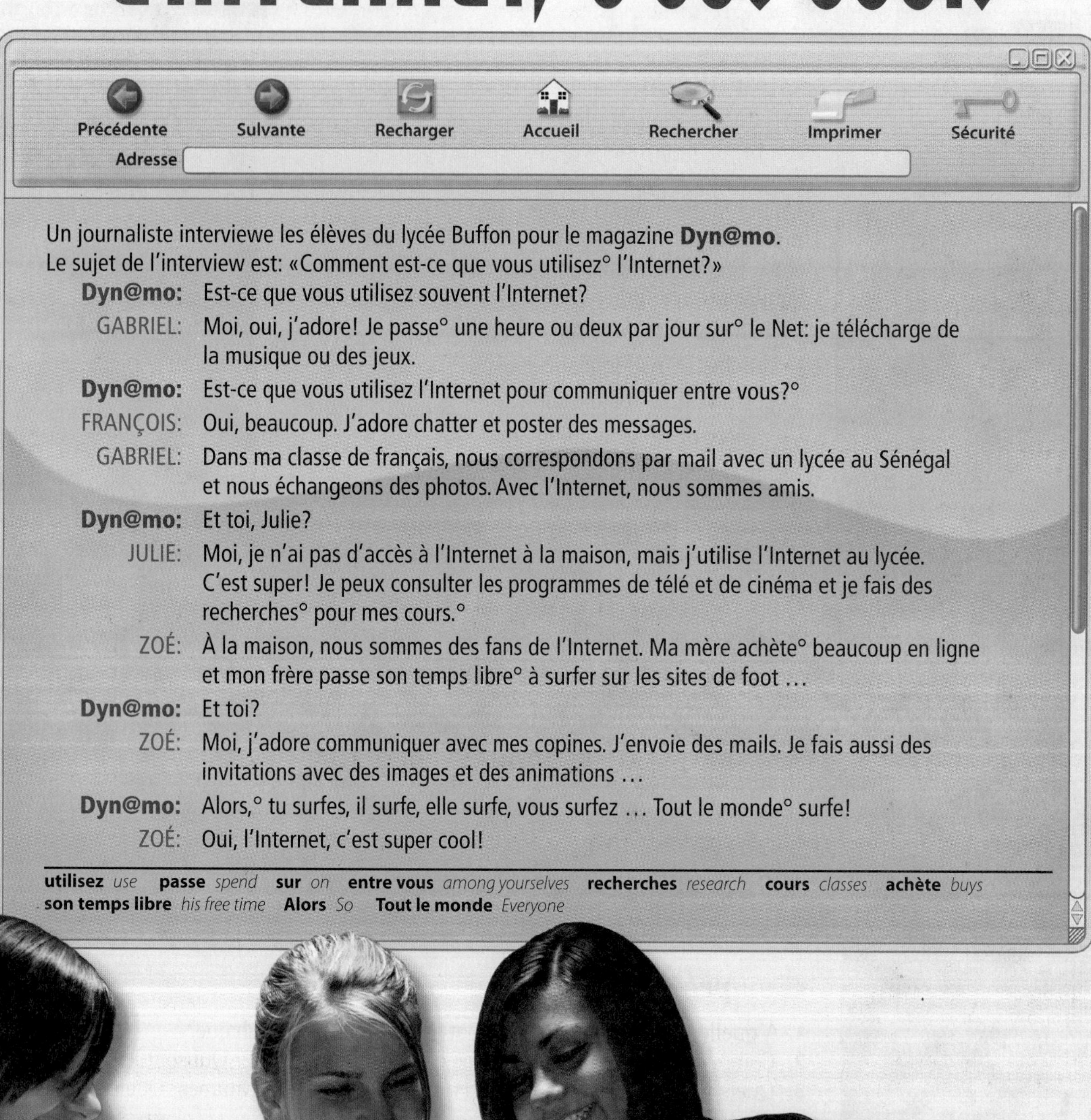

Un journaliste interviewe les élèves du lycée Buffon pour le magazine **Dyn@mo**.
Le sujet de l'interview est: «Comment est-ce que vous utilisez° l'Internet?»

Dyn@mo: Est-ce que vous utilisez souvent l'Internet?

GABRIEL: Moi, oui, j'adore! Je passe° une heure ou deux par jour sur° le Net: je télécharge de la musique ou des jeux.

Dyn@mo: Est-ce que vous utilisez l'Internet pour communiquer entre vous?°

FRANÇOIS: Oui, beaucoup. J'adore chatter et poster des messages.

GABRIEL: Dans ma classe de français, nous correspondons par mail avec un lycée au Sénégal et nous échangeons des photos. Avec l'Internet, nous sommes amis.

Dyn@mo: Et toi, Julie?

JULIE: Moi, je n'ai pas d'accès à l'Internet à la maison, mais j'utilise l'Internet au lycée. C'est super! Je peux consulter les programmes de télé et de cinéma et je fais des recherches° pour mes cours.°

ZOÉ: À la maison, nous sommes des fans de l'Internet. Ma mère achète° beaucoup en ligne et mon frère passe son temps libre° à surfer sur les sites de foot ...

Dyn@mo: Et toi?

ZOÉ: Moi, j'adore communiquer avec mes copines. J'envoie des mails. Je fais aussi des invitations avec des images et des animations ...

Dyn@mo: Alors,° tu surfes, il surfe, elle surfe, vous surfez ... Tout le monde° surfe!

ZOÉ: Oui, l'Internet, c'est super cool!

utilisez *use* **passe** *spend* **sur** *on* **entre vous** *among yourselves* **recherches** *research* **cours** *classes* **achète** *buys* **son temps libre** *his free time* **Alors** *So* **Tout le monde** *Everyone*

Additional readings @ **my.hrw.com**
FRENCH InterActive Reader

NOTE Culturelle

Les Français et la communication électronique

Today almost three-quarters of the French households have Internet. They use it principally to stay in touch with friends and family via e-mail and social networks. Adults turn to the Internet to make travel reservations and to shop online. Young people spend time on the Internet playing online games and downloading music.

The great majority of French young people have their own cell phones and communicate with one another via text messages (**un texto**). More and more have upgraded to smartphones allowing them also to share photos and videos.

PETIT DICTIONNAIRE DE LA COMMUNICATION ÉLECTRONIQUE

- **envoyer un mail (un mél)** = *to send an e-mail*
- **échanger des textos, des SMS** = *to text, exchange text messages*
- **partager une photo, une vidéo** = *to share a photo, a video*
- **chatter** = *to chat*
- **poster un message** = *to post a message*
- **regarder le profil des ses amis** = *to look at your friends' profiles*
- **être en ligne** = *to be online*

COMPARAISONS Culturelles

Read the Dyn@mo interview again and make a list of the different ways students at the lycée Buffon use the Internet. Then list the ways in which you use the Internet. Do you engage in some of the same activities as the French teenagers?

les jeunes Français	moi
•	•
•	•
•	•

Bonjour, Trinh!

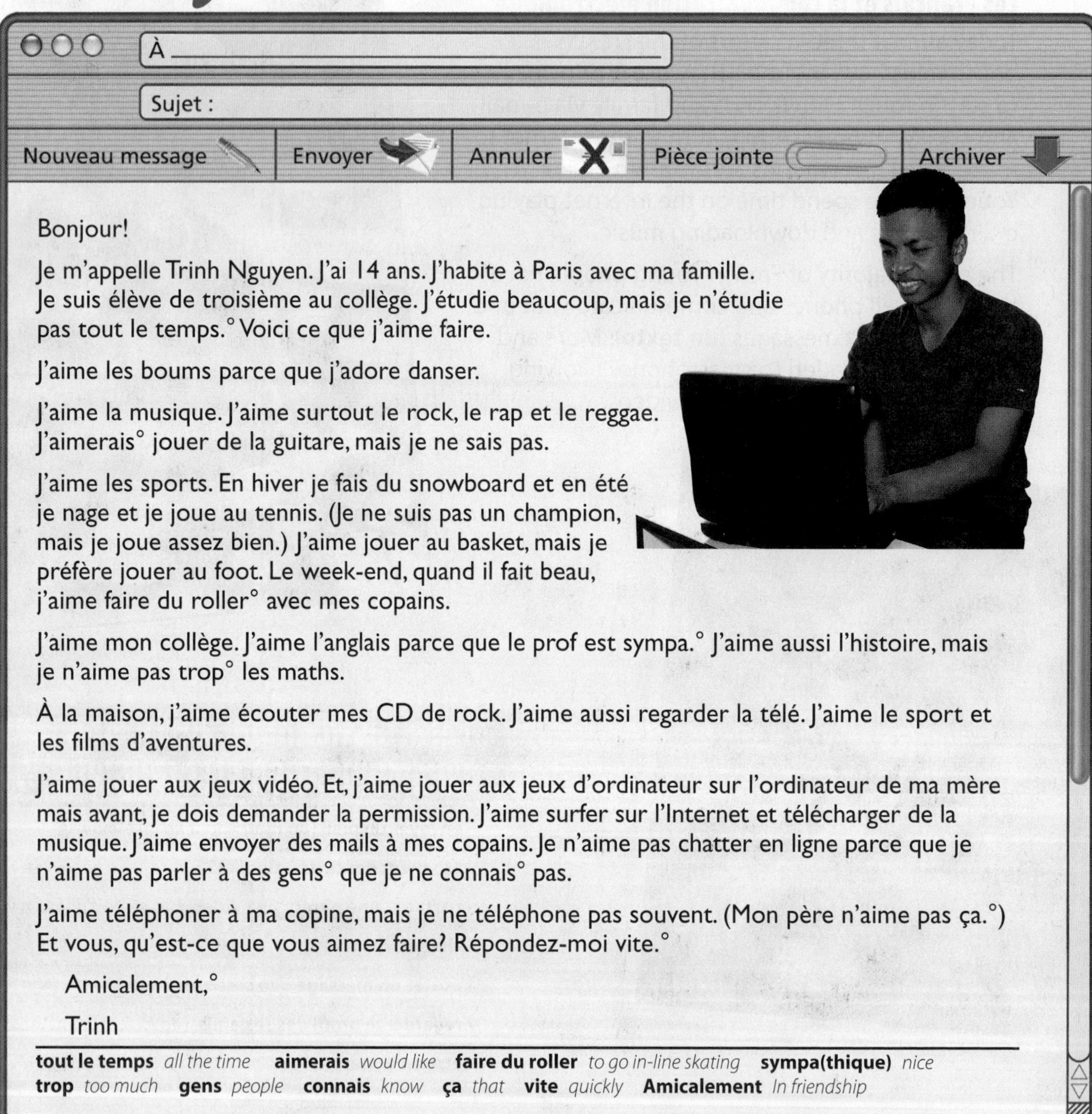

À

Sujet :

Nouveau message | Envoyer | Annuler | Pièce jointe | Archiver

Bonjour!

Je m'appelle Trinh Nguyen. J'ai 14 ans. J'habite à Paris avec ma famille. Je suis élève de troisième au collège. J'étudie beaucoup, mais je n'étudie pas tout le temps.° Voici ce que j'aime faire.

J'aime les boums parce que j'adore danser.

J'aime la musique. J'aime surtout le rock, le rap et le reggae. J'aimerais° jouer de la guitare, mais je ne sais pas.

J'aime les sports. En hiver je fais du snowboard et en été je nage et je joue au tennis. (Je ne suis pas un champion, mais je joue assez bien.) J'aime jouer au basket, mais je préfère jouer au foot. Le week-end, quand il fait beau, j'aime faire du roller° avec mes copains.

J'aime mon collège. J'aime l'anglais parce que le prof est sympa.° J'aime aussi l'histoire, mais je n'aime pas trop° les maths.

À la maison, j'aime écouter mes CD de rock. J'aime aussi regarder la télé. J'aime le sport et les films d'aventures.

J'aime jouer aux jeux vidéo. Et, j'aime jouer aux jeux d'ordinateur sur l'ordinateur de ma mère mais avant, je dois demander la permission. J'aime surfer sur l'Internet et télécharger de la musique. J'aime envoyer des mails à mes copains. Je n'aime pas chatter en ligne parce que je n'aime pas parler à des gens° que je ne connais° pas.

J'aime téléphoner à ma copine, mais je ne téléphone pas souvent. (Mon père n'aime pas ça.°) Et vous, qu'est-ce que vous aimez faire? Répondez-moi vite.°

Amicalement,°

Trinh

tout le temps *all the time* **aimerais** *would like* **faire du roller** *to go in-line skating* **sympa(thique)** *nice*
trop *too much* **gens** *people* **connais** *know* **ça** *that* **vite** *quickly* **Amicalement** *In friendship*

STRATEGY Reading

Cognates You have already discovered that there are many words in French that look like English words and have similar meanings. These are called cognates. Cognates let you increase your reading comprehension effortlessly. Be sure to pronounce them the French way!

- Sometimes the spelling is the same, or almost the same:

un champion	*champion*
la permission	*permission*

- Sometimes the spelling is a little different:

les maths	*math*

Additional readings @ **my.hrw.com**
FRENCH InterActive Reader

Activité écrite: Une lettre à Trinh

You are writing an e-mail to Trinh in which you introduce yourself and explain what you like to do. Be sure to use only vocabulary that you know in French. You may tell him:

- if you like music (and what kind)
- what sports you like to do in fall or winter
- what sports you like to do in spring or summer
- which school subjects you like and which you do not like
- what you like to do at home
- which programs you like to watch on TV
- what you like to do on the Internet and what you do not like to do

Writing Hint Use Trinh's letter as a model.

NOTE Culturelle

Les Vietnamiens en France

Vietnam and other Southeast Asian countries like Laos and Cambodia have a long civilization. For a period of about eighty years until the mid-1950s, these countries were occupied and administered by France which established schools and promoted the use of the French language among their populations.

In recent years, many Vietnamese people like Trinh's family have emigrated to France. Vietnamese restaurants are very popular with French students because of their fine yet inexpensive cuisine.

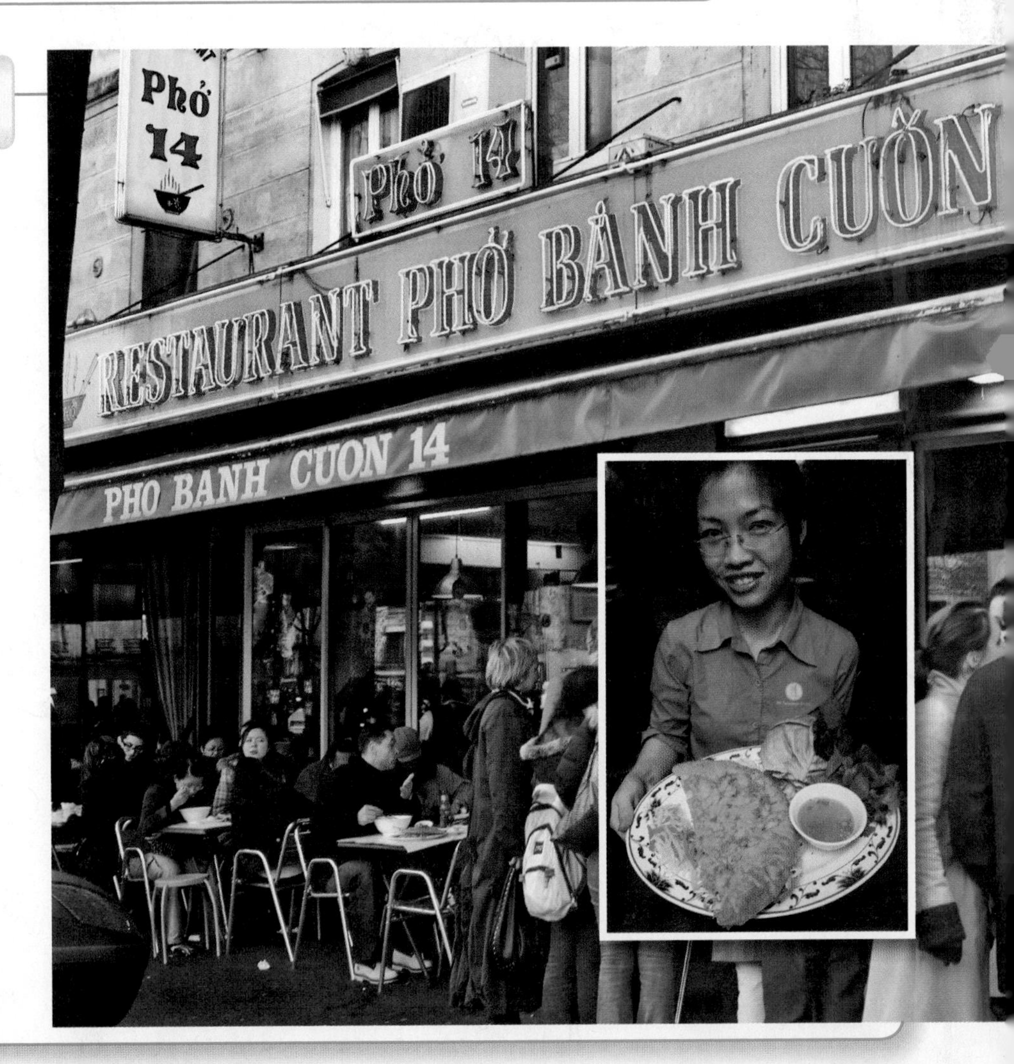

À l'école en France

Bonjour, Nathalie!

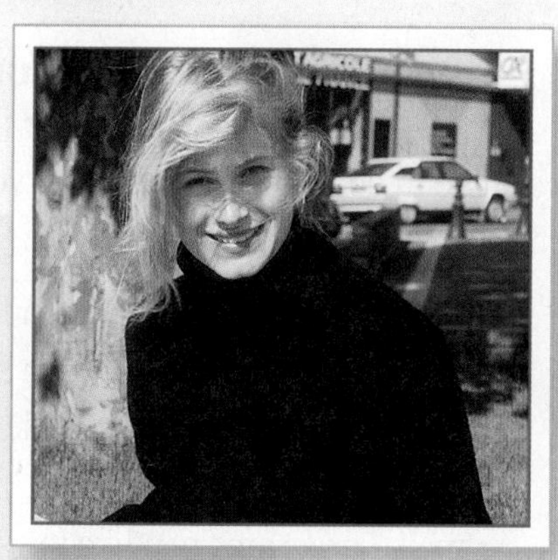

Bonjour!
Je m'appelle Nathalie Aubin.
J'ai 15 ans et j'habite à Savigny-sur-Orge avec ma famille. (Savigny est une petite° ville à 20 kilomètres au sud° de Paris.)
J'ai un frère, Christophe, 17 ans, et deux soeurs, Céline, 13 ans, et Florence, 7 ans.
Mon père est programmeur. (Il travaille à Paris.)
Ma mère est dentiste. (Elle travaille à Savigny.)
Je vais au lycée Jean-Baptiste Corot.
Je suis élève° de seconde°.
Et vous?

Nathalie

petite *small* **sud** *south* **élève** *student* **seconde** *tenth grade*

Les photos de Nathalie

Voici ma famille.

ma mère *ma soeur Céline*

mon père

moi

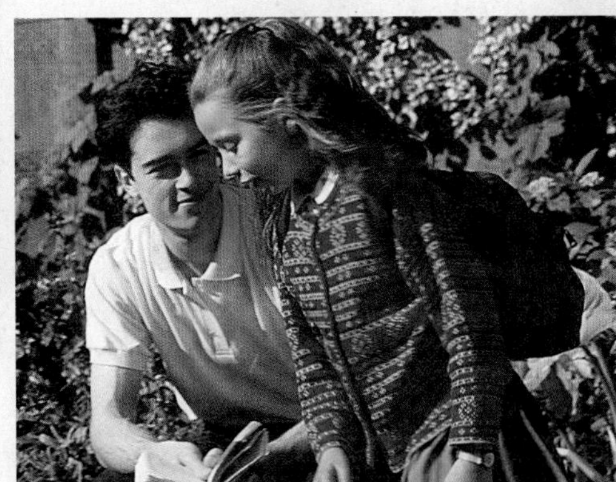

mon frère Christophe et ma soeur Florence

Voici ma maison. (C'est une maison confortable, mais ce n'est pas un château!)

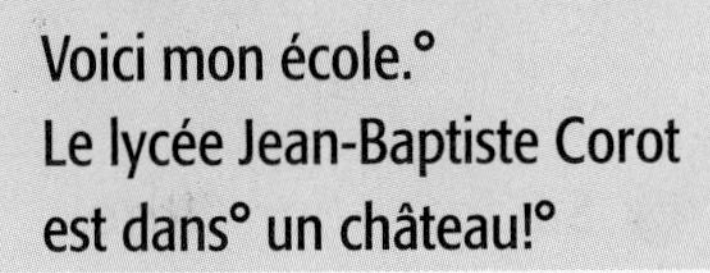

Voici mon école.°
Le lycée Jean-Baptiste Corot est dans° un château!°

école *school* **dans** *in* **château** *castle*

Le lycée Jean-Baptiste Corot

Jean-Baptiste Corot

The lycée Jean-Baptiste Corot is located in Savigny-sur-Orge, a small town about 12 miles south of Paris. Like many French schools, it is named after a famous French person. Jean-Baptiste Corot was a 19th century painter, remembered especially for his landscapes.

The lycée Jean-Baptiste Corot is both old and modern. It was created in the 1950s on the grounds of a historical castle dating from the 12th century. The castle, which serves as the administrative center, is still surrounded by a moat. The lycée itself has many modern facilities which include:

- **les salles de classe** *(classrooms)*
- **la cantine** *(cafeteria)*
- **le stade** *(stadium)* **et**
  le terrain de sport *(playing field)*

un pastel de Corot

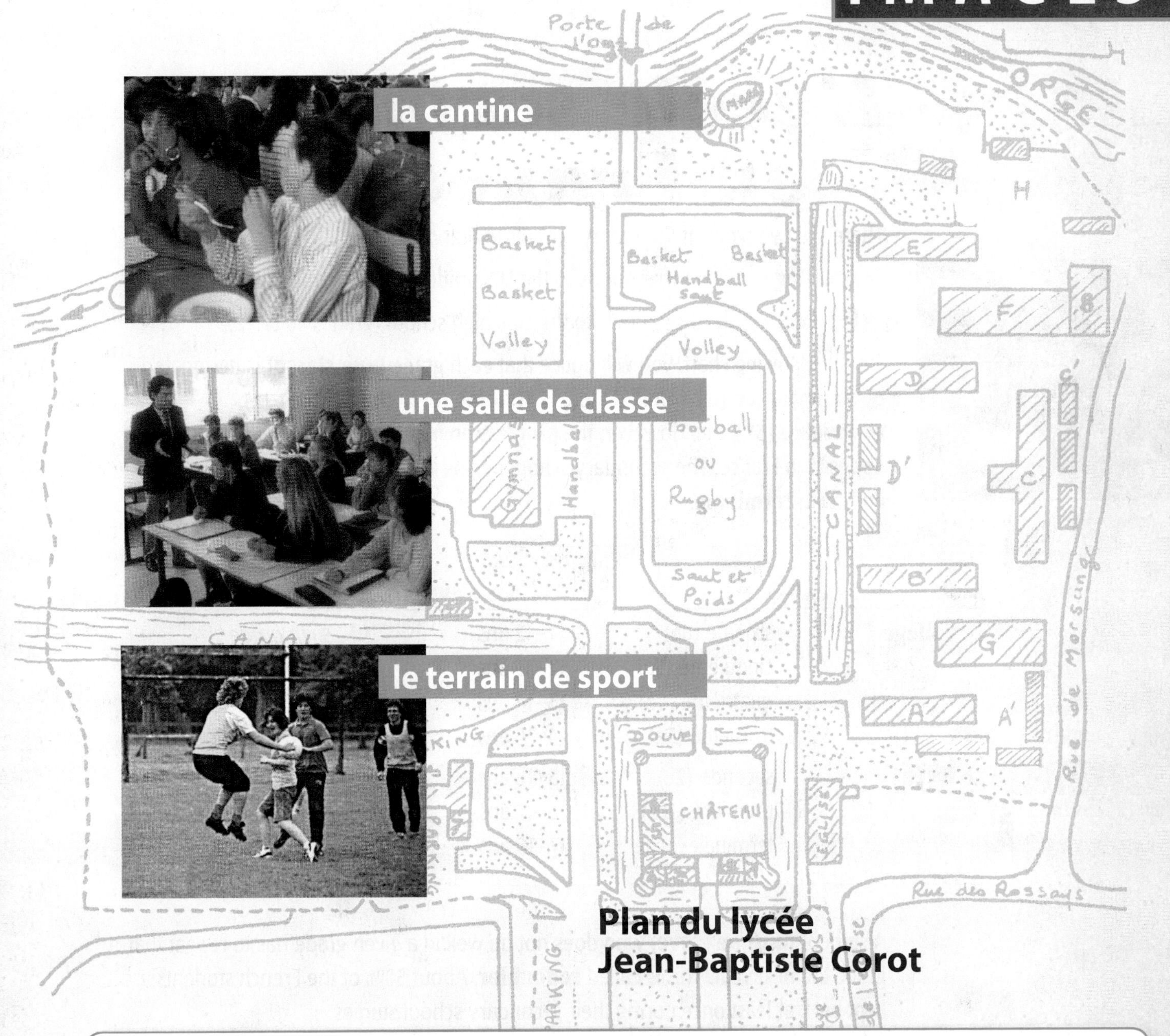

Plan du lycée Jean-Baptiste Corot

Comparaisons Culturelles

1. Compare your school to the lycée Jean-Baptiste Corot.

- Is your school named after somebody? If so, why is this person famous?
- Is your school older or more modern than the lycée Jean-Baptiste Corot? When was it built (approximately)?
- Does your school have the same facilities as the lycée Jean-Baptiste Corot? Does it have other facilities?

2. Make a map of your school, giving French names to its facilities. (Ask for your teacher's help for words you do not know.)

L'école secondaire en France

There are two types of secondary schools in France:

- **le collège,** which corresponds to the U.S. middle school (grades 6 to 9)
- **le lycée,** which corresponds to the U.S. high school (grades 10 to 12)

On the following chart, you will notice that each grade **(une classe)** is designated by a number (as in the United States): **sixième (6e), cinquième (5e), quatrième (4e),** etc. However, the progression from grade to grade is the opposite in France. The secondary school begins in France with **sixième** and ends with **terminale**.

École	Classe	Âge des élèves	Équivalent américain
Le collège	sixième (6e)	11–12 ans	*sixth grade*
	cinquième (5e)	12–13 ans	*seventh grade*
	quatrième (4e)	13–14 ans	*eighth grade*
	troisième (3e)	14–15 ans	*ninth grade*
Le lycée	seconde (2e)	15–16 ans	*tenth grade*
	première (1re)	16–17 ans	*eleventh grade*
	terminale	17–18 ans	*twelfth grade*

A student **(un/une élève)** who does not do well in a given grade has to repeat that grade the next year. This is called **redoubler**. About 50% of the French students are kept back at least once during their secondary school studies.

At the end of high school, French students take a two-part national examination called **le baccalauréat,** or **le bac** for short, which they have to pass in order to enter the university.

- The first part, which focuses on the French language, is administered at the end of **première**.
- The second part, which is given at the end of **terminale**, offers students over twenty options reflecting their area of specialization.

Only 75% of the students who take the **bac** in a given year pass the exam. Of those who are successful, about 85% continue their studies either at the university or at a specialized professional school. Since education in France is considered a responsibility of the government, tuition is free at all public universities.

Des élèves vous parlent

David Souliac, 14 ans

J'habite à Bergerac, une petite ville
dans le sud-ouest° de la France. — *southwest*
Je suis élève de 4e au collège Jacques Prévert.
Là, j'étudie l'anglais et l'espagnol.

Antoine Restaut, 14 ans

J'habite à Paris.
Je suis élève au collège Jeannine Manuel.
C'est un collège international.
J'aime les maths et les sciences.
Je voudrais être pilote comme° mon père. — *like*

Pauline Lescure, 16 ans

Je suis élève de première au lycée Schoelcher
à Fort-de-France en Martinique.
J'étudie les sciences.
Je veux être médecin.° — *doctor*
Je voudrais aller° à l'université à Paris. — *to go*
Mais d'abord,° je dois être reçue° au bac. — *first/pass*

Le programme scolaire *(School curriculum)*

At the middle school **(au collège)**, all French students take certain required subjects **(des matières obligatoires)**. In **quatrième,** for instance, these subjects include French, math, one foreign language, history and geography, science **(sciences de la vie et de la terre** – life and earth sciences), and art. Depending on their preferences and career plans, they can also choose among a certain number of electives **(des matières facultatives)**. Many opt for a second foreign language **(une langue).**

Here is a list of subjects taught in French middle schools. (Note that no school offers all the languages listed, but most schools offer three or four.) How many of the subjects can you identify?

Matières obligatoires	Matières facultatives	Langues modernes
français	latin	allemand
maths	grec	anglais
1ère langue moderne	2ème langue moderne	arabe
histoire		espagnol
géographie		hébreu
physique-chimie		italien
sciences de la vie et de la terre		portugais
technologie		russe
éducation civique		
éducation physique et sportive		
arts plastiques		
éducation musicale		

Comparaisons Culturelles

Compare the curriculum of an eighth grader in the United States with that of a French teenager in the equivalent grade **(quatrième)**. You may first want to list the subjects offered in your school system for grades six through nine.

a) Matières obligatoires
b) Matières facultatives
c) Langues modernes

Do you prefer the French or the American curriculum? Explain.

L'emploi du temps de Nathalie

Nathalie Aubin est en seconde au lycée Jean-Baptiste Corot. Voici son emploi du temps.

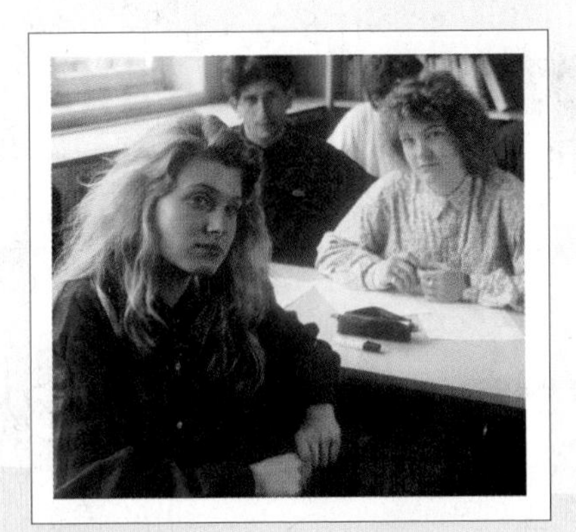

LYCÉE JEAN-BAPTISTE COROT

Étudiante: AUBIN, Nathalie

	LUNDI	MARDI	MERCREDI	JEUDI	VENDREDI	SAMEDI
8h30 à 9h30	Histoire	Allemand		Informatique°		Français
9h30 à 10h30	Anglais	Français	Anglais	Physique	Allemand	Français
10h30 à 11h30	Sport	Français	Informatique	Maths	Latin	Latin
11h30 à 12h30	Français	Latin	Maths		Sciences vie et terre	Histoire ou civilisation
13h00 à 14h00						
14h00 à 15h00	Sciences vie et terre	Maths		Allemand		
15h00 à 16h00	Géographie	Maths				
16h00 à 17h00	Physique	Anglais		Sport		

informatique *computer science*

Comparaisons Culturelles

Compare Nathalie's schedule with that of an American student in the same grade (tenth grade). You may want to make a chart:

	France	United States
number of classes per week		
number of foreign languages		
number of hours per week for sports		
other differences		

On the basis of your comparisons, do you prefer the French system or the American system? Explain.

Mon emploi du temps
Write out your own school schedule in French.

Expressions pour la classe

Le professeur dit ...

à une élève / à un élève	à la classe
Regarde! *(Look!)* Regarde la vidéo.	**Regardez!** Regardez la vidéo.
Écoute! *(Listen!)* Écoute le CD.	**Écoutez!** Écoutez le CD.
Parle! *(Speak!)* Parle plus fort *(louder)*.	**Parlez!** Parlez plus fort.
Réponds! *(Answer!)* Réponds à la question.	**Répondez!** Répondez à la question.
Répète! *(Repeat!)* Répète la phrase *(sentence)*.	**Répétez!** Répétez la phrase.
Lis! *(Read!)* Lis l'exercice.	**Lisez!** Lisez l'exercice.
Écris! *(Write!)* Écris dans ton cahier.	**Écrivez!** Écrivez dans vos cahiers.
Prends *(Take)* une feuille de papier. / un crayon	**Prenez** une feuille de papier. / un crayon
Ouvre *(Open)* ton livre. / la porte	**Ouvrez** vos livres. / la porte
Ferme *(Close)* ton cahier. / la fenêtre	**Fermez** vos cahiers. / la fenêtre
Viens! *(Come!)* Viens ici.	**Venez!** Venez ici.
Va! *(Go!)* Va au tableau.	**Allez!** Allez au tableau.
Lève-toi! *(Stand up!)*	**Levez-vous!**
Assieds-toi! *(Sit down!)*	**Asseyez-vous!**
Apporte-moi *(Bring me)* / **Donne-moi** *(Give me)* / **Montre-moi** *(Show me)* ton devoir.	**Apporte-moi** / **Donne-moi** / **Montre-moi** vos devoirs.

Quelques objets

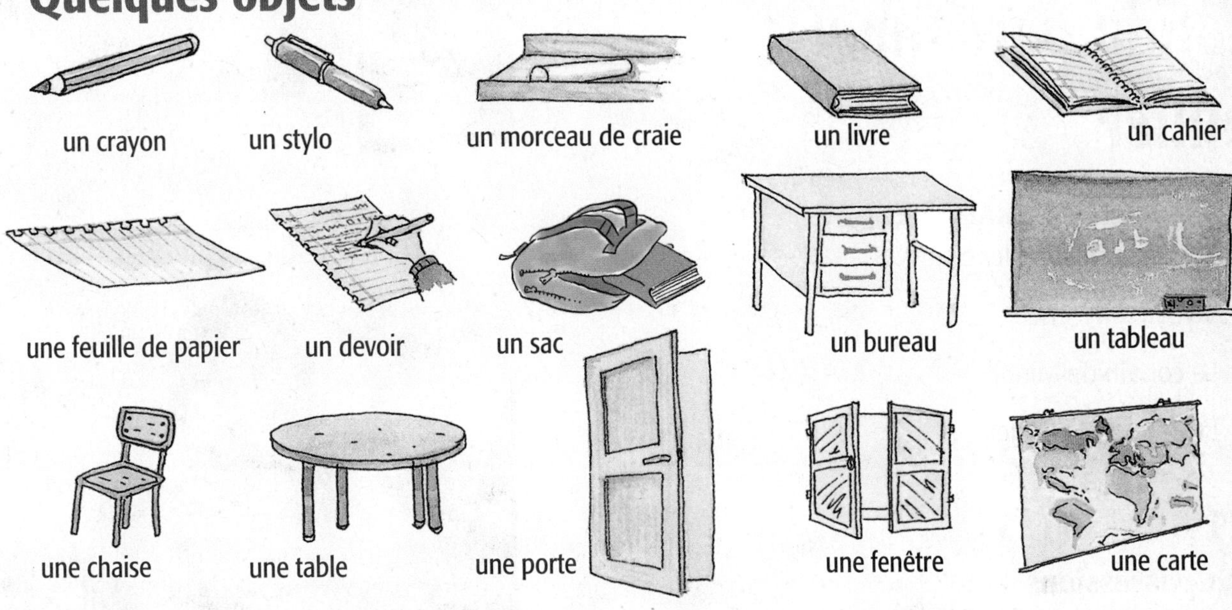

Tu dis ...

I know.

I don't know.

I don't understand.

What does ... mean?

How does one say ... in French?

Écoutez bien!

Imagine you are in a school in France. Listen carefully to what different French teachers ask you to do and carry out their instructions. If you have trouble understanding the commands, your teacher will mime the actions for you.

Unité 4

Le monde personnel et familier

THÈME ET OBJECTIFS

People and possessions

When you meet French teenagers, you will want to share information about yourself, your friends, and your possessions.

In this unit, you will learn ...

- to talk about yourself: your personality and what you look like
- to describe your friends and how old they are
- to describe your room
- to talk about everyday objects that you own or use
- to describe these objects: their size and color

Leçon 9

LE FRANÇAIS PRATIQUE

DVD AUDIO

Les personnes et les objets

Accent sur ... les jeunes Français

France is a young country. One quarter of the population is under the age of twenty. In their daily lives outside school, young people in France are not that different from their counterparts in the United States. They enjoy listening to music and going to the movies. On weekends, they go to the mall or into the city to check out the newest teen fashions and the latest in video games. As computers become more and more widespread, French young people often spend their free time surfing the Internet and participating in chat rooms and forums.

Since almost everyone studies English in school, French teenagers are very much aware of the American way of life. They have a generally positive attitude towards the United States and many would like to visit our country.

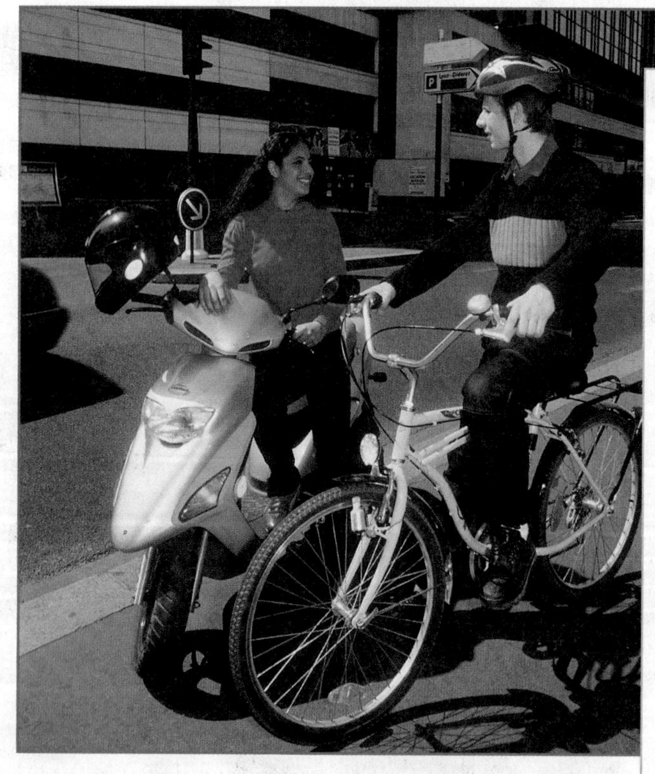

Thomas a un vélo. C'est un vélo anglais.
Michèle n'a pas de vélo. Elle a un scooter.

Élodie et Paul font une promenade en ville. Paul a un MP3. Il écoute de la musique. Élodie a un portable. Elle téléphone à une copine.

@HOMETUTOR
my.hrw.com

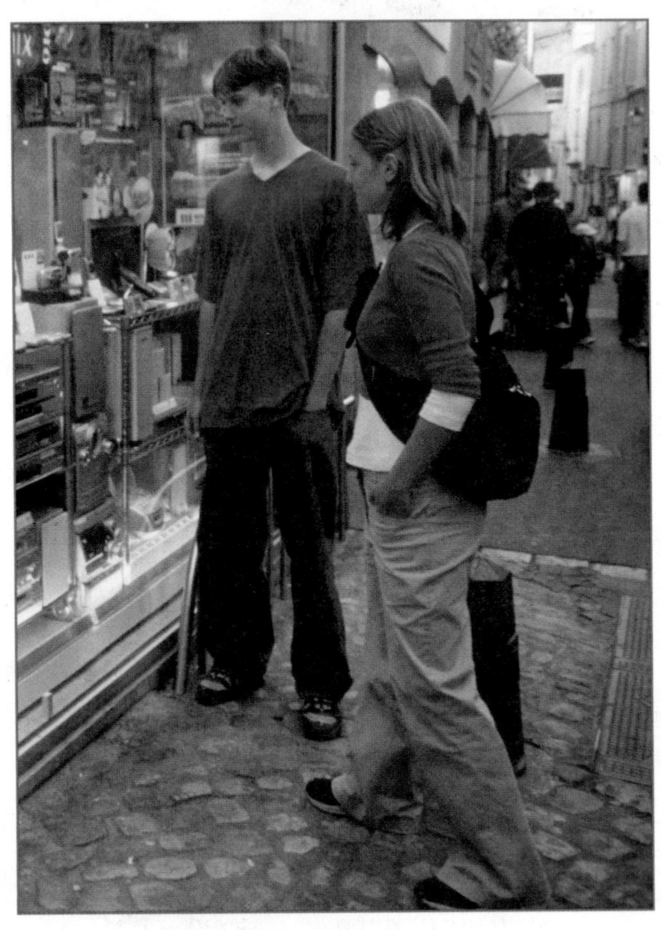
Jean-Marc et Valérie sont devant un magasin d'équipement hi-fi. Ils regardent des mini-chaînes.

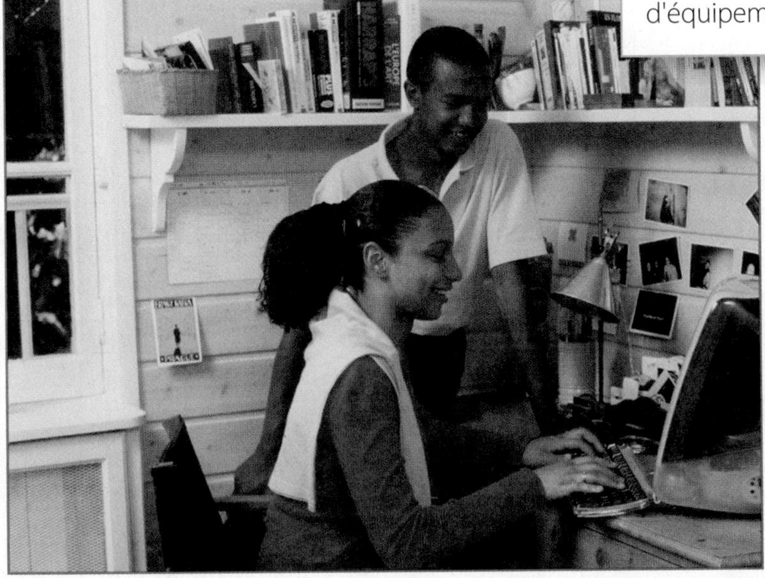
Zaïna a un ordinateur. Elle surfe sur l'Internet. Elle aime aussi jouer aux jeux d'ordinateur avec Ousmane.

A VOCABULAIRE La description des personnes

Qui est-ce?

C'est un copain.

▶ How to describe someone:

Qui est-ce?
C'est un copain.

Comment s'appelle-t-il?
Il s'appelle Marc.

Quel âge a-t-il?
Il a seize ans.

Comment est-il?
Il est petit.
Il est blond.

Qui est-ce?
C'est une copine.

Comment s'appelle-t-elle?
Elle s'appelle Sophie.

Quel âge a-t-elle?
Elle a quinze ans.

Comment est-elle?
Elle est grande.
Elle est brune.

Les personnes

une **personne**

une **personne**

un **étudiant**	*student*	une **étudiante**	
un **élève**	*pupil*	une **élève**	
un **camarade**	*classmate*	une **camarade**	
un **homme**	*man*	une **femme**	*woman*
un **professeur**, un **prof**	*teacher*	un **professeur**, une **prof**	
un **voisin**	*neighbor*	une **voisine**	

→ **Une personne** is always feminine whether it refers to a male or female person.

→ **Un professeur** is always masculine whether it refers to a male or female teacher. However, in casual French, one distinguishes between **un prof** (male) and **une prof** (female).

La description physique

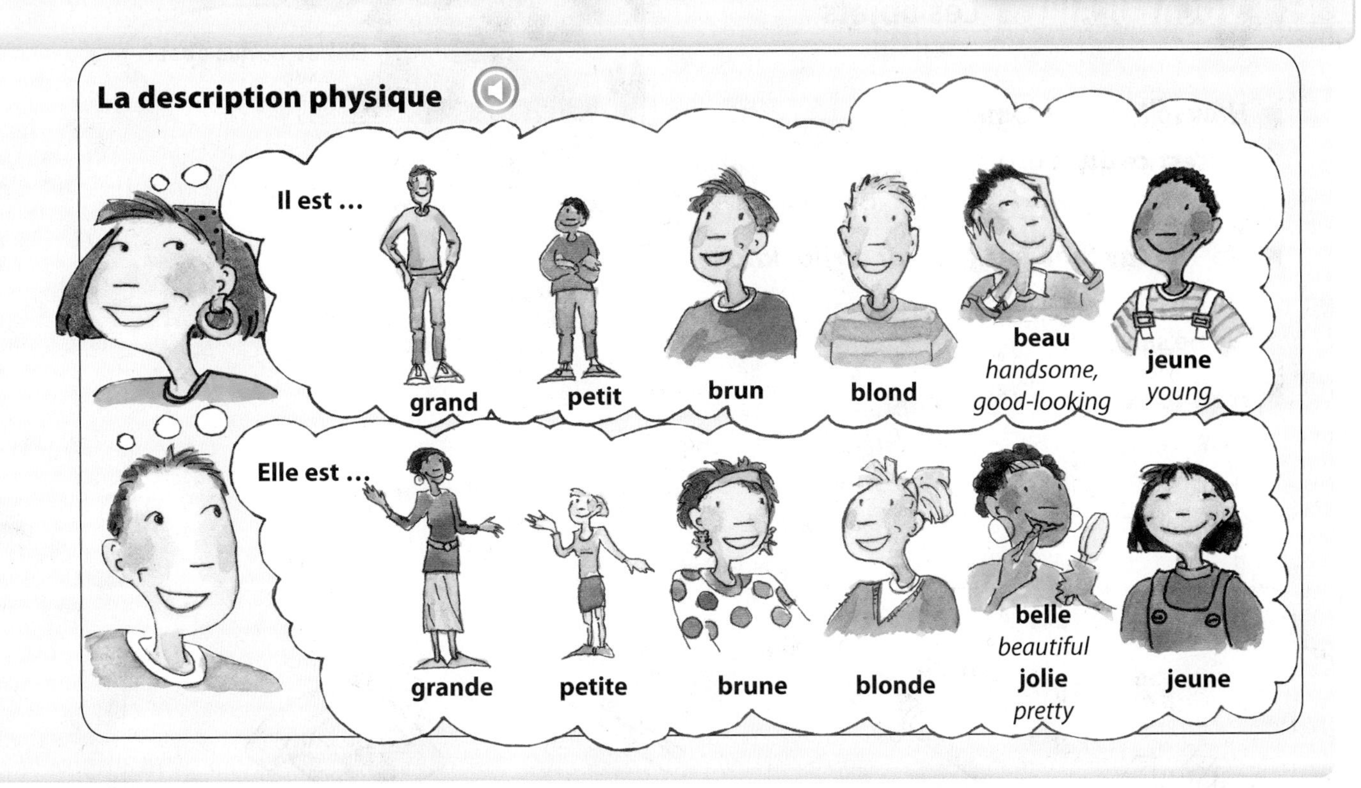

1 Oui ou non?

PARLER Describe the people below in affirmative or negative sentences.

▶ Frankenstein / beau?
Frankenstein n'est pas beau.

1. Shaquille O'Neal / grand?
2. Brad Pitt / brun?
3. Dracula / beau?
4. mon copain / blond?
5. mon père / petit?
6. mon voisin / jeune?
7. Britney Spears / belle?
8. le président / jeune?
9. Oprah Winfrey / grande?
10. ma copine / petite?
11. ma mère / brune?
12. ma voisine / jolie?

2 Vacances à Québec

PARLER/ÉCRIRE You spent last summer in Quebec and have just had your photographs developed. Describe each of the people, giving name, approximate age, and two or three characteristics.

Alain

blond(e)	petit(e)
brun(e)	beau (belle)
grand(e)	jeune

▶ **Il s'appelle Alain.
Il est blond.
Il a seize ans.
Il n'est pas grand.
Il est petit.**

1. Anne-Marie

2. Jean-Pierre

3. Claire

4. Mademoiselle Lévêque

5. Madame Paquette

6. Monsieur Beliveau

B VOCABULAIRE Les objets

Qu'est-ce que c'est?

▶ How to identify something:

Qu'est-ce que c'est?	*What is it? What's that?*	**—Qu'est-ce que c'est?**
C'est …	*It's …, That's …*	**—C'est** un livre.

▶ How to say that you know or do not know:

Je sais.	*I know.*
Je ne sais pas.	*I don't know.*

▶ How to point out something:

—Regarde ça.	*Look at that.*
—Quoi?	*What?*
—Ça, là-bas.	*That, over there.*

RAPPEL

In French, the names of objects are MASCULINE or FEMININE.

Masculine objects can be introduced by **un** or **le (l')**: **un stylo, le stylo, l'objet.**

Feminine objects can be introduced by **une** or **la (l')**: **une montre, la montre, l'affiche.**

3 *Qu'est-ce que c'est?*

PARLER Ask a classmate to identify the following objects.

▶ **Qu'est-ce que c'est?**
C'est un stylo.

4 *S'il te plaît*

PARLER Ask a classmate to give you the following objects.

▶ **—S'il te plaît, donne-moi le livre.**
—Voilà le livre.
—Merci.

C VOCABULAIRE Les affaires personnelles *(personal belongings)*

▶ *How to talk about things you have:*

Est-ce que tu as ... ?	*Do you have ... ?*	—**Est-ce que tu as** une moto?
Oui, j'ai ...	*Yes, I have ...*	—**Oui, j'ai** une moto.

Quelques objets

un portable (un smartphone)

un appareil-photo

un MP3 (un lecteur MP3)

une tablette

une télé

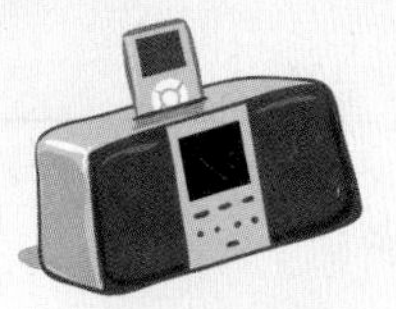
une radio (un dock)

un ordinateur

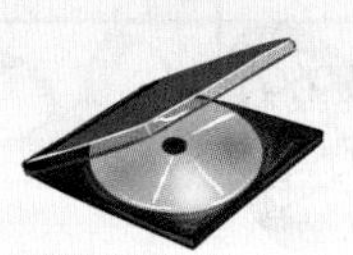
un CD

un DVD

une voiture (une auto)

un vélo (une bicyclette)

une mobylette

un scooter

une moto

▶ *How to ask if an object works:*

—Est-ce que la radio **marche?**	*Does the radio work?*
—Oui, elle **marche.**	*Yes, it works.*

➔ The verb **marcher** has two meanings:

for people:	*to walk*	Nous **marchons.**
for things:	*to work, to run*	Le scooter ne **marche** pas bien.

RAPPEL

Masculine nouns can be replaced by **il.**

Le vélo marche.

Il marche bien.

Feminine nouns can be replaced by **elle.**

La voiture marche.

Elle marche bien.

@HOMETUTOR
my.hrw.com

5 Et toi?

PARLER

1. J'ai … *(Name 3 objects you own.)*
2. Je voudrais … *(Name 3 things you would like to have.)*
3. Pour Noël / Hanoukka, je voudrais … *(Name 2 gifts you would like to receive.)*

6 Joyeux anniversaire *(Happy birthday)*

PARLER/ÉCRIRE For your birthday, a rich aunt is giving you the choice between different possible gifts. Indicate your preferences.

▶ vélo ou scooter?

1. mobylette ou moto?
2. portable ou MP3?
3. appareil-photo ou radio?
4. tablette ou smartphone?
5. télé ou ordinateur?
6. DVD ou montre?

7 Qu'est-ce que tu as?

PARLER Éric asks Léa if she has the following objects. She says that she does. Play both roles.

▶ 

▶ ÉRIC: **Est-ce que tu as une guitare?**

LÉA: **Oui, j'ai une guitare.**

8 Est-ce qu'il marche bien?

PARLER Tell your classmates that you own the following objects. They will ask you if the objects are working. Answer according to the illustrations.

▶ **—J'ai un vélo.**
—Est-ce qu'il marche bien?
—Non, il ne marche pas bien.

▶ **—J'ai une télé.**
—Est-ce qu'elle marche bien?
—Oui, elle marche très bien.

D VOCABULAIRE Ma chambre *(My room)*

▶ *How to talk about what there is in a place:*

il y a	*there is*	Dans *(In)* ma chambre, **il y a** une télé.
	there are	Dans le garage, **il y a** deux voitures.
est-ce qu'il y a ... ?	*is/are there ... ?*	**Est-ce qu'il y a** un ordinateur dans la classe?
qu'est-ce qu'il y a ... ?	*what is there ... ?*	**Qu'est-ce qu'il y a** dans le garage?

Dans ma chambre

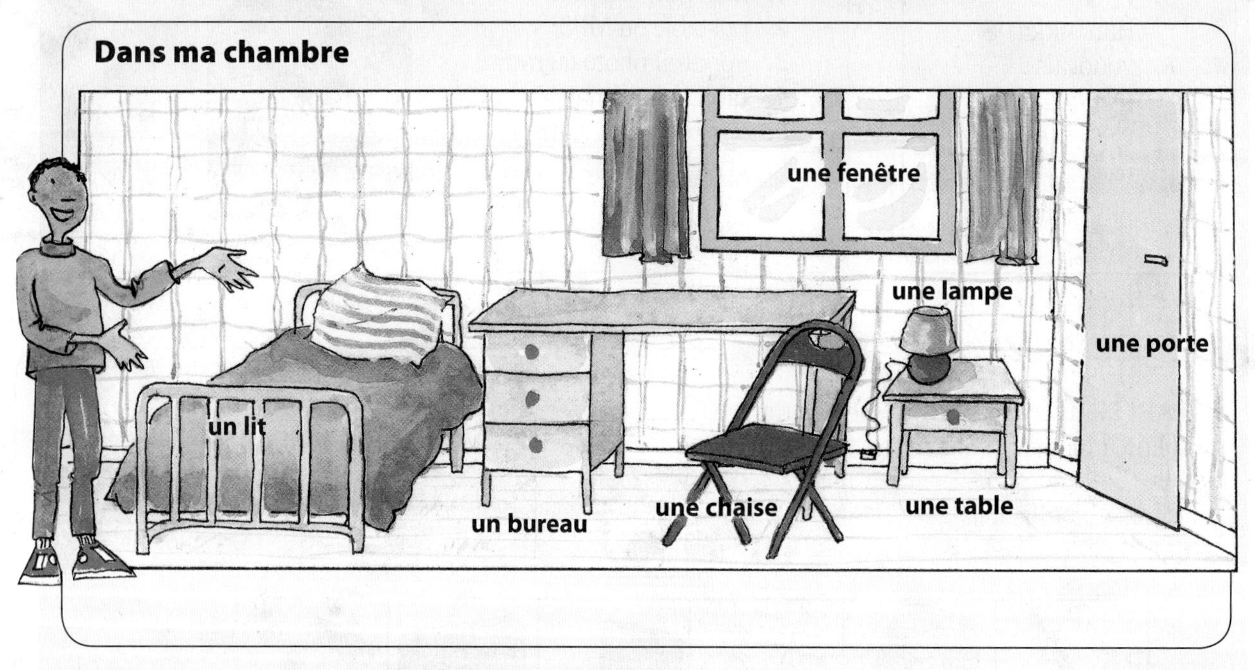

▶ *How to say where something or someone is:*

@HOMETUTOR
my.hrw.com

9 Qu'est-ce qu'il y a?

PARLER Describe the various objects that are in the pictures.

1. Sur la table, il y a …
2. Sous le lit, il y a …
3. Dans le garage, il y a …

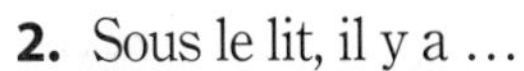

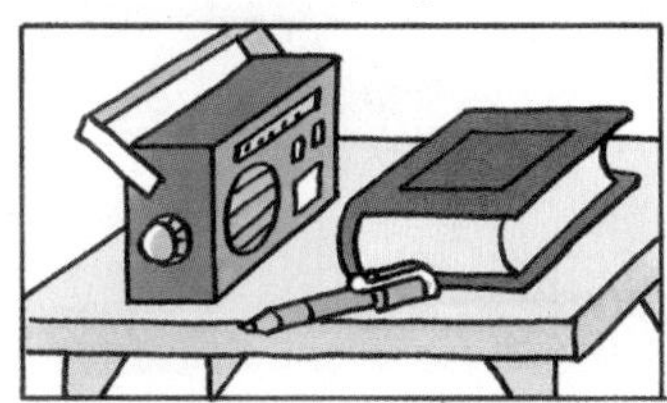

10 Ma chambre

PARLER/ÉCRIRE Describe the various objects (pieces of furniture and personal belongings) that are in your room.

▶ **Dans ma chambre, il y a une radio, …**
Il y a aussi …

11 Où est le téléphone?

PARLER Michèle is looking for the telephone. Jean-Claude tells her where it is.

▶ MICHÈLE: **Où est le téléphone?**
JEAN-CLAUDE: **Il est sur la table.**

12 C'est étrange! *(It's strange!)*

PARLER/ÉCRIRE Funny things sometimes happen. Describe these curious happenings by selecting an item from Column A and putting it in one of the places listed in Column B.

▶

▶ Il y a …

A	B
un rhinocéros	dans la classe
un éléphant	sur le bureau
une girafe	sous la table
un crabe	sous le lit
une souris *(mouse)*	derrière la porte
un ami de King Kong	sur la tour Eiffel
un extra-terrestre	dans le jardin *(garden)*
	devant le restaurant

13 La chambre de Nicole 

PARLER Florence wants to borrow a few things from Nicole's room. Nicole tells her where each object is.

▶ la télé
FLORENCE: **Où est la télé?**
NICOLE: **Elle est sur la table.**

1. la raquette
2. la guitare
3. le livre
4. le vélo
5. l'ordinateur
6. le sac
7. la radio
8. le CD
9. le portable

14 Pauvre Monsieur Vénard *(Poor Mr. Vénard)*

PARLER/ÉCRIRE Today Monsieur Vénard left on vacation, but he soon ran out of luck. Describe the four cartoons by completing the sentences below.

Le voyage de Monsieur Vénard

1. M. Vénard est ____ la voiture.

2. M. Vénard est ____ la voiture.

3. M. Vénard est ____ la voiture.

4. La contractuelle° est ____ la voiture.

la contractuelle *meter maid*

E VOCABULAIRE L'équipement électronique

un dock (avec enceintes)	*docking station (with speakers)*
chatter	*to chat*
envoyer un mail (un mél)	*to send an e-mail*
envoyer un texto, un SMS	*to send a text message*
poster un message	*to post a message*
surfer sur l'Internet (le Net)	*to surf the Internet*
télécharger de la musique	*to download music*

COMPARAISONS INTERPERSONNELLES

Here is a list of various activities that you can do with a computer. List the four activities you like to do best, ranking them in order of preference. Compare your lists with your classmates.

- chatter
- faire mes devoirs *(homework)*
- écouter de la musique
- envoyer un mail à un copain / une copine
- surfer sur le Net
- regarder les nouvelles *(news)*
- télécharger de la musique
- faire des recherches *(research)* pour la classe de français
- jouer aux jeux d'ordinateur

UN SONDAGE

Conduct a poll in your class to determine which two of the above computer activities students like the best and which two they like the least.

OBJECTIFS

Now you can . . .
- describe your belongings
- talk about people and give their ages

1 Écoutez bien!

ÉCOUTER You will hear a series of sentences. In each one an object is mentioned. If you see the object only in Léa's room, mark A. If you see the object only in Pierre's room, mark B. If you see the object in the two rooms, mark both A and B.

A. La chambre de Léa

B. La chambre de Pierre

	A Léa	B Pierre
1.		
2.		
3.		
4.		
5.		
6.		
7.		
8.		
9.		
10.		
11.		
12.		
13.		
14.		
15.		
16.		
17.		
18.		

2 Conversation dirigée 

PARLER André is visiting his cousin Marie. Act out the dialogue according to the instructions.

André		Marie
asks Marie if she has a computer	→ ↙	answers affirmatively
asks her if it works well	→ ↙	says that it works very well and asks why
says he would like to send an e-mail to a friend	→	says that the computer is on the desk in her room

3 Créa-dialogue  

PARLER Daniel is showing Nathalie his recent photographs, and she is asking questions about the various people. Create similar dialogues and act them out in class.

▶ un copain

Éric/14

▶ —Qui est-ce?
—C'est un copain.
—Comment s'appelle-t-il?
—Il s'appelle Éric.
—Quel âge a-t-il?
—Il a quatorze ans.

1. une cousine	2. un camarade	3. une camarade	4. un voisin	5. une voisine	6. un professeur
Valérie/20	Philippe Boucher/13	Nathalie Masson/15	Monsieur Dumas/70	Madame Smith/51	Monsieur Laval/35

4 Mes affaires 

ÉCRIRE Imagine that your family is going to move to another city. Prepare for the move by making a checklist of your things. Write out your list by hand or on a computer.

Mes affaires:
- **un lit**
-
-

5 Ma chambre 

ÉCRIRE A French student is going to spend two weeks at your house. Write him/her a short e-mail describing your room. In your note, mention …

- *at least 3 pieces of furniture*
- *at least 3 school-related objects*
- *4 personal belongings*

If you wish, you can add some descriptive comments.

6 Un ordinateur 

ÉCRIRE Imagine that you have just won a brand new computer in a contest at your school. Write a short paragraph in which you …

- *describe its various components*
- *mention 3 ways in which you want to use it*

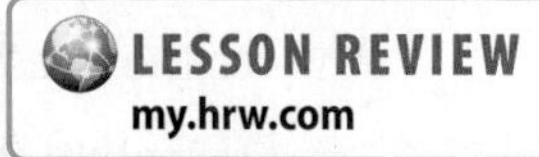

Leçon 10

Conversation et Culture

Vive la différence!

AUDIO

We are not necessarily like our friends. Léa describes herself and her best friend Céline. Both of them live in Paris and are quite different.

Léa

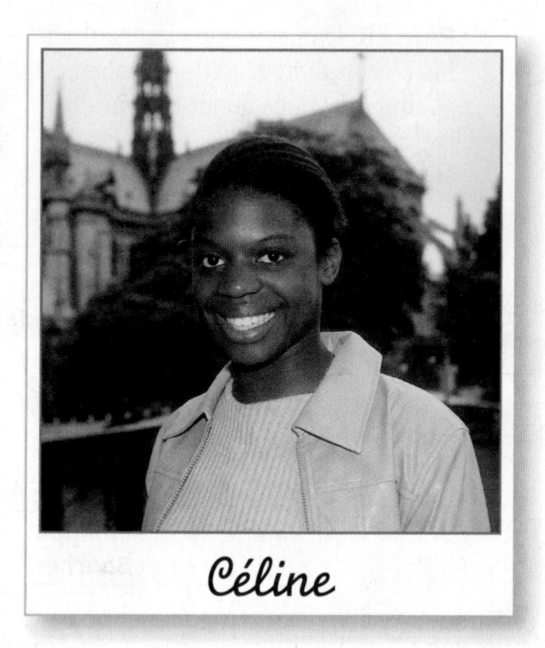

Céline

Je m'appelle Léa.

Je suis française.

J'ai des frères, mais je n'ai pas de soeur.

J'ai un chien.

J'ai un scooter.

J'aime la musique classique.

J'aime le basket et le tennis.

Elle s'appelle Céline.

Elle est haïtienne.

Elle n'a pas de frère, mais elle a deux soeurs.

Elle n'a pas de chien, mais elle a un chat très mignon.

Elle a un vélo.

Elle préfère le compas.

Elle préfère le foot.

Céline et moi, nous sommes très différentes ... mais nous sommes copines. C'est l'essentiel, non?

Compréhension

Answer the questions below with the appropriate names: **Léa, Céline,** or **Léa et Céline**.

1. Qui habite en France?
2. Qui a deux soeurs?
3. Qui n'a pas de frère?
4. Qui a un vélo?
5. Qui aime la musique classique?
6. Qui aime les sports?

NOTE Culturelle

Haïti
Port-au-Prince

EN BREF: Haïti

Capitale: Port-au-Prince
Population: 10 millions d'habitants
Langues: créole, français

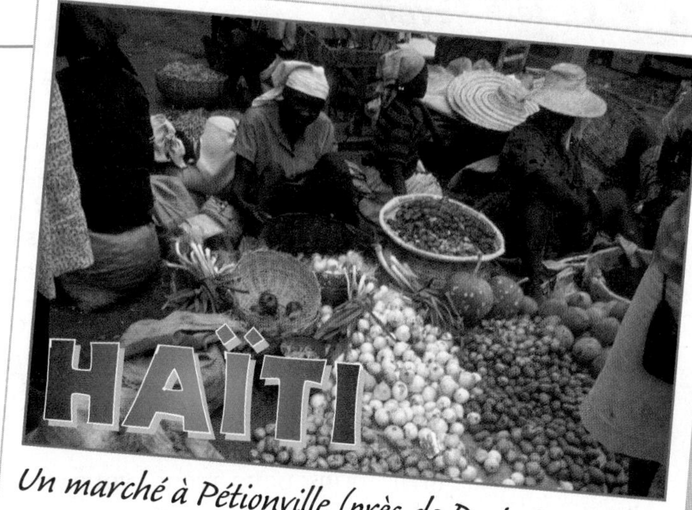

Un marché à Pétionville (près de Port-au-Prince)

Une peinture haïtienne

Haiti occupies the western part of the large Caribbean island on which the Dominican Republic is also located. Its inhabitants are of African origin. Their enslaved ancestors revolted against their French masters in 1805 and established the first independent Black nation in modern history. Today many Haitians have emigrated to France, Canada, and especially to the United States. There are sizable Haitian communities in Florida and in cities along the northeastern seaboard.

Haitians are friendly, industrious, and artistic people. In the twentieth century, Haitian painters developed their own widely appreciated folk art style and Haitian paintings are now in collections around the world. The Haitians also love music, especially **compas** or **kompas** which highlights a variety of instruments including conga drums, guitar, and keyboard. Its creole lyrics are expressed against a background of African, Caribbean, reggae, and rock rhythms.

Haitian creole cuisine, which features rice dishes, pork, and shellfish, is often quite spicy. Typical Haitian dishes include **griots** (fried pork), **riz djon-djon** (rice with mushrooms), and **pain patate** (sweet potato cake).

CONNEXIONS Haïti

Learn more about Haiti. Divide the class into several groups, each with a different assignment. For example:

- Create a bulletin board display with pictures, maps, and newspaper clippings about Haiti.
- Find books on Haitian paintings and Haitian artists and make a presentation to the class.
- Find examples of **compas** music and play a selection for the class.

A Le verbe *avoir*

The verb **avoir** *(to have, to own)* is irregular. Note the forms of this verb in the present tense.

avoir	*to have*	
j'**ai**	*I have*	J'**ai** une copine à Québec.
tu **as**	*you have*	Est-ce que tu **as** un frère?
il/elle **a**	*he/she has*	Philippe **a** une cousine à Paris.
nous **avons**	*we have*	Nous **avons** un ordinateur.
vous **avez**	*you have*	Est-ce que vous **avez** une moto?
ils/elles **ont**	*they have*	Ils n'**ont** pas ton appareil-photo.

→ There is liaison in the forms: **nous avons, vous avez, ils ont, elles ont.**

VOCABULAIRE Expressions avec *avoir*

avoir faim	*to be hungry*	**J'ai faim.** Et toi, est-ce que tu **as faim?**
avoir soif	*to be thirsty*	Paul **a soif.** Sylvie n'**a** pas **soif.**
avoir ... ans	*to be ... (years old)*	**J'ai** 14 **ans.** Le prof **a** 35 **ans.**

1 Qu'est-ce qu'ils ont?

PARLER From what the people are doing, say which object in the box they have.

un MP3
un ordinateur
un portable
une raquette
une télé

▶ Léa regarde un film.
Elle a une télé.

1. Tu joues au tennis.
2. Éric écoute du rock.
3. Je regarde un film.
4. Vous téléphonez.
5. Nous écoutons de la musique.
6. Vous envoyez un mail.
7. Elles jouent au tennis.
8. Ils surfent sur le Net.

2 Expression personnelle

PARLER/ÉCRIRE How old are the following people? Complete the sentences below. If you don't know their ages, guess.

1. J'ai ...
2. *(A classmate)* Tu as ...
3. *(The teacher)* Vous ...
4. Mon copain ...
5. Ma copine ...
6. La voisine ...

3 Faim ou soif? 

PARLER You are at a party with your classmates. Offer them the following foods and beverages. They will accept or refuse by saying whether they are hungry or thirsty.

▶ un sandwich

1. une crêpe
2. un soda
3. un hamburger
4. un jus d'orange
5. un croissant
6. un jus de raisin
7. une pizza
8. une limonade

@HOMETUTOR
my.hrw.com

B Les noms et les articles: masculin et féminin

NOUNS

- Nouns designating PEOPLE

  Nouns that designate male persons are almost always *masculine:*

  un garçon **un ami**

  Nouns that designate female persons are almost always *feminine:*

  une fille **une amie**

→ EXCEPTIONS:

une personne is always feminine (even when it refers to a male)

un professeur is always masculine (even when it refers to a woman)

- Nouns designating ANIMALS, OBJECTS, and THINGS

  There is no systematic way to determine whether these nouns are masculine or feminine. Therefore, it is very important to learn these nouns with their articles.

MASCULINE:	**un** portable	**un** vélo	**un** ordinateur
FEMININE:	**une** tablette	**une** moto	**une** affiche

LEARNING ABOUT LANGUAGE

NOUNS are words that designate people, animals, objects, and things.

In French, all nouns have GENDER: they are either MASCULINE or FEMININE.

ARTICLES

Note the forms of the articles in the chart below.

	MASCULINE		FEMININE			
INDEFINITE ARTICLE	**un**	*a, an*	**une**	*a, an*	**un** garçon	**une** fille
DEFINITE ARTICLE	**le**	*the*	**la**	*the*	**le** garçon	**la** fille

→ Both **le** and **la** become **l'** before a vowel sound:

le garçon **l'ami**

la fille **l'amie**

LEARNING ABOUT LANGUAGE

Nouns are often introduced by ARTICLES. In French, ARTICLES have the *same* gender as the nouns they introduce.

PRONOUNS

Note the forms of the pronouns in the chart below.

MASCULINE	**il**	*he* *it*	Où est **le** garçon? Où est **le** portable?	**Il** est en classe. **Il** est sur la table.
FEMININE	**elle**	*she* *it*	Où est **la** fille? Où est **la** voiture?	**Elle** est en ville. **Elle** est là-bas.

LEARNING ABOUT LANGUAGE

Nouns may be replaced by PRONOUNS. In French, PRONOUNS have the *same* gender as the nouns they replace.

4 Les célébrités 

PARLER You and Jean-Pierre have been invited to a benefit attended by many celebrities. Jean-Pierre asks you who each person is. Answer him using **un** or **une**, as appropriate.

▶ Katie Couric/journaliste
—**Tiens, voilà Katie Couric!**
—**Qui est-ce?**
—**Une journaliste.**

1. Anderson Cooper/journaliste
2. Julia Roberts/actrice
3. Brad Pitt/acteur
4. Usher/chanteur *(singer)*
5. Britney Spears/chanteuse
6. Taylor Lautner/acteur
7. Venus Williams/athlète
8. Whoopi Goldberg/comédienne

5 Sur la table ou sous la table?

PARLER Caroline is looking for the following objects. Cécile tells her where each one is: on or under the table.

▶ portable
CAROLINE: **Où est le portable?**
CÉCILE: **Le portable?**
Il est sur la table.

1. ordinateur
2. sac
3. affiche
4. calculatrice
5. raquette
6. appareil-photo
7. télé
8. lecteur MP3

C Les noms et les articles: le pluriel

Compare the singular and plural forms of the articles and nouns in the sentences below.

SINGULAR	PLURAL
Tu as **le livre?**	Tu as **les livres?**
Qui est **la fille** là-bas?	Qui sont **les filles** là-bas?
Voici **un sac.**	Voici **des sacs.**
J'invite **une copine.**	J'invite **des copines.**

PLURAL NOUNS

In written French, the plural of most nouns is formed as follows:

SINGULAR NOUN + s = PLURAL NOUN

→ If the noun ends in **-s** in the singular, the singular and plural forms are the same.

Voici **un Français.** Voici **des Français.**

→ In spoken French, the final **-s** of the plural is always silent.

→ NOTE: **des gens** *(people)* is always plural. Compare:

une personne	*person*	Qui est **la personne** là-bas?
des gens	*people*	Qui sont **les gens** là-bas?

SINGULAR AND PLURAL ARTICLES

The forms of the articles are summarized in the chart below.

	SINGULAR		PLURAL			
DEFINITE ARTICLE	**le (l')** **la (l')**	*the*	**les**	*the*	**les** garçons **les** filles	**les** ordinateurs **les** affiches
INDEFINITE ARTICLE	**un** **une**	*a, an*	**des**	*some*	**des** garçons **des** filles	**des** ordinateurs **des** affiches

→ There is liaison after **les** and **des** when the next word begins with a vowel sound.
→ **Des** corresponds to the English article *some*. While *some* is often omitted in English, **des** must be expressed in French. Contrast:

Il y a	**des**	**livres sur la table.**
There are	*some*	*books on the table.*

Je dîne avec	**des**	**amis.**
I'm having dinner with	*...*	*friends.*

6 Pluriel, s'il vous plaît

PARLER/ÉCRIRE Give the plurals of the following nouns.

▶ une copine
des copines

▶ l'ami
les amis

1. un copain
2. une amie
3. un homme
4. une femme
5. un euro
6. une affiche
7. le voisin
8. l'élève
9. la cousine
10. le livre
11. l'ordinateur
12. la voiture

7 Shopping

PARLER You are in a department store looking for the following items. Ask the salesperson if he or she has these items. The salesperson will answer affirmatively.

▶ **—Pardon, monsieur (madame).**
Est-ce que vous avez des sacs?
—Bien sûr, nous avons des sacs.

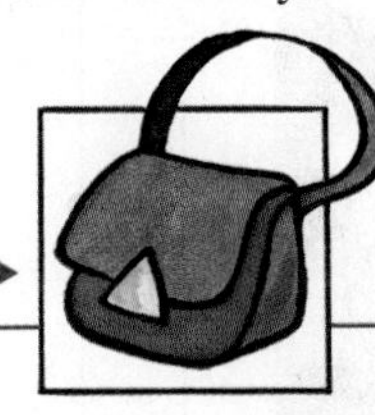

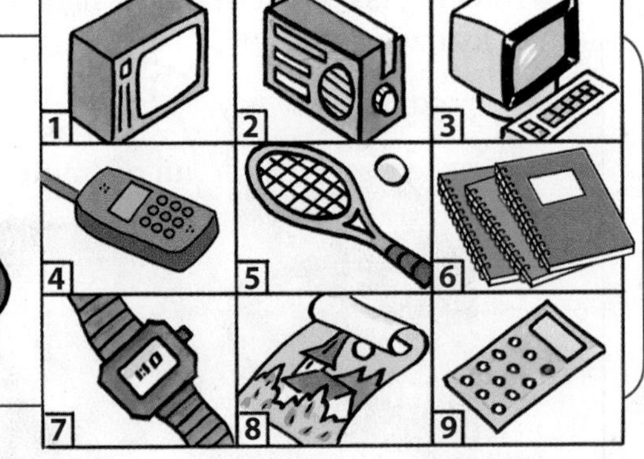

8 Qu'est-ce qu'il y a?

PARLER/ÉCRIRE Explain what there is in the following places. Complete the sentences with **il y a** and at least two nouns of your choice. Be sure to use the appropriate articles: **un, une, des.**

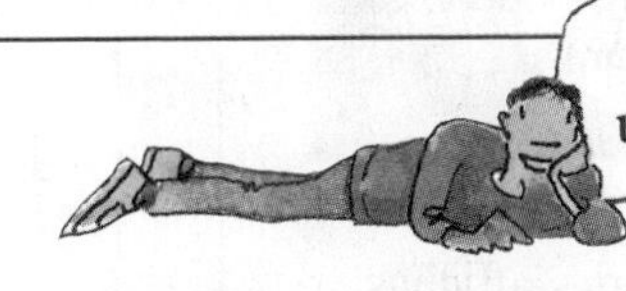

Dans le garage, il y a une moto (des voitures ...).

▶ Dans le garage, ...

1. Sur le bureau, ...
2. À la boum, ...
3. Dans la classe, ...
4. Au café, sur la table, ...
5. Dans ma chambre, ...
6. Dans mon sac, ...

D L'article indéfini dans les phrases négatives

Compare the forms of the indefinite article in affirmative and negative sentences.

AFFIRMATIVE	NEGATIVE	
Tu as **un** vélo?	Non, je n'ai **pas de** vélo.	*No, I don't have a bike.*
Est-ce que Paul a **une** radio?	Non, il n'a **pas de** radio.	*No, he doesn't have a radio.*
Vous invitez **des** copains demain?	Non, nous n'invitons **pas de** copains.	*No, we are not inviting any friends.*

After a NEGATIVE verb:

pas + un, une, des becomes **pas de**

→ Note that **pas de** becomes **pas d'** before a vowel sound.

Alice a un ordinateur. — Paul n'a **pas d'**ordinateur.
J'ai des amis à Québec. — Je n'ai **pas d'**amis à Montréal.

→ The negative form of **il y a** is **il n'y a pas:**

Dans ma chambre,
il y a une radio. — **Il n'y a pas de** télé. — *There is no TV.*
il y a des affiches. — **Il n'y a pas de** photos. — *There are no photographs.*

→ After **être**, the articles **un, une,** and **des** do not change.

Philippe est un voisin. — Éric n'est **pas un** voisin.
Ce sont des vélos. — Ce ne sont **pas des** mobylettes.

9 Possessions

PARLER Ask your classmates if they own the following.

▶ un ordinateur

1. un appareil-photo
2. une moto
3. une mobylette
4. une clarinette
5. des jeux vidéo
6. des affiches
7. un boa
8. un alligator
9. des hamsters
10. un portable

10 Oui et non

PARLER/ÉCRIRE One cannot have everything. Say that the following people do not have what is indicated in parentheses.

▶ Paul a un vélo. (un scooter)
Il n'a pas de scooter.

1. Julien a un scooter. (une voiture)
2. J'ai une radio. (une télé)
3. Vous avez un MP3. (un smartphone)
4. Léa a une calculatrice. (un ordinateur)
5. Vous avez des frères. (une soeur)
6. Nous avons un chien. (des chats)
7. Tu as des copains à Bordeaux. (des copains à Lyon)
8. Marc a un oncle à Québec. (un oncle à Montréal)
9. Nathalie a des cousins à Paris. (des cousins à Lille)

11 Le grenier *(The attic)*

PARLER Your friend is cleaning the attic. Ask if the following items are up there. Your friend (a classmate) will answer according to the illustration.

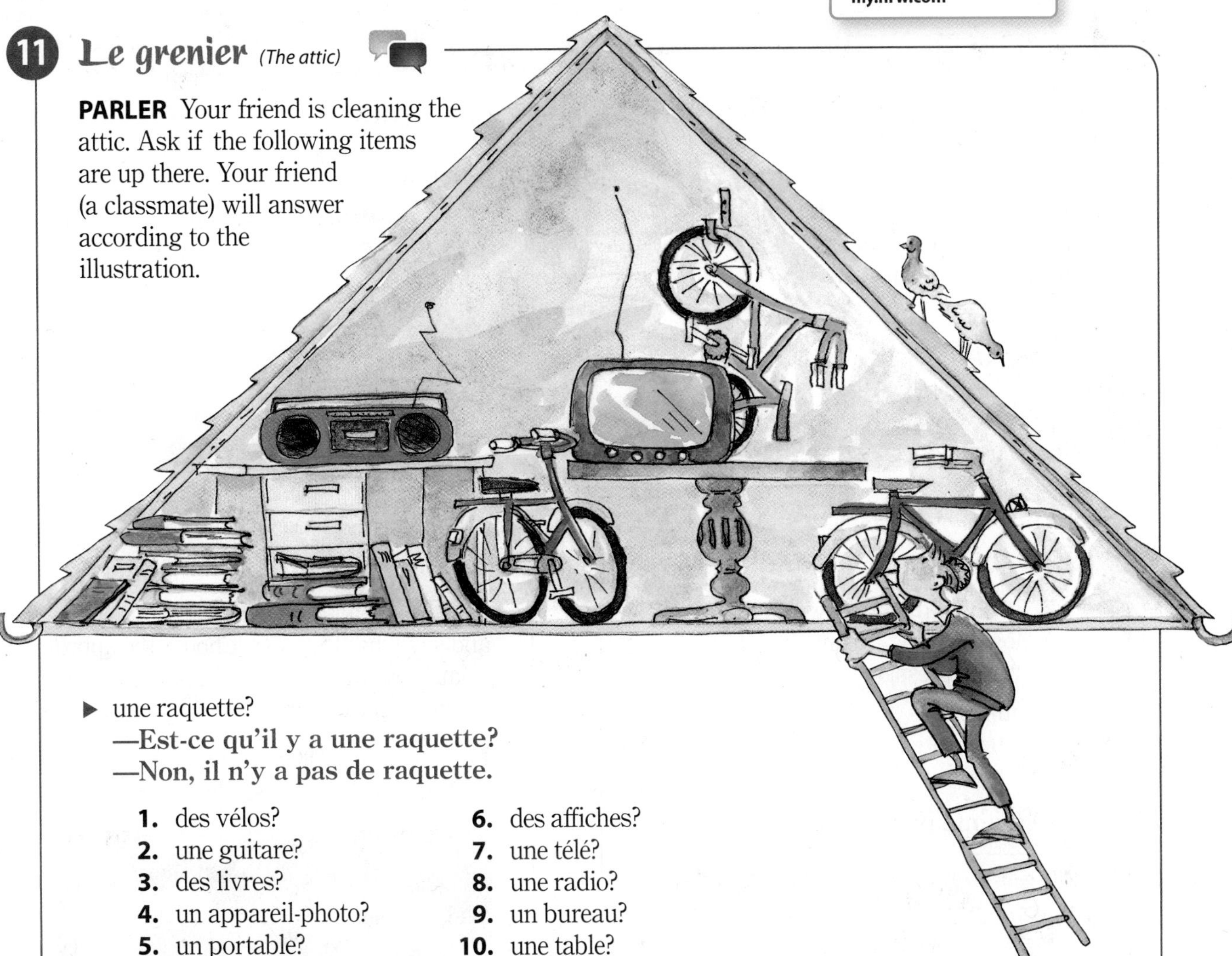

▶ une raquette?
—Est-ce qu'il y a une raquette?
—Non, il n'y a pas de raquette.

1. des vélos?
2. une guitare?
3. des livres?
4. un appareil-photo?
5. un portable?
6. des affiches?
7. une télé?
8. une radio?
9. un bureau?
10. une table?

VOCABULAIRE Expression pour la conversation

▶ ***How to contradict a negative statement or question:***

Si! *Yes!* —Tu n'as pas de télé?
—**Si!** J'ai une télé.

12 Contradictions!

PARLER/ÉCRIRE Contradict all of the following negative statements.

▶ Tu ne parles pas anglais! **Si, je parle anglais!**

1. Tu ne parles pas français!
2. Tu n'étudies pas!
3. Tu ne joues pas au basket!
4. Tu n'aimes pas les sports!
5. Tu n'aimes pas la musique!
6. Tu n'écoutes pas le professeur!

E L'usage de l'article défini dans le sens général

In French, the definite article **(le, la, les)** is used more often than in English. Note its use in the following sentences.

J'aime **la musique.**	*(In general) I like* ***music.***
Tu préfères **le tennis** ou **le golf?**	*(Generally) do you prefer* ***tennis*** *or* ***golf?***
Julie aime **les jeux vidéo.**	*(In general) Julie likes* ***video games.***
Nous aimons **la liberté.**	*(In general) we love* ***liberty.***

LANGUAGE COMPARISONS

In contrast with English, French uses the definite article (**le, la, les**) to introduce ABSTRACT nouns, or nouns used in a GENERAL or COLLECTIVE sense.

13 Expression personnelle

PARLER/ÉCRIRE Say how you feel about the following things, using one of the suggested expressions.

Je n'aime pas ...
J'aime un peu ...
J'aime beaucoup ...

▸ **Je n'aime pas la violence.**

la musique	le français	la violence	le théâtre
la nature	les maths	l'injustice	le cinéma
les sports	les sciences	la liberté	la danse
le camping			la photo *(photography)*

14 C'est évident! *(It's obvious!)*

PARLER Read about the following people and say what they like. Choose the appropriate item from the list. (Masculine nouns are in blue. Feminine nouns are in red.)

▸ Yvette écoute son MP3.
Yvette aime la musique.

art cinéma danse français musique nature tennis

1. Jean-Claude a une raquette.
2. Léa fait une promenade dans la forêt.
3. Nous visitons un musée *(museum)*.
4. Tu regardes un film.
5. Vous étudiez en classe de français.
6. Véronique et Roger sont dans une discothèque.

@HOMETUTOR
my.hrw.com

F L'usage de l'article défini avec les jours de la semaine

Compare the following sentences.

REPEATED EVENTS
Le samedi, je dîne avec des copains.
(On) Saturdays *(in general), I have dinner with friends.*

SINGLE EVENT
Samedi, je dîne avec mon cousin.
(On) Saturday *(that is, this Saturday), I am having dinner with my cousin.*

To indicate a repeated or habitual event, French uses the construction:

le + DAY OF THE WEEK

→ When an event happens only once, no article is used.

15 Questions personnelles PARLER

1. Est-ce que tu étudies le samedi?
2. Est-ce que tu dînes au restaurant le dimanche? Si *(If)* oui, avec qui?
3. Est-ce que tu as une classe de français le lundi? le mercredi?
4. Est-ce que tu regardes les matchs de football américain le samedi? le dimanche?
5. Est-ce que tu travailles? Où? *(Name of place or store)* Quand?

16 L'emploi du temps

PARLER/ÉCRIRE

	LUNDI	MARDI	MERCREDI	JEUDI	VENDREDI
9 h	français	physique	sciences	biologie	
10 h		histoire		maths	anglais
11 h	maths	sciences	anglais		français

The following students all have the same morning schedule. Complete the sentences accordingly.

▶ **Nous avons une classe de français <u>le lundi</u> ...**

1. J'ai une classe de maths ______.
2. Tu as une classe de sciences ______.
3. Jacques a une classe de physique ______.
4. Thérèse a une classe d'histoire ______.
5. Vous avez une classe de biologie ______.
6. Les élèves ont une classe d'anglais ______.

Prononciation

Les articles *le* et *les*

le /lə/ les /le/

Be sure to distinguish between the pronunciation of **le** and **les.** In spoken French, that is often the only way to tell the difference between a singular and a plural noun.

le sac **les sacs**

Répétez:						
/lə/	**le**	**le sac**	**le vélo**	**le portable**	**le copain**	**le voisin**
/le/	**les**	**les sacs**	**les vélos**	**les portables**	**les copains**	**les voisins**

OBJECTIFS

Now you can . . .
- talk about what you have and do not have
- describe in general what you like and do not like

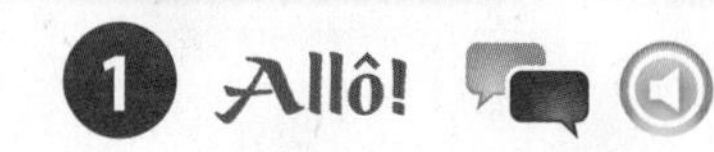

1 Allô!

PARLER Jean-Marc is phoning some friends. Match his questions on the left with his friends' answers on the right.

1. Quel âge a ton copain?
2. Est-ce qu'Éric a un scooter?
3. Où est l'appareil-photo?
4. Tu as un smartphone?
5. Est-ce que tu aimes étudier l'anglais?
6. Tu as soif?

a. Oui, mais je n'ai pas de tablette.
b. Il est sur la table.
c. Quatorze ans.
d. Oui, je voudrais une limonade.
e. Oui, mais je préfère l'espagnol.
f. Non, mais il a une moto.

2 Un sondage

PARLER/ÉCRIRE A French consumer research group wants to know what things American teenagers own. Conduct a survey in your class asking who has the objects on the list. Count the number of students who raise their hands for each object, and report your findings on a separate piece of paper.

Qui a un portable? ... Quinze élèves ont des portables.

3 Créa-dialogue  

PARLER Ask your classmates if they like the following things. Then ask if they own the corresponding object.

le tennis	1. échanger des textos	2. le jogging	3. les maths	4. la photo	5. les matchs de baseball	6. l'exercice

▶ —Tu aimes <u>le tennis</u>?
—Oui, j'aime <u>le tennis</u>.
(Non, je n'aime pas <u>le tennis</u>.)

—Tu as <u>une raquette</u>?
—Oui, j'ai <u>une raquette</u>.
(Non, je n'ai pas <u>de raquette</u>.)

4 Quelle est la différence?

PARLER/ÉCRIRE Sophie went away with her family for the weekend and she took some of her belongings with her. Describe what is in her room on Friday and what is missing on Saturday.

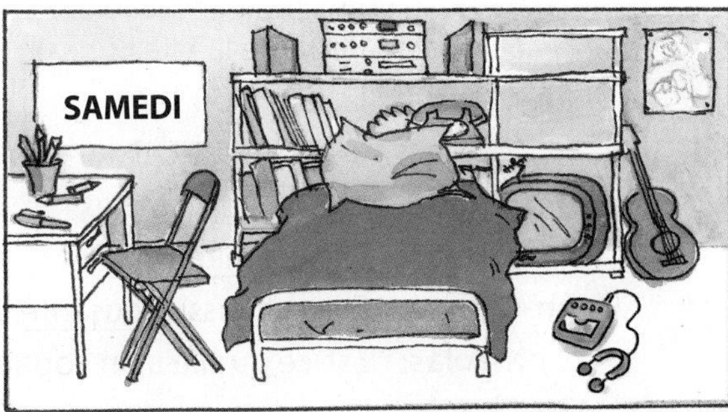

▶ **Il y a ...**

▶ **Il n'y a pas de ...**

5 Composition: Ma semaine 

ÉCRIRE In a short paragraph, describe what you do (or do not do) regularly on various days of the week. Select three days and two different activities for each day. Use only vocabulary that you know. Perhaps you might want to exchange paragraphs with a friend by e-mail.

Le lundi, j'ai une classe de français ...

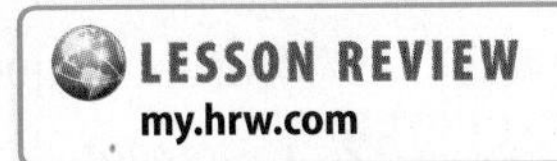

Le copain de Mireille

DVD AUDIO

Nicolas and Jean-Claude are having lunch at the school cafeteria. Nicolas is looking at the students seated at the other end of their table.

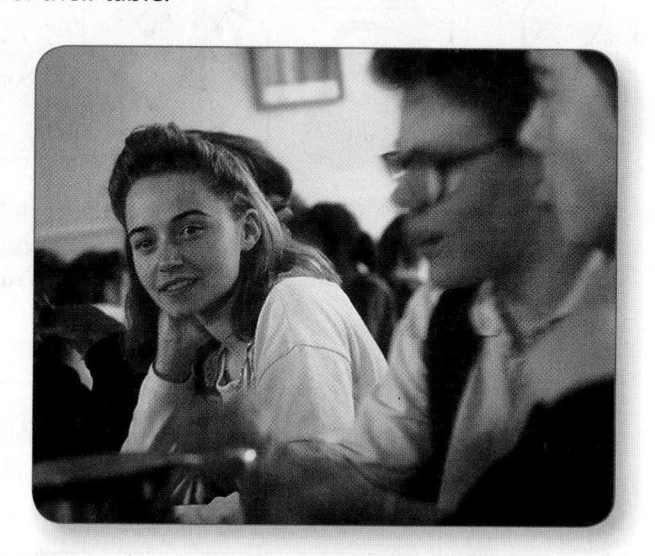

Nicolas: Regarde la fille là-bas!
Jean-Claude: La fille blonde?
Nicolas: Oui! Qui est-ce?
Jean-Claude: C'est Mireille Labé.
Nicolas: Elle est mignonne! — *cute*
Jean-Claude: Elle est aussi amusante, intelligente et sympathique. — *fun/nice*
Nicolas: Est-ce qu'elle a un copain?
Jean-Claude: Oui, elle a un copain.
Nicolas: Il est sympathique?
Jean-Claude: Oui ... Très sympathique!
Nicolas: Et intelligent?
Jean-Claude: Aussi!
Nicolas: Dommage! ... Qui est-ce?
Jean-Claude: C'est moi!
Nicolas: Euh ... oh ... Excuse-moi et félicitations! — *congratulations*

Compréhension

1. Qui est-ce que Nicolas regarde?
2. Comment s'appelle la fille?
3. Est-ce qu'elle est jolie?
4. Est-ce qu'elle a d'autres *(other)* qualités?
5. Est-ce qu'elle a un copain?
6. Qui est le copain de Mireille *(Mireille's boyfriend)?*

NOTE *Culturelle*

L'amitié et la bande de copains

French people believe in friendship (**l'amitié**) and family life and rank these values far above money, material comfort, and personal success. The friendships they establish at an early age tend to be durable. Since French people move much less frequently than Americans, and since distances are much smaller, they remain in close contact with their high school friends throughout their entire lives.

French teenagers, like their American counterparts, are very sociable. They have a close-knit group of friends, known as **la bande de copains**, with whom they share common interests. They go out together, especially to movies, concerts, and parties. This group may include classmates, cousins, other young people whom they have met during vacations, as well as the children of family friends. When young people invite their friends to the house, it is customary to introduce them to their parents.

COMPARAISONS *Culturelles*

What similarities and differences do you see between the French and American attitudes towards friendship?

- **les similarités**
- **les différences**

In your opinion, are these attitudes basically the same? Explain.

OPINION *Personnelle*

Rank the following values mentioned in the text from 1 (the highest) to 5.

- **l'amitié**
- **l'argent** *(money)*
- **le confort matériel**
- **la famille**
- **le succès personnel**

Compare your rankings with your classmates.

A Les adjectifs: masculin et féminin

Compare the forms of the adjectives in heavy print as they describe masculine and feminine nouns.

MASCULINE	FEMININE
Le scooter est **petit**.	La voiture est **petite**.
Patrick est **intelligent**.	Caroline est **intelligente**.
L'ordinateur est **moderne**.	La télé est **moderne**.

In written French, feminine adjectives are usually formed as follows:

MASCULINE ADJECTIVE + **-e** = FEMININE ADJECTIVE

→ If the masculine adjective ends in **-e,** there is no change in the feminine form.

Jérôme est **timide**. Juliette est **timide**.

→ Adjectives that follow the above patterns are called REGULAR adjectives. Those that do not are called IRREGULAR adjectives. For example:

Marc est **beau**. Sylvie est **belle**.
Paul est **canadien**. Marie est **canadienne**.

NOTE French dictionaries list adjectives by their masculine forms. For irregular adjectives, the feminine form is indicated in parentheses.

LEARNING ABOUT LANGUAGE

ADJECTIVES are words that describe people, places, and things.

In French, MASCULINE adjectives are used with masculine nouns, and FEMININE adjectives are used with feminine nouns. This is called NOUN-ADJECTIVE AGREEMENT.

NOTES DE PRONONCIATION:

- If the masculine form of an adjective ends in a silent consonant, that consonant is pronounced in the feminine form.
- If the masculine form of an adjective ends in a vowel or a pronounced consonant, the masculine and feminine forms sound the same.

DIFFERENT PRONUNCIATION		SAME PRONUNCIATION	
petit	peti**t**e	timide	timide
blond	blon**d**e	joli	jolie
français	françai**s**e	espagnol	espagnole

1 Vive la différence!

PARLER/ÉCRIRE People can be friends and yet be quite different. Describe the girls named in parentheses, indicating that they are not like their friends.

▶ Jean-Marc est blond. (Mélanie) **Mélanie n'est pas blonde.**

1. Jean-Louis est blond. (Carole)
2. Paul est petit. (Mireille)
3. Éric est beau. (Marthe)
4. Jérôme est grand. (Louise)
5. Michel est riche. (Émilie)
6. André est français. (Lisa)
7. Antonio est espagnol. (Céline)
8. Bill est américain. (Julie)

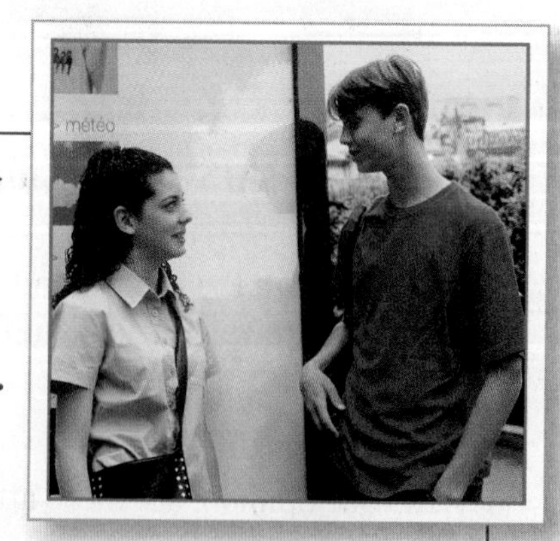

@HOMETUTOR
my.hrw.com

VOCABULAIRE La description 

ADJECTIFS		Voici Olivier.	Voici Sophie.
amusant	*amusing, fun*	Il est **amusant.**	Elle est **amusante.**
intelligent	*intelligent*	Il est **intelligent.**	Elle est **intelligente.**
intéressant	*interesting*	Il est **intéressant.**	Elle est **intéressante.**
méchant	*mean, nasty*	Il n'est pas **méchant.**	Elle n'est pas **méchante.**
bête	*silly, dumb*	Il n'est pas **bête.**	Elle n'est pas **bête.**
sympathique	*nice, pleasant*	Il est **sympathique.**	Elle est **sympathique.**
timide	*timid*	Il est **timide.**	Elle n'est pas **timide.**
gentil (gentille)	*nice, kind*	Il est **gentil.**	Elle est **gentille.**
mignon (mignonne)	*cute*	Il est **mignon.**	Elle est **mignonne.**
sportif (sportive)	*athletic*	Il est **sportif.**	Elle est **sportive.**

ADVERBES

assez	*rather*	Nous sommes **assez** intelligents.
très	*very*	Vous n'êtes pas **très** sportifs!

2 Oui ou non?

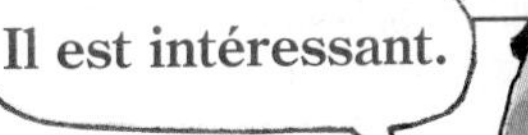

PARLER In your opinion, do the following people have the suggested traits? (Note: These traits are given in the masculine form only.)

▶ le prince William / intéressant?

1. le Président / sympathique?
2. Venus Williams / sportif?
3. ma copine / gentil?
4. Britney Spears / mignon?
5. Oprah Winfrey / intelligent?
6. Einstein / bête?
7. Jay Leno / amusant?
8. le prof / méchant?

3 Descriptions

PARLER Select one of the following characters. Using words from the **Vocabulaire**, describe this character in two affirmative or negative sentences.

▶ Frankenstein
Il est très méchant.
Il n'est pas très mignon.

1. Tarzan
2. King Kong
3. Big Bird
4. Batman
5. Miss Piggy
6. Wonder Woman
7. Charlie Brown
8. Blanche-Neige *(Snow White)*
9. Garfield
10. Snoopy

4 L'idéal

PARLER/ÉCRIRE Now you have the chance to describe your ideal people. Use two adjectives for each one.

1. Le copain idéal est … et …
2. La copine idéale est … et …
3. Le professeur idéal est … et …
4. L'étudiant idéal est … et …
5. L'étudiante idéale est … et …

B Les adjectifs: le pluriel

Compare the forms of the adjectives in heavy print as they describe singular and plural nouns.

SINGULAR	PLURAL
Paul est **intelligent** et **timide.**	Paul et Éric sont **intelligents** et **timides.**
Alice est **intelligente** et **timide.**	Alice et Claire sont **intelligentes** et **timides.**

In written French, plural adjectives are usually formed as follows:

SINGULAR ADJECTIVE + **-s** = PLURAL ADJECTIVE

→ If the masculine singular adjective already ends in **-s**, there is no change in the plural form.

Patrick est **français.**	Patrick et Daniel sont **français.**
BUT: Anne est **française.**	Anne et Alice sont **françaises.**

NOTE DE PRONONCIATION: Because the final **-s** of plural adjectives is silent, singular and plural adjectives sound the same.

SUMMARY: Forms of regular adjectives

	MASCULINE	FEMININE	*also:*	
SINGULAR	- **grand**	-e **grande**	timide	timide
PLURAL	-s **grands**	-es **grandes**	français	français**es**

5 Une question de personnalité

PARLER/ÉCRIRE Indicate whether or not the following people exhibit the personality traits in parentheses. (These traits are given in the masculine singular form only. Make the necessary agreements.)

▶ Alice et Thérèse aiment parler en public. (timide?)

1. Claire et Valérie sont très populaires. (amusant?)
2. Robert et Jean-Luc n'aiment pas danser. (timide?)
3. Catherine et Martine aiment jouer au foot. (sportif?)
4. Laure et Léa ont un «A» en français. (intelligent?)
5. Thomas et Vincent n'aiment pas le jogging. (sportif?)
6. Les voisins n'aiment pas parler avec nous. (sympathique?)

@HOMETUTOR
my.hrw.com

VOCABULAIRE Les adjectifs de nationalité

américain	*American*	**italien (italienne)**	*Italian*
mexicain	*Mexican*	**canadien (canadienne)**	*Canadian*
français	*French*	**japonais**	*Japanese*
anglais	*English*	**chinois**	*Chinese*
espagnol	*Spanish*		
suisse	*Swiss*		

→ Words that describe nationality are adjectives and take adjective endings.

Monsieur Katagiri est **japonais.**
Kumi et Michiko sont **japonaises.**

VOCABULAIRE Expression pour la conversation

▶ ***How to introduce a conclusion:***

alors *so, then* —J'habite à Québec.
—Alors, tu es canadien!

6 Quelle nationalité? 

PARLER Ask where the following people live and what their nationalities are. A friend will answer you.

▶ **—Où habitent Lois et Kim?**
—Elles habitent à Miami.
—Alors, elles sont américaines?
—Mais oui, elles sont américaines.

▶ Lois et Kim	1. Jim et Bob	2. Léa et Aline
Miami	Liverpool	Toulouse
américain	anglais	français

3. Clara et Tere	4. Luc et Paul	5. ??
Madrid	Montréal	??
espagnol	??	??

7 Les nationalités

PARLER/ÉCRIRE Give the nationalities of the following people.

▶ Silvia et Maria sont de Rome.
Elles sont italiennes.

1. Lise et Nathalie étudient à Québec.
2. Michael et Dennis sont de Liverpool.
3. Luis et Paco étudient à Madrid.
4. Isabel et Carmen travaillent à Acapulco.
5. Yoko et Kumi sont de Tokyo.
6. Monsieur et Madame Chen habitent à Beijing.
7. Jean-Pierre et Claude sont de Genève.
8. Françoise et Sylvie travaillent à Paris.

C La place des adjectifs

Note the position of the adjectives in the sentences on the right.

Philippe a une voiture.	Il a une voiture **anglaise.**
Denise invite des copains.	Elle invite des copains **américains.**
Voici un livre.	Voici un livre **intéressant.**
J'ai des amies.	J'ai des amies **sympathiques.**

In French, adjectives usually come AFTER the noun they modify, according to the pattern:

ARTICLE +	NOUN +	ADJECTIVE
une	voiture	**française**
des	copains	**intéressants**

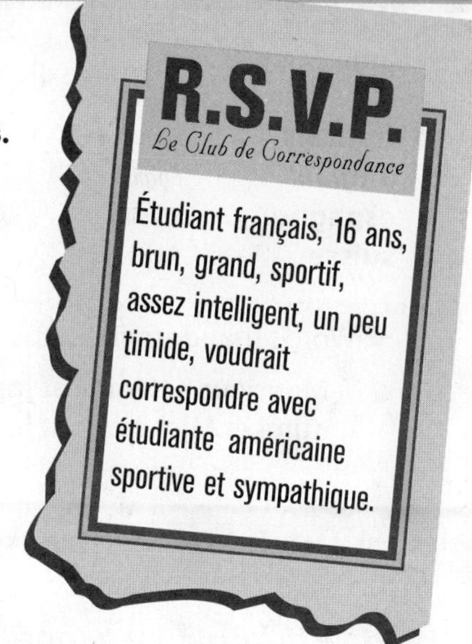

8 Préférences personnelles

PARLER For each person or object below, choose among the characteristics in parentheses. Indicate your preference.

▶ avoir un copain (sympathique, intelligent, sportif)
Je préfère avoir un copain intelligent.

1. avoir une copine (amusante, mignonne, intelligente)
2. avoir un professeur (gentil, intelligent, amusant)
3. avoir des voisins (sympathiques, intéressants, riches)
4. avoir une voiture (moderne, confortable, rapide)
5. avoir une calculatrice (japonaise, américaine, française)
6. avoir une montre (suisse, japonaise, française)
7. dîner dans un restaurant (italien, chinois, français)
8. regarder un film (intéressant, amusant, intelligent)
9. travailler avec des personnes (gentilles, amusantes, sérieuses)
10. faire un voyage avec des gens (amusants, riches, sympathiques)

9 Qui se ressemble ...

(Birds of a feather ...)

PARLER Say that the following people have friends, relatives, or acquaintances with the same personality or nationality.

▶ Claire est anglaise. (un copain)
Elle a un copain anglais.

1. Jean-Pierre est sympathique. (des cousines)
2. La prof est intelligente. (des étudiants)
3. Madame Simon est intéressante. (des voisines)
4. Alice est américaine. (des copines)
5. Véronique est amusante. (un frère)
6. Michel est sportif. (une soeur)
7. Pedro est espagnol. (des camarades)
8. Antonio est mexicain. (une copine)
9. Bernard est sportif. (un voisin)

Birds of a feather flock together.

@HOMETUTOR
my.hrw.com

10 Préférences internationales

PARLER/ÉCRIRE Choose an item from Column A and indicate your preference as to country of origin by choosing an adjective from Column B. Be sure to make the necessary agreement.

	A	B
	la musique	anglais
	la cuisine	américain
	les voitures	français
Je préfère …	les ordinateurs	mexicain
	les appareils-photo	chinois
	les CD	japonais
	les restaurants	italien

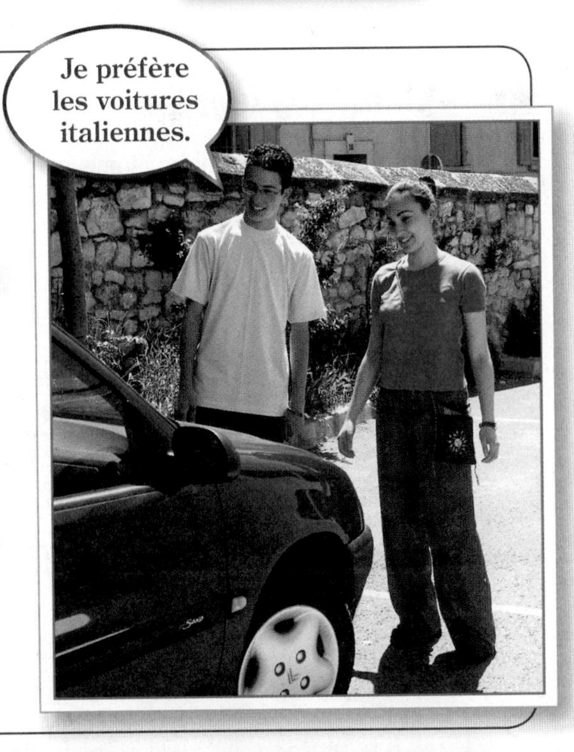

Prononciation

Les consonnes finales

/-/ /d/

blond

blonde

As you know, when the last letter of a word is a consonant, that consonant is often silent. But when a word ends in "**e**," the consonant before it is pronounced. As you practice the following adjectives, be sure to distinguish between the masculine and the feminine forms.

	MASCULINE ADJECTIVE *(no final consonant sound)*		FEMININE ADJECTIVE *(final consonant sound)*
Répétez:	**blond**	/d/	**blonde**
	grand		**grande**
	petit	/t/	**petite**
	amusant		**amusante**
	français	/z/	**française**
	anglais		**anglaise**
	américain	/n/	**américaine**
	canadien		**canadienne**

À votre tour!

OBJECTIFS

Now you can . . .
- describe your personality
- describe other people: their nationality, their physical appearance and their personality

 Allô!  

PARLER Valérie is phoning some friends. Match her questions on the left with her friends' answers on the right.

1. Ton frère aime jouer au foot?
2. Cécile et Sophie sont mignonnes, n'est-ce pas?
3. Pourquoi est-ce que tu invites Olivier?
4. Tu aimes la classe?
5. Tu as des cousins?

a. Oui, et intelligentes aussi!
b. Parce qu'il est amusant et sympathique.
c. Oui, j'ai un professeur très intéressant.
d. Oui, il est très sportif.
e. Oui, mais ils ne sont pas très sympathiques.

2 Créa-dialogue  

PARLER With your classmates, talk about the people of different nationalities you may know or objects you may own.

▶ 

▶ —J'ai des cousins mexicains.
—Ils sont mignons?
—Oui, ils sont très mignons.

1. une voisine	2. un prof	3. des copines	4. un livre	5. une voiture
blond?	sympathique?	sportif?	intéressant?	grand?

3 Avis de recherche *(Missing person's bulletin)*

ÉCRIRE The two people in the pictures to the right have been reported missing. Describe each one as well as you can, using your imagination. Mention:

- the (approximate) age of the person
- the way he/she looks
- personality traits
- other features or characteristics

4 Descriptions

PARLER Give an oral presentation describing your favorite actor **(un acteur)** and actress **(une actrice)**. In your descriptions, include:

- the person's name
- approximate age
- nationality
- physical appearance
- personality traits
- a film he/she plays in (Il/elle joue dans ...)

Voici une photo de mon acteur favori. Il s'appelle ...

Voici mon actrice favorite. Elle s'appelle ...

You may wish to show photos of the two actors you have chosen to talk about.

5 Composition: Fête d'anniversaire

ÉCRIRE You have invited Jean-Pierre, a French exchange student, to your upcoming birthday party. Write him an e-mail describing two of the guests that he will meet at the party: a boy and a girl. For each person (who may be real or imaginary), provide such information as name, age, nationality, physical appearance, and personality traits.

Il y a un garçon qui s'appelle ...

Il y a une fille qui s'appelle ...

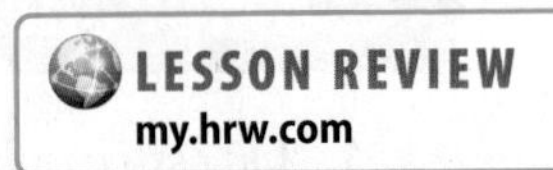

Leçon 12

Conversation et Culture

La voiture de Roger

DVD  AUDIO 

	Dans la rue, il y a une voiture rouge.	*street/red*
	C'est une petite voiture. C'est une voiture de sport.	
	Dans la rue, il y a aussi un café. Au café, il y a un jeune homme.	
	Il s'appelle Roger.	
	C'est le propriétaire de la voiture rouge.	*owner*
	Une jeune fille entre dans le café.	*enters*
	Elle s'appelle Véronique.	
	C'est l'amie de Roger.	*Roger's friend*
	Véronique parle à Roger.	
Véronique:	Tu as une nouvelle voiture, n'est-ce pas?	*new*
Roger:	Oui, j'ai une nouvelle voiture.	
Véronique:	Est-ce qu'elle est grande ou petite?	
Roger:	C'est une petite voiture.	
Véronique:	De quelle couleur est-elle?	
Roger:	C'est une voiture rouge.	
Véronique:	Est-ce que c'est une voiture italienne?	
Roger:	Oui, c'est une voiture italienne. Mais dis donc, Véronique, tu es vraiment très curieuse!	*hey there* / *really*
Véronique:	Et toi, tu n'es pas assez curieux!	*curious enough*
Roger:	Ah bon? Pourquoi?	
Véronique:	Pourquoi?! … Regarde la contractuelle là-bas!	*meter maid*
Roger:	Ah, zut alors!	

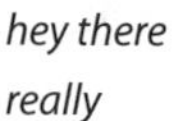
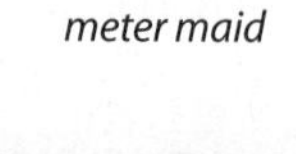

Compréhension

1. Qu'est-ce qu'il y a dans la rue?
2. Est-ce que la voiture est grande?
3. Comment s'appelle le jeune homme?
4. Où est-il?
5. Comment s'appelle la jeune fille?
6. De quelle couleur est la voiture?

NOTE Culturelle

Les Français et la voiture

France is one of the leading producers of automobiles in the world. The two automakers, **Renault** and **Peugeot-Citroën,** manufacture a variety of models ranging from sports cars to mini-vans and buses.

To obtain a driver's license **(un permis de conduire)** in France, you must be eighteen years old and pass a very difficult driving test. French teenagers can, however, begin to drive at the age of sixteen, as long as they take lessons at an accredited driving school **(auto-école)** and are accompanied by an adult. Lessons in these schools are expensive and it may cost you 300 euros before you pass the exam and get your official license.

The French driver's license is a **permis à points** (license with points). A new license carries with it 12 points. When a driver commits a traffic violation, such as speeding or not wearing a seat belt, a corresponding number of points is subtracted from the license. If a driver loses all 12 points, the license is revoked and that person can no longer drive.

OPINION Personnelle

Do you think that the **permis à points** is a good idea? Explain your position.

A Les couleurs

Note the form and position of the color words in the following sentences:

Alice a un vélo **bleu.**	*Alice has a **blue** bicycle.*
Nous avons des chemises **bleues.**	*We have **blue** shirts.*

Names of colors are ADJECTIVES and take adjective ENDINGS. They come *after* the noun.

VOCABULAIRE Les couleurs 

De quelle couleur ... ? *What color ... ?* —**De quelle couleur** est la moto?
—Elle est rouge.

blanc	noir	bleu	rouge	jaune	vert	gris	marron	orange	rose
(blanche)	(noire)	(bleue)	(rouge)	(jaune)	(verte)	(grise)	(marron)	(orange)	(rose)

→ The colors **orange** and **marron** are INVARIABLE. They do not take any endings.

un sac **orange**	des sacs **orange**
un tee-shirt **marron**	une chemise **marron**

1 De quelle couleur? 

PARLER Ask your classmates to name the colors of things they own. (They may invent answers.)

▶ ta chambre?

1. ta bicyclette?
2. ton tee-shirt?
3. ton appareil-photo?
4. ta montre?
5. ta raquette de tennis?
6. ton livre de français?
7. ton chien (chat)?

2 Possessions 

PARLER Ask what objects or pets the following people own. A classmate will answer, giving the color.

▶ —Est-ce que Léa a un chat?
—Oui, elle a un chat jaune.

▶ Léa

1. Mme Mercier

2. Marc

3. Delphine

4. Sophie

5. Éric

3 L'arche de Noé

PARLER/ÉCRIRE Noah's ark has just landed. Give the colors of the animals as they get off the ship.

▶ le chien **Le chien est blanc.**

1. le chat
2. l'éléphant *(m.)*
3. la panthère
4. le zèbre
5. le flamant
6. le cardinal
7. le lion
8. le perroquet

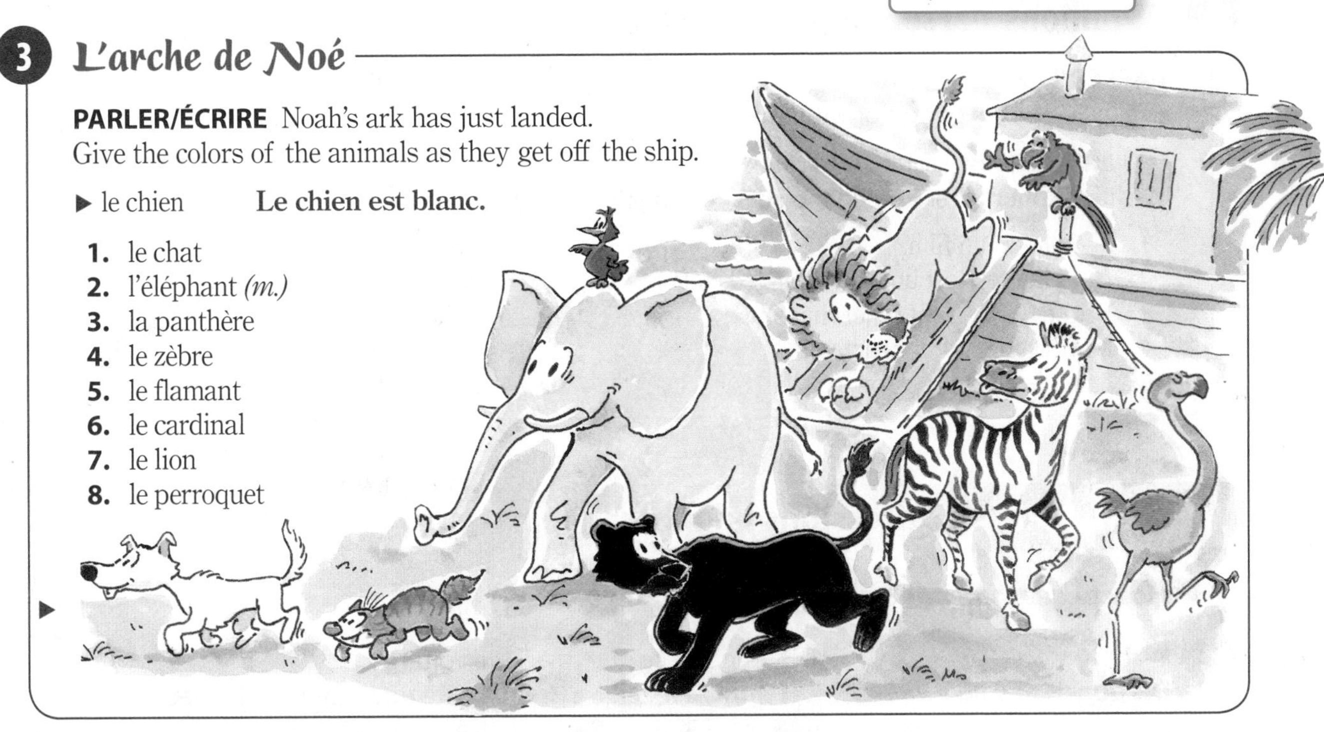

B La place des adjectifs avant le nom

Compare the position of the adjectives in the following sentences.

Voici une voiture **française.** Voici une **petite** voiture.
Paul est un garçon **intelligent.** Pierre est un **beau** garçon.

A few adjectives like **petit** and **beau** come BEFORE the noun they modify.

➔ The article **des** often becomes **de** before an adjective. Compare:

des voitures → **de** petites voitures

VOCABULAIRE Les adjectifs qui précèdent le nom

beau (belle)	*beautiful, handsome*	Regarde la **belle** voiture!
joli	*pretty*	Qui est la **jolie** fille avec André?
grand	*big, large, tall*	Nous habitons dans un **grand**‿appartement. (t)
petit	*little, small, short*	Ma soeur a un **petit**‿ordinateur. (t)
bon (bonne)	*good*	Tu es un **bon** copain.
mauvais	*bad*	Patrick est un **mauvais**‿élève. (z)

➔ There is a LIAISON after the above adjectives when the noun which follows begins with a vowel sound. Note that in liaison:

- the **"d"** of **grand** is pronounced /t/: **un grand‿appartement** (t)
- **bon** is pronounced like **bonne: un bon‿élève** (n)

4 Opinions personnelles

PARLER/ÉCRIRE Give your opinion about the following people and things, using the adjectives **bon** or **mauvais.**

▶ Julia Roberts est (une) actrice *(actress)*.
Julia Roberts est une bonne actrice (une mauvaise actrice).

1. *Titanic* est un film.
2. «60 Minutes» est un programme de télé.
3. Britney Spears est (une) chanteuse.
4. Matt Damon est (un) acteur.
5. Dracula est une personne.
6. Les Yankees sont une équipe *(team)* de baseball.
7. Les Lakers sont une équipe de basket.
8. Je suis un(e) élève.
9. *Discovering French* est un livre.

VOCABULAIRE Expressions pour la conversation

▶ ***How to get someone's attention:***

Dis!	*Say! Hey!*	**Dis,** Éric, est-ce que tu as une voiture?
Dis donc!	*Hey there!*	**Dis donc,** est-ce que tu veux faire une promenade avec moi?

5 Dialogue

PARLER Christine asks her cousin Thomas if he has certain things. He responds affirmatively, describing each one. Play both roles.

▶ une radio (petite) ▶ un scooter (italien)

1. une télé (petite)
2. une guitare (espagnole)
3. un vélo (rouge)
4. une calculatrice (petite)
5. un sac (grand)
6. des livres (intéressants)
7. une copine (amusante)
8. une mobylette (bleue)
9. une montre (belle)
10. un copain (bon)
11. une cousine (jolie)
12. une radio (japonaise)

@HOMETUTOR
my.hrw.com

C Il est ou c'est?

When describing a person or thing, French speakers use two different constructions, **il est (elle est)** and **c'est**.

		Il est + ADJECTIVE **Elle est** + ADJECTIVE	**C'est** + ARTICLE + NOUN (+ ADJECTIVE)
Roger	*He is ...*	**Il est** amusant.	**C'est** un copain. **C'est** un copain amusant.
Véronique	*She is ...*	**Elle est** sportive.	**C'est** une amie. **C'est** une bonne amie.
un scooter	*It is ...*	**Il est** joli.	**C'est** un scooter français. **C'est** un bon scooter.
une voiture	*It is ...*	**Elle est** petite.	**C'est** une voiture anglaise. **C'est** une petite voiture.

→ Note the corresponding plural forms:

(Pierre et Marc)	*They are ...*	**Ils sont** amusants.	**Ce sont** des copains.
(Claire et Anne)	*They are ...*	**Elles sont** timides.	**Ce sont** des copines.

→ In negative sentences, **c'est** becomes **ce n'est pas.**

Ce n'est pas un mauvais élève. *He's **not** a bad student.*
Ce n'est pas une Peugeot. *It's **not** a Peugeot.*

→ **C'est** is also used with names of people

C'est Véronique. **C'est** Madame Lamblet.

6 Descriptions 

PARLER/ÉCRIRE Complete the following descriptions with **Il est, Elle est,** or **C'est,** as appropriate.

A. Roger
1. ____ grand.
2. ____ brun.
3. ____ un garçon sympathique.
4. ____ un mauvais élève.

B. Véronique
5. ____ une fille brune.
6. ____ une amie sympathique.
7. ____ très amusante.
8. ____ assez grande.

C. La voiture de Roger
9. ____ une voiture moderne.
10. ____ une petite voiture.
11. ____ rouge.
12. ____ très rapide.

D. Le scooter de Véronique
13. ____ bleu et blanc.
14. ____ très économique.
15. ____ un joli scooter.
16. ____ assez confortable.

D Les expressions impersonnelles avec *c'est*

Note the use of **c'est** in the following sentences.

J'aime parler français.	**C'est** intéressant.	*It's interesting.*
Je n'aime pas travailler le week-end.	**Ce n'est pas** amusant.	*It's no(t) fun.*

To express an opinion on a general topic, French speakers use the construction:

C'est
Ce n'est pas } + MASCULINE ADJECTIVE

VOCABULAIRE Opinions

C'est ... *It's ..., That's ...*
Ce n'est pas ... *It's not ..., That's not ...*

vrai	*true*	**chouette**	*neat*
faux	*false*	**super**	*great*
		génial	*terrific*
facile	*easy*	**pénible**	*a pain, annoying*
difficile	*hard, difficult*	**drôle**	*funny*

→ To express an opinion, French speakers also use adverbs like **bien** and **mal.**

C'est bien.	*That's good.*	Tu étudies? **C'est bien.**
C'est mal.	*That's bad.*	Alain n'étudie pas. **C'est mal.**

7 Vrai ou faux?

PARLER Imagine that your little sister is talking about where certain cities are located. Tell her whether her statements are right or wrong.

1. Paris est en Italie.
2. Los Angeles est en Californie.
3. Genève est en Italie.
4. Dakar est en Afrique.
5. Fort-de-France est au Canada.
6. Québec est en France.
7. Port-au-Prince est en Haïti.
8. Montréal est au Canada.

8 Opinion personnelle

PARLER Ask your classmates if they like to do the following things. They will answer, using an expression from the **Vocabulaire**.

▶ nager

1. téléphoner
2. parler en public
3. parler français
4. danser
5. voyager
6. dîner en ville
7. jouer aux jeux vidéo
8. étudier le week-end
9. écouter la musique classique
10. surfer sur l'Internet
11. télécharger de la musique

Prononciation  ch /ʃ/

Les lettres «ch»

The letters **"ch"** are usually pronounced like the English *"sh."*

chien

Répétez: **chien chat chose marche**
chouette chocolat affiche
Michèle a un chat et deux chiens.

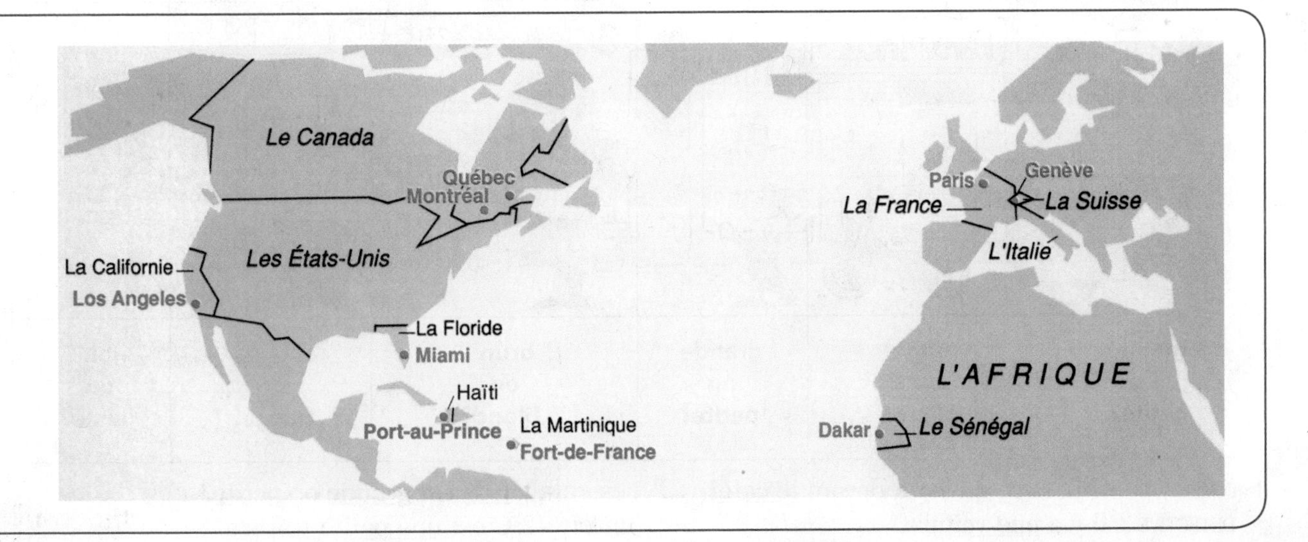

À votre tour!

OBJECTIFS

Now you can . . .
- express your opinions about people and activities
- describe everyday objects: their size and color

1 Allô!

PARLER Christophe is phoning some friends. Match his questions on the left with his friends' answers on the right.

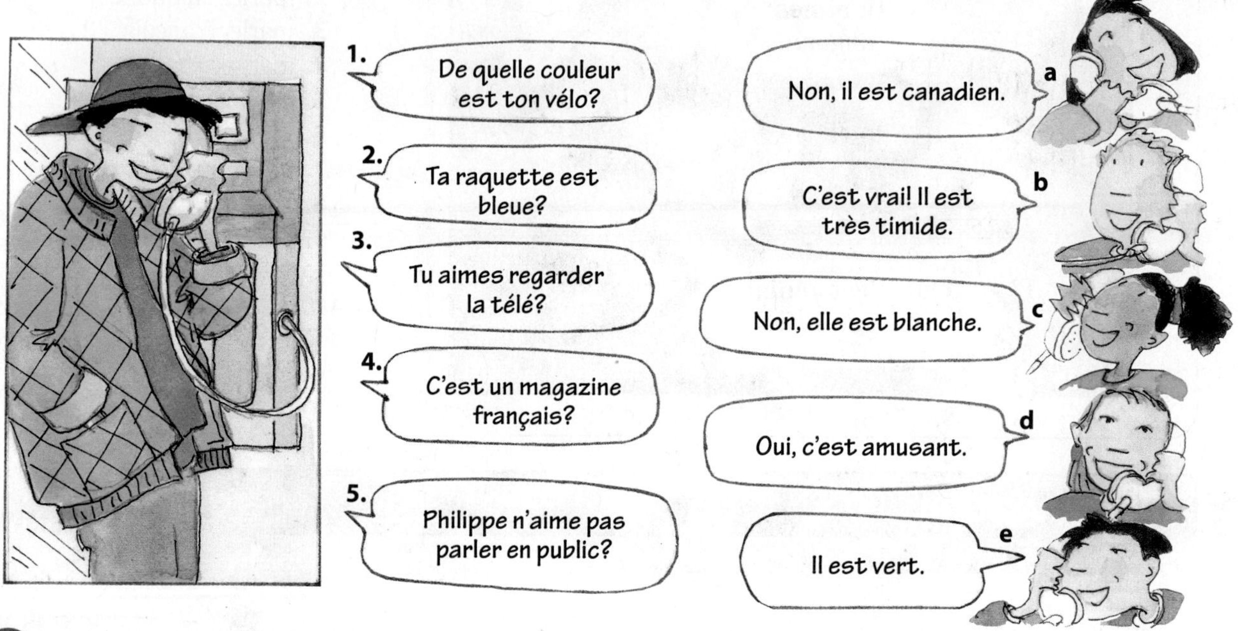

2 Créa-dialogue

PARLER There has been a burglary in the rue Saint-Pierre. By walkie-talkie, two detectives are describing what they see. Play both roles.

► (le)	1. (la)	2. (la)	3. (le)	4. (le)	5. (la)
grande ou petite?	rouge ou bleue?	grande ou petite?	brun ou blond?	anglais ou français?	noir ou jaune?

► DÉTECTIVE 1: Qu'est-ce qu'il y a devant le café?
DÉTECTIVE 2: Il y a une voiture.

DÉTECTIVE 1: Elle est grande ou petite?
DÉTECTIVE 2: C'est une petite voiture.

3 Faisons connaissance! 

PARLER Try to find out which students have the same interests you do. Select two activities you enjoy from Column A and ask a classmate if he/she likes to do them. Your classmate will answer yes or no, using an appropriate expression from Column B.

A	B
téléphoner	chouette
envoyer des mails	super
surfer sur l'Internet	génial
jouer aux jeux vidéo	amusant
jouer au foot	intéressant
voyager	pénible
organiser des boums	drôle
parler avec les voisins	difficile
parler français en classe	facile
étudier pour l'examen	
travailler dans le jardin	

4 Dialogue: Un chien! 

PARLER Imagine that your classmate has just received a dog for his/her birthday. You want to know more about this new pet. Ask your classmate ...

- what the dog's name is
- how old he is
- what color he is
- if he is a small dog or a big dog
- if he is cute
- if he is a mean dog (*un chien méchant*)

5 Composition: Une voiture 

ÉCRIRE Describe your parents' car or any other car you have seen recently. Provide the following information, writing a sentence for each of these points.

- make/model
- color
- age
- country of origin
- size (*petit? grand?*)
- other characteristics (*confortable? rapide? économique?*)

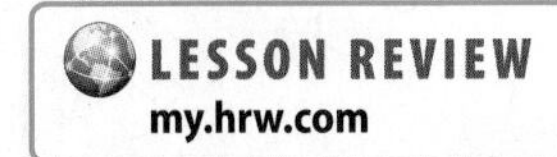

Tests de contrôle

By taking the following tests, you can check your progress in French and also prepare for the unit test. Write your answers on a separate sheet of paper.

Review...
- names of objects: pp. 140, 142, and 144

1 The right object

Name the following objects. Make sure to use the appropriate article: **un** or **une.**

Review...
- **être** and **avoir:** pp. 84 and 152

2 Être and avoir

Complete the following sentences with the appropriate forms of **être** or **avoir.**

1. Tu — une montre.
2. Tu — français.
3. Céline — quinze ans.
4. Nous — soif.
5. Thomas — sympathique.
6. Mes copains — amusants.
7. Vous — un portable.
8. Est-ce que vous — faim?

Review...
- adjectives: pp. 164-165, 166-167

3 The right adjectives

Complete the following descriptions with the appropriate forms of the adjectives in parentheses.

1. (français)	une amie ...	des copains ...
2. (américain)	des filles ...	des garçons ...
3. (sympathique)	une copine ...	des personnes ...
4. (intelligent)	une personne ...	des amies ...
5. (sportif)	une fille ...	des copines ...
6. (gentil)	des amies ...	des copains ...
7. (rouge)	une voiture ...	un vélo ...
8. (blanc)	une moto ...	des bicyclettes ...
9. (japonais)	une télé ...	des ordinateurs ...

4 The right choice

Complete the following sentences with the appropriate option suggested in parentheses.

(Note: + means that no word is needed.)

1. Qui est — fille là-bas? **(le, la, l')**
2. — ordinateur est sur la table. **(L', Le, La)**
3. Jean-Paul aime — musique classique. **(+, la, une)**
4. Léa a — copines canadiennes. **(+, une, des)**
5. Philippe n'a pas — portable. **(+, un, de)**

Review...
- definite and indefinite articles: pp. 153-156, 158

6. Ma mère a une voiture — . **(jaune, jolie, grande)**
7. Nous avons un — professeur. **(bon, sympathique, intéressant)**

Review...
- position of adjectives: pp. 168, 175

8. Voici Catherine. — une amie sympathique. **(Il est, Elle est, C'est)**
9. Voici Marc. — canadien. **(Il est, Elle est, C'est)**

Review...
- il est or c'est: p. 177

5 Composition: Mon cousin / Ma cousine

Digital performance space

Write a paragraph of five or six sentences describing one of your cousins, real or imaginary. Give your cousin's name, nationality and age, plus a brief description. Say why your cousin is interesting (or not interesting). Use only vocabulary and expressions that you know in French.

STRATEGY Writing

a) Make a list of the things you want to say about your cousin.

b) Organize your ideas and write your description.

c) Check that all the adjectives have the right endings.

nom: __________

nationalité: __________

âge: __________

description physique: __________

personnalité: __________

intéressant(e)? (pourquoi) __________

Vocabulaire

POUR COMMUNIQUER

Talking about people

Qui est-ce?	*Who is it?*
Comment est il/elle?	*What is he/she like?*
Quel âge a-t-il/elle?	*How old is he/she?*

Talking about things

Qu'est-ce que c'est?	*What is it? What's that?*
C'est ...	*It's ...*
Est-ce que tu as ...?	*Do you have ...?*
Oui, j'ai ...	*Yes, I have ...*
Regarde ça.	*Look at that.*
Quoi?	*What?*
Ça, là-bas.	*That, over there.*
Il y a ...	*There is ..., There are ...*
Est-ce qu'il y a ...?	*Is there ...? Are there ...?*
Qu'est-ce qu'il y a ...?	*What is there ...?*
De quelle couleur ...?	*What color ...?*

Expressing opinions

C'est ... *It's ...*

bien	*good*
chouette	*neat*
difficile	*hard, difficult*
drôle	*funny*
facile	*easy*
faux	*false*
génial	*terrific*
mal	*bad*
pénible	*a pain, annoying*
super	*great*
vrai	*true*

MOTS ET EXPRESSIONS

Les personnes

un camarade	*classmate*
un élève	*pupil, student*
un étudiant	*student*
une camarade	*classmate*
une élève	*pupil, student*
une étudiante	*student*
un prof	*teacher*
un professeur	*teacher*
un voisin	*neighbor*
une prof	*teacher*
une personne	*person*
une voisine	*neighbor*

Quelques possessions

un appareil-photo	*camera*
un cahier	*notebook*
un CD	*CD*
un crayon	*pencil*
un dock	*docking station*
un DVD	*DVD*
un livre	*book*
un MP3 (un lecteur MP3)	*MP3 player*
un objet	*object*
un ordinateur	*computer*
un portable (un smartphone)	*cell phone (smartphone)*
un sac	*bag*
un scooter	*motor scooter*
un stylo	*pen*
une tablette	*tablet (computer)*
un téléphone	*phone*
un vélo	*bicycle, bike*
une affiche	*poster*
une auto	*car*
une bicyclette	*bicycle*
une calculatrice	*calculator*
une chose	*thing*
une guitare	*guitar*
une mobylette	*motorbike, moped*
une montre	*watch*
une moto	*motorcycle*
une radio	*radio*
une raquette	*tennis racket*
une télé	*TV set*
une voiture	*car*

La chambre

un bureau	*desk*	**une chaise**	*chair*	**une porte**	*door*
un lit	*bed*	**une fenêtre**	*window*	**une table**	*table*
		une lampe	*lamp*		

Où?

dans	*in*	**devant**	*in front of*	**sur**	*on, on top of*
derrière	*behind, in back of*	**sous**	*under*		

La description

amusant(e)	*amusing, fun*	**jeune**	*young*		
beau (belle)*	*beautiful, handsome*	**joli(e)***	*pretty*		
bête	*silly, dumb*	**mauvais(e)***	*bad*		
blond(e)	*blonde*	**méchant(e)**	*mean, nasty*		
bon (bonne)*	*good*	**mignon (mignonne)**	*cute*	**assez**	*rather*
brun(e)	*brown, dark-haired*	**petit(e)***	*small, little, short*	**très**	*very*
gentil (gentille)	*nice, kind*	**sportif (sportive)**	*athletic*		
grand(e)*	*big, large, tall*	**sympathique**	*nice, pleasant*		
intelligent(e)	*intelligent, smart*	**timide**	*timid, shy*		
intéressant(e)	*interesting*				

** Adjectives that come before the noun*

Les adjectifs de nationalité

américain(e)	*American*	**espagnol(e)**	*Spanish*	**mexicain(e)**	*Mexican*
anglais(e)	*English*	**français(e)**	*French*	**suisse**	*Swiss*
canadien (canadienne)	*Canadian*	**italien (italienne)**	*Italian*		
chinois(e)	*Chinese*	**japonais(e)**	*Japanese*		

Les couleurs

blanc (blanche)	*white*	**jaune**	*yellow*	**orange***	*orange*	**vert(e)**	*green*
bleu(e)	*blue*	**marron***	*brown*	**rose**	*pink*		
gris(e)	*grey*	**noir(e)**	*black*	**rouge**	*red*		

** Invariable adjectives*

Verbes réguliers en *-er*

marcher	*to work, to run (to function)*
	to walk

Verbes irréguliers

avoir	*to have*
avoir faim	*to be hungry*
avoir soif	*to be thirsty*
avoir … ans	*to be … (years old)*

Expressions utiles

Dis!	*Say! Hey!*	**Je sais.**	*I know.*	**lundi**	*on Monday*
Dis donc!	*Hey there!*	**Je ne sais pas.**	*I don't know.*	**le lundi**	*on Mondays*
alors	*so, then*	**Si!**	*Yes!*	**le week-end**	*on weekends*

VOCABULAIRE SUPPLÉMENTAIRE: L'informatique

un clavier	*keyboard*	**une imprimante**	*printer*	**chatter**	*to chat (online)*
un dock (avec enceintes)	*docking station (with speakers)*	**un ordinateur portable**	*laptop*	**envoyer un mail**	*to send an e-mail*
				poster un message	*to post a message*
un écran	*screen*	**un PC**	*PC*	**un SMS**	*text message*
un jeu d'ordinateur	*computer game*	**une souris**	*mouse*	**surfer sur l'Internet**	*to surf the Internet*
un mail (un mél)	*e-mail*			**télécharger**	*to download*
				un texto	*text message*

Petit catalogue des compliments ... et des insultes

Language Comparisons

Over the centuries, French and English have influenced one another.

- Which of the compliments and insults did French borrow from English? Which word has English borrowed from French? Sometimes French and English express themselves in different ways.
- Which of the animal comparisons on the next page are the same in French and English? Which are different?

Additional readings @ **my.hrw.com**
FRENCH InterActive Reader

LES ANIMAUX et LE LANGAGE

Selon° toi, est-ce que les animaux ont une personnalité? Pour les Français, les animaux ont des qualités et des défauts,° comme° nous. Devine° comment on° complète les phrases suivantes° en français.

1 Philippe n'aime pas étudier. Il préfère dormir.° Il est paresseux° comme° …

un tigre

un chat

un lézard

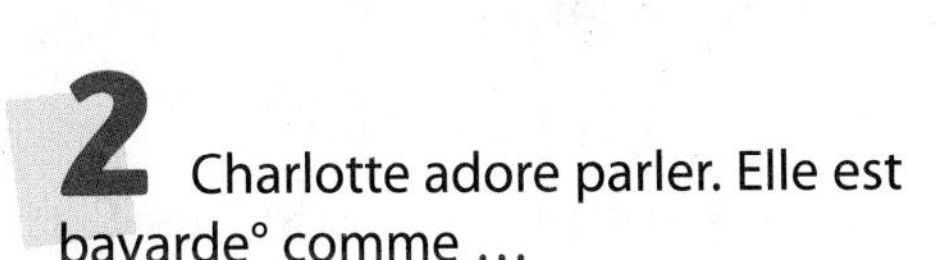

2 Charlotte adore parler. Elle est bavarde° comme …

une poule

une pie

un lion

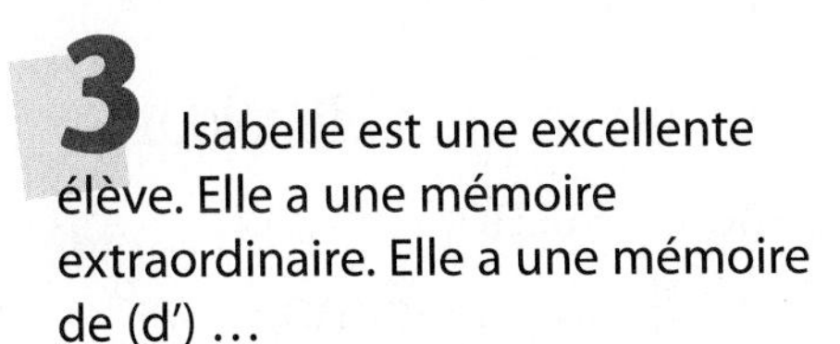

3 Isabelle est une excellente élève. Elle a une mémoire extraordinaire. Elle a une mémoire de (d') …

éléphant

hippopotame

kangourou

4 Le petit frère de Christine est jeune, mais il est très intelligent. Il est malin° comme …

un cheval

un singe

une girafe

5 Où est Jacques? Il n'est pas prêt!° Oh là là! Il est lent° comme …

une tortue

un poisson

un rhinocéros

6 Nicole a très, très faim. Elle a une faim de (d') …

lion

ours

loup

Selon *According to* **défauts** *shortcomings* **comme** *like* **Devine** *Guess* **on** *one* **phrases suivantes** *following sentences* **dormir** *to sleep* **paresseux** *lazy* **comme** *as* **bavarde** *talkative* **malin** *clever* **prêt** *ready* **lent** *slow*

Voici les réponses:
1. *un lézard* **2.** *une pie* **3.** *éléphant* **4.** *un singe* **5.** *une tortue* **6.** *loup*

Le scooter, c'est génial!

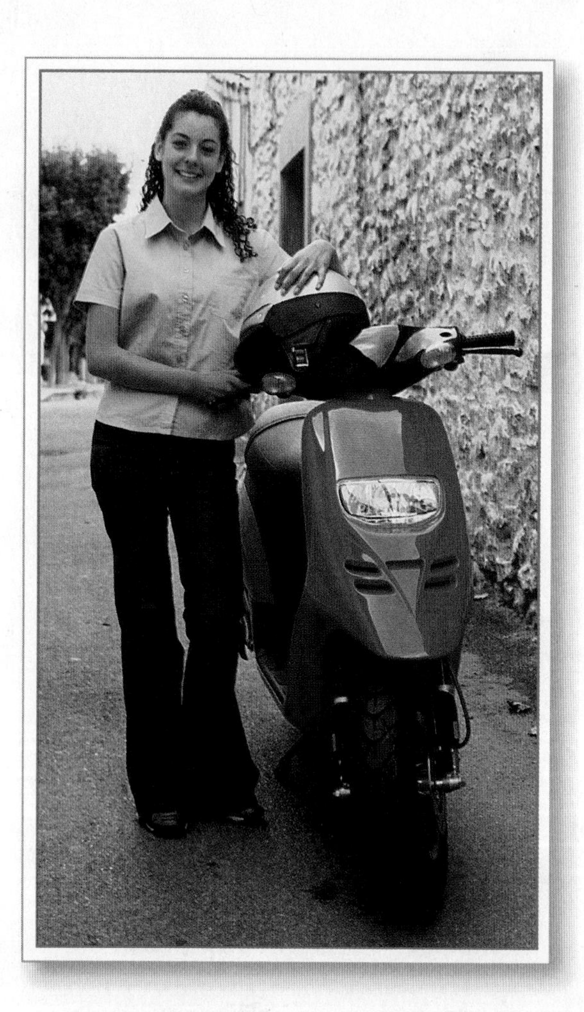

Je m'appelle Mélanie et j'ai 15 ans. J'ai un scooter. C'est un cadeau° d'anniversaire de ma grand-mère. Il est rouge et il est très confortable.

Ma copine Élodie a une mobylette. C'est une MBK. Nous allons° au collège ensemble.° Nous avons le BSR et nous sommes prudentes.° Nous portons° un casque° et nous respectons la limite de vitesse:° 45 kilomètres l'heure.

Le week-end, nous allons au centre-ville. Nous n'avons pas de problème de stationnement.° Quand il fait beau, nous allons à la campagne.° Quand nous sommes sur nos° petites machines, nous avons l'impression de liberté. Le scooter, c'est génial!

cadeau *gift* **allons** *go* **ensemble** *together* **prudentes** *careful* **portons** *wear* **casque** *helmet* **vitesse** *speed* **stationnement** *parking* **campagne** *country* **nos** *our*

Compréhension: vrai ou faux

1. Mélanie a un scooter.
2. Élodie a un scooter aussi.
3. Quand Mélanie est en scooter, elle porte un casque.
4. Avec un scooter, on a souvent un problème de stationnement.
5. En scooter, Mélanie a l'impression de liberté.

Et vous?

1. What are the advantages or disadvantages of owning a moped or a scooter?
2. What would you do if you had a motor scooter? How would this change your habits?

CONNEXIONS

Go to the Internet site of a French manufacturer of mopeds and scooters and make a poster showing some of the products you find.

Additional readings @ **my.hrw.com**
FRENCH InterActive Reader

Mobylette . . . ou scooter?

Couleurs: noir, gris, rouge
Prix: 680 €

Couleurs: rouge, bleu, noir
Prix: 1 600 €

Et vous?

1. Which of the above would you choose? Use the following in your response:

   couleur *prix en €* *prix en $*

2. Is it expensive? *(cher, chère)*
3. Why did you choose it?

NOTE Culturelle

La mobylette et le scooter

Mopeds and motor scooters are very popular among French teenagers. To drive one, you must be at least 14 years old. If you are under 16, you cannot go over 45 kilometers (about 30 miles) per hour. You must also have a license known as the **BSR** or **Brevet de Sécurité Routière** *(Certificate of Highway Safety)* which you get after a short course of driver's education. And, of course, whenever you are riding, you must wear a helmet!

The most popular makes of mopeds and scooters include Peugeot, Renault, and MBK, all manufactured in France. The term **mobylette** was originally a brand name which French students shortened to **mob.** It now is used to refer to any type of moped.

French teens love their mopeds and their scooters, and they take great care of them. During the week, many students ride them to school. On weekends, they use them to go into town, to get to their sports clubs, or to go for a ride in the country with their friends.

Bonjour, Brigitte!

Chers° copains américains,

Je m'appelle Brigitte Lavie. J'ai quatorze ans. Voici ma photo. Je ne suis pas très grande, mais je ne suis pas petite. Je suis de taille° moyenne.° Je suis brune, mais j'ai les yeux verts. Je suis sportive. J'aime le ski, le jogging et la danse moderne.

J'habite à Toulouse avec ma famille. Mon père travaille dans l'industrie aéronautique. Il est ingénieur.° Ma mère travaille dans une banque. Elle est directrice° du personnel.

J'ai une soeur et un frère. Ma petite soeur s'appelle Élodie. Elle a cinq ans. Elle est très mignonne. Mon frère s'appelle Mathieu. Il a treize ans. Il est pénible. J'ai un chien. Il s'appelle Attila mais il est très gentil. (Il est plus gentil que° mon frère!) J'ai aussi deux poissons rouges.° Ils n'ont pas de nom.°

J'ai un lecteur MP3 et j'adore écouter de la musique. J'ai un ordinateur. C'est un cadeau° de ma marraine.° Je surfe sur l'Internet et j'envoie des mails. Je n'ai pas de scooter mais j'ai une mob.

J'ai beaucoup de copains, mais je n'ai pas de «petit copain».° Ça n'a pas d'importance!° Je suis heureuse° comme ça.°

Amitiés,
Brigitte

Chers *Dear* **taille** *size* **moyenne** *average* **ingénieur** *engineer* **directrice** *director*
plus gentil que *nicer than* **poissons rouges** *goldfish* **nom** *name* **cadeau** *gift* **marraine** *godmother*
petit copain *boyfriend* **Ça n'a pas d'importance!** *It doesn't matter!* **heureuse** *happy* **comme ça** *like that*

Additional readings @ my.hrw.com
FRENCH InterActive Reader

STRATEGY Reading

Guessing from context As you read French, try to guess the meanings of unfamiliar words before you look at the English equivalents. Often the context provides good hints. For example, Brigitte writes:

Je ne suis pas très grande, mais je ne suis pas petite.
Je suis de taille moyenne.

She is neither tall nor short. She must be about average:
de taille moyenne = *of medium height or size*

Sometimes you know what individual words in an expression mean, but the phrase does not seem to make sense. Then you have to guess at the real meaning. For example, Brigitte writes that she has:
deux poissons rouges *?? red fish??*
If you guessed that these are most likely goldfish, you are right!

Activité écrite: Une lettre à Brigitte

Write a letter to Brigitte in which you describe yourself and your family. You may tell her:

- your name and how old you are
- if you are tall or short
- if you like sports, and which ones
- if you have brothers and sisters (and if so, their names and ages)
- if you have pets (and if so, give their names)
- a few things you own
- a few things you like to do

Writing Hint Use Brigitte's letter as a model.

Pour écrire une lettre

To write to a boy, begin with:	**Cher**	**Cher Patrick,**
To write to a girl, begin with:	**Chère**	**Chère Brigitte,**
End your letter with:	**Amicalement,** *(In friendship,)* **Amitiés,** *(Best regards,)*	

NOTE Culturelle

Toulouse

Toulouse, with a population of nearly one million people, is the center of the French aeronautic and space industry. It is in Toulouse that the Airbus planes and the Ariane rockets are being built in cooperation with other European countries.

Tête à tête Pair Activities

CONTENTS

L'École franco-américaine — Élève B

You and your partner are both enrolled in a French-American school, but you are in different classes and have different friends.

- The pictures on the right show your two best friends: one a girl, the other a boy.
- Your partner has pictures of his/her two best friends.

▶ Ask each other questions to find out more about each other's friends:

- name
  Comment s'appelle ton ami(e)?
- age
  Quel âge a ton ami(e)?
- nationality
  Il est français ou américain?
  Elle est française ou américaine?

Do any of your friends have the same name? the same age? the same nationality?

Alice — 15 ans

David — 14 ans

L'École franco-américaine — Élève A

You and your partner are both enrolled in a French-American school, but you are in different classes and have different friends.

- The pictures on the right show your two best friends: one a girl, the other a boy.
- Your partner has pictures of his/her two best friends.

▶ Ask each other questions to find out more about each other's friends:

- name
  Comment s'appelle ton ami(e)?
- age
  Quel âge a ton ami(e)?
- nationality
  Il est français ou américain?
  Elle est française ou américaine?

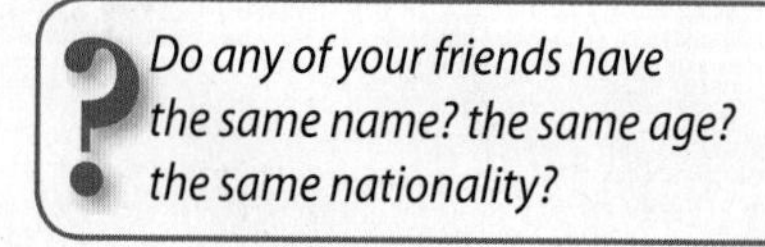

Do any of your friends have the same name? the same age? the same nationality?

Pauline — 16 ans

Patrick — 15 ans

Au restaurant — Élève B

You are at a French restaurant with your partner.

- Your menu has the prices for the beverages.
- Your partner's menu has the prices for the food items.

▶ Ask each other questions to find out the cost of the various foods and beverages.

Élève A: Combien coûte le café?
Élève B: Le café coûte deux euros dix.

Élève B: Combien coûte la pizza?
Élève A: La pizza coûte ...

What is the most expensive food?
What is the least expensive food?

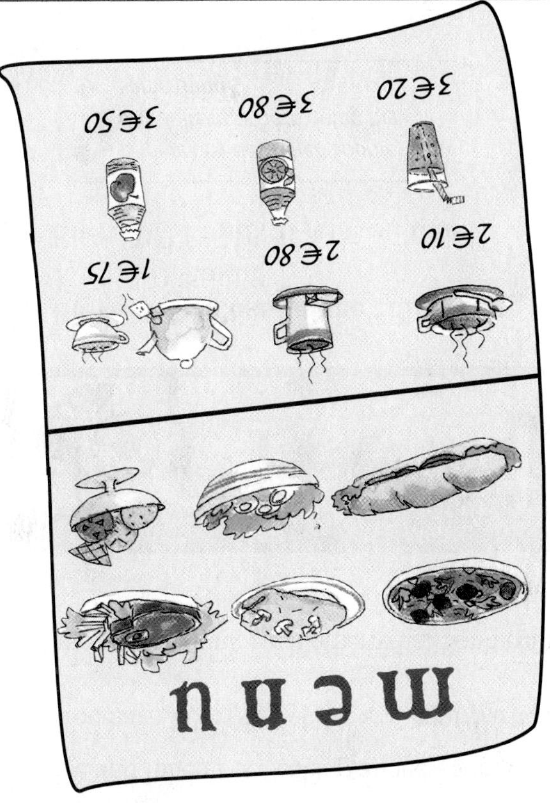

Au restaurant — Élève A

You are at a French restaurant with your partner.

- Your menu has the prices for the food items.
- Your partner's menu has the prices for the beverages.

▶ Ask each other questions to find out the cost of the various foods and beverages.

Élève A: Combien coûte le café?
Élève B: Le café coûte deux euros dix.

Élève B: Combien coûte la pizza?
Élève A: La pizza coûte ...

menu
5€40
4€80
10€80
3€70
3€30
2€50

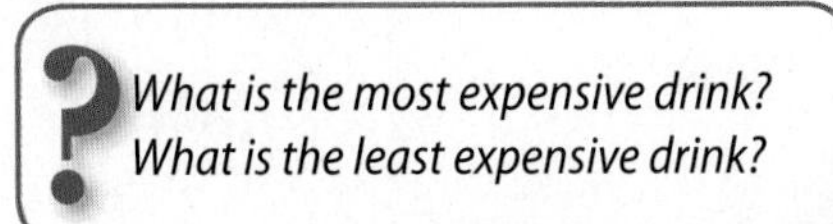

Activités de la semaine — Élève B

Sophie and Julien have each planned their activities for the week.

- You have Julien's calendar and your partner has Sophie's calendar.

▶ Take turns asking each other what Sophie and Julien are doing each day.

La semaine de Julien

Élève A: Qu'est-ce que Julien fait lundi?
Élève B: Lundi, il joue au foot.

Élève B: Et Sophie, qu'est-ce qu'elle fait lundi?
Élève A: Elle joue au tennis.

Is there any day when Sophie and Julien are both doing the same thing?

Activités de la semaine — Élève A

Sophie and Julien have each planned their activities for the week.

- You have Sophie's calendar and your partner has Julien's calendar.

▶ Take turns asking each other what Sophie and Julien are doing each day.

La semaine de Sophie

Élève A: Qu'est-ce que Julien fait lundi?
Élève B: Lundi, il joue au foot.

Élève B: Et Sophie, qu'est-ce qu'elle fait lundi?
Élève A: Elle joue au tennis.

Is there any day when Sophie and Julien are both doing the same thing?

Deux chambres — Élève B

Mélanie and Marc are brother and sister.

- You have a picture of Marc's room. Your partner has a picture of Mélanie's room.

La chambre de Marc

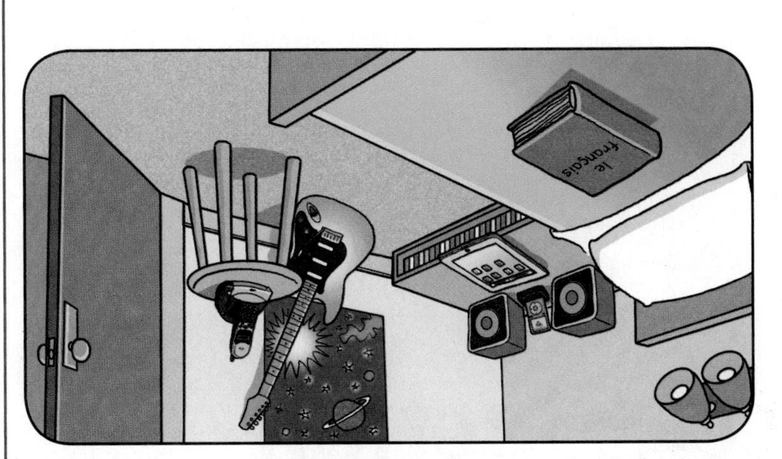

▶ Take turns asking each other questions to determine which objects or furniture can be found in each of the rooms.

Élève A: **Est-ce que Marc a un bureau?**
Élève B: **Non, il n'a pas de bureau.**

Élève B: **Est-ce que Mélanie a une radio?**
Élève A: **Non, elle n'a pas de radio.**

Which items are the same in both rooms?

Deux chambres — Élève A

Mélanie and Marc are brother and sister.

- You have a picture of Mélanie's room. Your partner has a picture of Marc's room.

▶ Take turns asking each other questions to determine which objects or furniture can be found in each of the rooms.

La chambre de Mélanie

Élève A: **Est-ce que Marc a un bureau?**
Élève B: **Non, il n'a pas de bureau.**

Élève B: **Est-ce que Mélanie a une radio?**
Élève A: **Non, elle n'a pas de radio.**

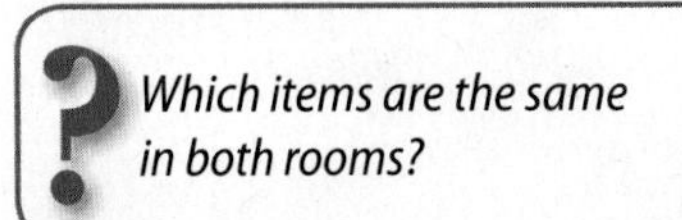

Which items are the same in both rooms?

Reference Section

CONTENTS

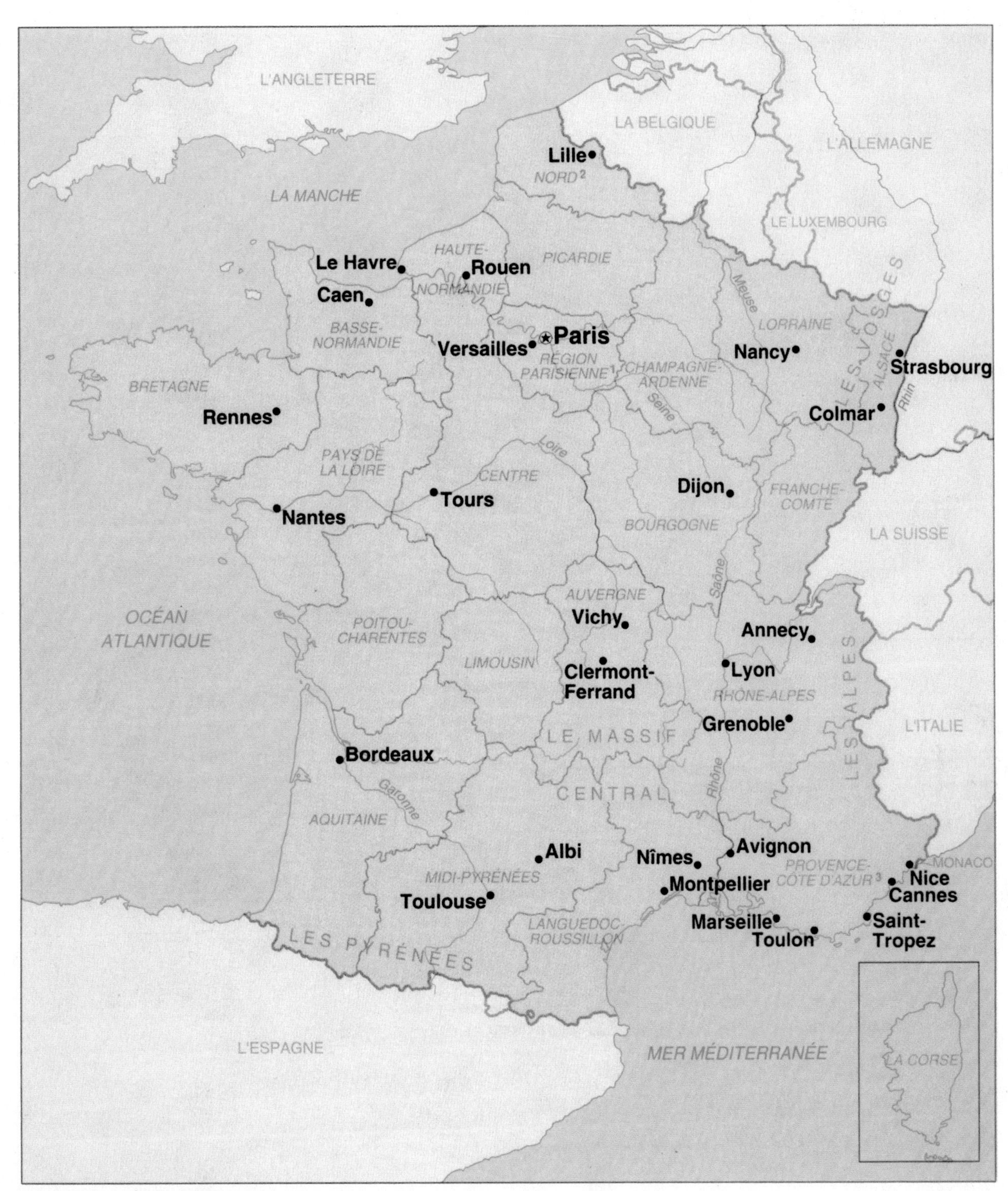

[1]Also known as Île-de-France
[2]Also known as Nord-Pas-de-Calais
[3]Also known as Provence-Alpes-Côte d'Azur *(Bottin 1989)*

APPENDIX 1

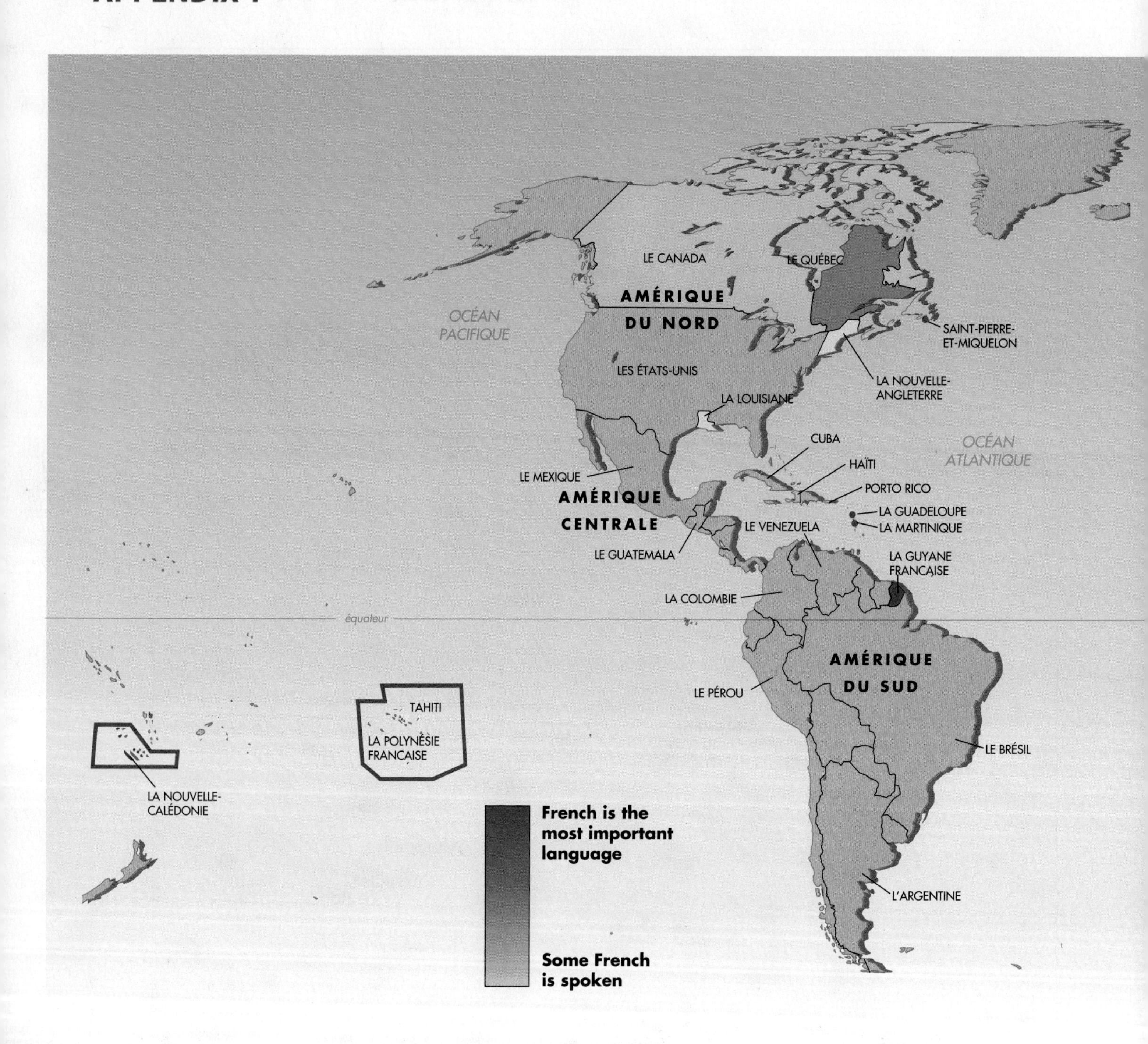

LE CANADA
LE QUÉBEC
AMÉRIQUE
DU NORD
OCÉAN
PACIFIQUE
SAINT-PIERRE-
ET-MIQUELON
LES ÉTATS-UNIS
LA NOUVELLE-
ANGLETERRE
LA LOUISIANE
CUBA
OCÉAN
ATLANTIQUE
HAÏTI
LE MEXIQUE
PORTO RICO
AMÉRIQUE
CENTRALE
LA GUADELOUPE
LA MARTINIQUE
LE VENEZUELA
LE GUATEMALA
LA GUYANE
FRANÇAISE
LA COLOMBIE
équateur
AMÉRIQUE
DU SUD
LE PÉROU
TAHITI
LA POLYNÉSIE
FRANÇAISE
LE BRÉSIL
LA NOUVELLE-
CALÉDONIE
French is the
most important
language
L'ARGENTINE
Some French
is spoken

MAP *The French Speaking World*

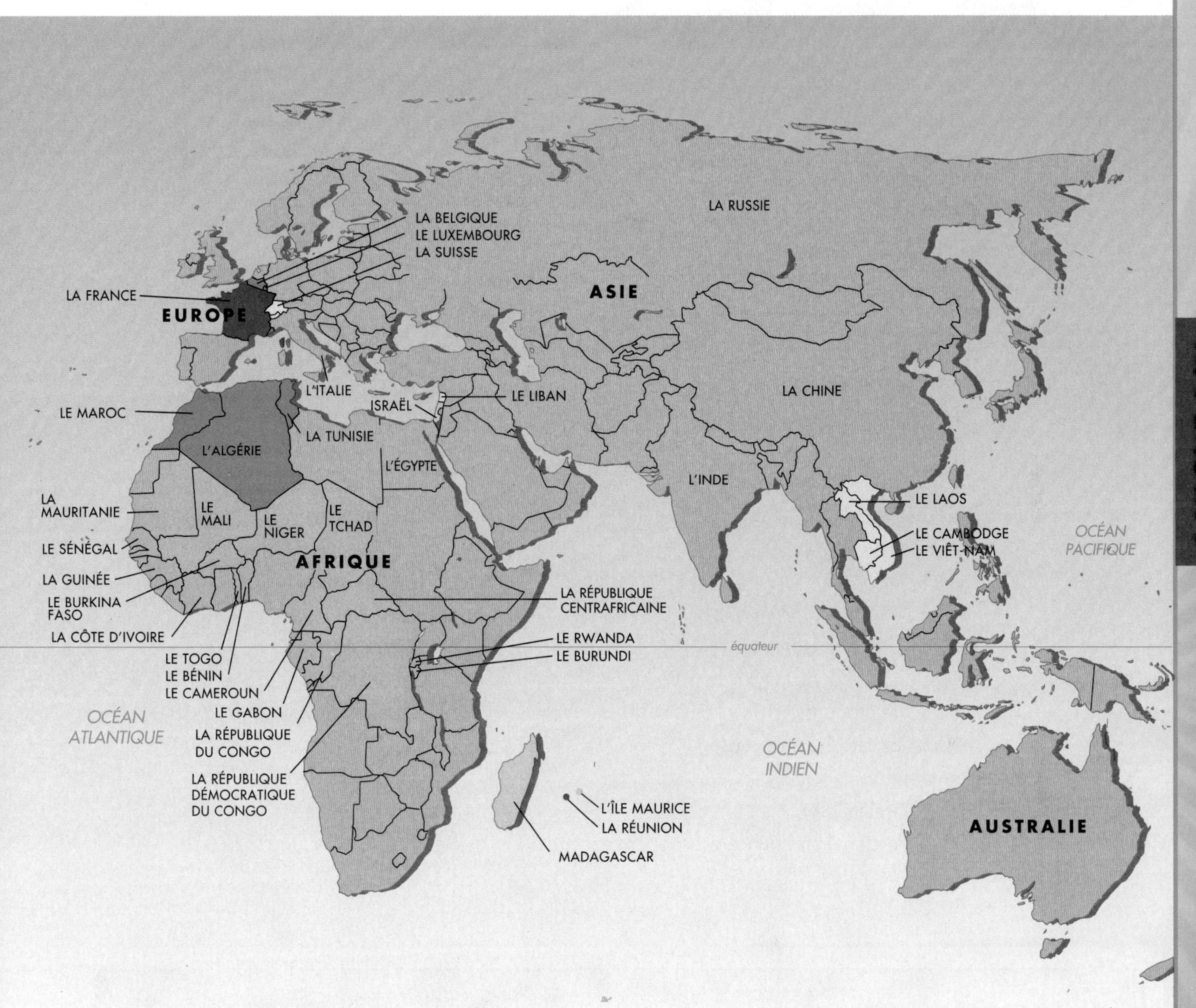

APPENDIX 1

APPENDIX 2 SOUND-SPELLING CORRESPONDENCES

VOWELS

Sound	*Spelling*	*Examples*
/a/	**a, à, â**	Madame, là-bas, théâtre
/i/	**i, î**	visite, Nice, dîne
	y (initial, final, or between consonants)	Yves, Guy, style
/u/	**ou, où, oû**	Toulouse, où, août
/y/	**u, û**	tu, Luc, sûr
/o/	**o** (final or before silent consonant)	piano, idiot, Margot
	au, eau	jaune, Claude, beau
	ô	hôtel, drôle, Côte d'Ivoire
/ɔ/	**o**	Monique, Noël, jolie
	au	Paul, restaurant, Laure
/e/	**é**	Dédé, Québec, télé
	e (before silent final **z, t, r**)	chez, et, Roger
	ai (final or before final silent consonant)	j'ai, mai, japonais
/ɛ/	**è**	Michèle, Ève, père
	ei	seize, neige, tour Eiffel
	ê	tête, être, Viêt-nam
	e (before two consonants)	elle, Pierre, Annette
	e (before pronounced final consonant)	Michel, avec, cher
	ai (before pronounced final consonant)	française, aime, Maine
/ə/	**e** (final or before single consonant)	je, Denise, venir
/ø/	**eu, oeu**	deux, Mathieu, euro, oeufs
	eu (before final **se**)	nerveuse, généreuse, sérieuse
/œ/	**eu,** (before final pronounced consonant except /z/)	heure, neuf, Lesieur,
	oeu	soeur, coeur, oeuf
	oe	oeil

NASAL VOWELS

Sound	*Spelling*	*Examples*
/ɑ̃/	**an, am**	France, quand, lampe
	en, em	Henri, pendant, décembre
/ɔ̃/	**on, om**	non, Simon, bombe
/ɛ̃/	**in, im**	Martin, invite, impossible
	yn, ym	syndicat, sympathique, Olympique
	ain, aim	Alain, américain, faim
	(o) + in	loin, moins, point
	(i) + en	bien, Julien, viens
/œ̃/	**un, um**	un, Lebrun, parfum

SEMI - VOWELS

Sound	Spelling	Examples
/j/	**i, y** (before vowel sound)	bien, piano, Lyon
	-il, -ill (after vowel sound)	oeil, travaille, Marseille, fille
/ɥ/	**u** (before vowel sound)	lui, Suisse, juillet
/w/	**ou** (before vowel sound)	oui, Louis, jouer
/wa/	**oi, oî,**	voici, Benoît
	oy (before vowel)	voyage

CONSONANTS

Sound	Spelling	Examples
/b/	**b**	Barbara, banane, Belgique
/k/	**c** (before **a, o, u,** or consonant)	casque, cuisine, classe
	ch(r)	Christine, Christian, Christophe
	qu, q (final)	Québec, qu'est-ce que, cinq
	k	kilo, Kiki, ketchup
/ʃ/	**ch**	Charles, blanche, chez
/d/	**d**	Didier, dans, médecin
/f/	**f**	Félix, franc, neuf
	ph	Philippe, téléphone, photo
/g/	**g** (before **a, o, u,** or consonant)	Gabriel, gorge, légumes, gris
	gu (before **e, i, y**)	vague, Guillaume, Guy
/ɲ/	**gn**	mignon, champagne, Allemagne
/ʒ/	**j**	je, Jérôme, jaune
	g (before **e, i, y**)	rouge, Gigi, gymnastique
	ge (before **a, o, u**)	orangeade, Georges, nageur
/l/	**l, ll**	Lise, elle, cheval
/m/	**m**	Maman, moi, tomate
/n/	**n**	banane, Nancy, nous
/p/	**p**	peu, Papa, Pierre
/r/	**r, rr**	arrive, rentre, Paris
/s/	**c** (before **e, i, y**)	ce, Cécile, Nancy
	ç (before **a, o, u**)	ça, garçon, déçu
	s (initial or before consonant)	sac, Sophie, reste
	ss (between vowels)	boisson, dessert, Suisse
	t (before **i** + vowel)	attention, Nations Unies, natation
	x	dix, six, soixante
/t/	**t**	trop, télé, Tours
	th	Thérèse, thé, Marthe
/v/	**v**	Viviane, vous, nouveau
/gz/	**x**	examen, exemple, exact
/ks/	**x**	Max, Mexique, excellent
/z/	**s** (between vowels)	désert, Louise, télévision
	z	Suzanne, zut, zéro

APPENDIX 2

APPENDIX 3 Numbers

A VOCABULAIRE CARDINAL NUMBERS

0 to 19

0	**zéro**	10	**dix**
1	**un (une)**	11	**onze**
2	**deux**	12	**douze**
3	**trois**	13	**treize**
4	**quatre**	14	**quatorze**
5	**cinq**	15	**quinze**
6	**six**	16	**seize**
7	**sept**	17	**dix-sept**
8	**huit**	18	**dix-huit**
9	**neuf**	19	**dix-neuf**

20 to 59

20	**vingt**	31	**trente et un (une)**
21	**vingt et un (une)**	32	**trente-deux**
22	**vingt-deux**	40	**quarante**
23	**vingt-trois**	41	**quarante et un (une)**
30	**trente**	50	**cinquante**

60 to 99

60	**soixante**	81	**quatre-vingt-un (une)**
70	**soixante-dix**	82	**quatre-vingt-deux**
71	**soixante et onze**	90	**quatre-vingt-dix**
72	**soixante-douze**	91	**quatre-vingt-onze**
80	**quatre-vingts**		

100 to 1 000 000

100	**cent**	600	**six cents**
101	**cent un (une)**	700	**sept cents**
102	**cent deux**	800	**huit cents**
200	**deux cents**	900	**neuf cents**
201	**deux cent un**	1 000	**mille**
300	**trois cents**	2 000	**deux mille**
400	**quatre cents**	1 000 000	**un million**
500	**cinq cents**		

Notes:

1. The word **et** occurs only in the numbers 21, 31, 41, 51, 61, and 71: **vingt et un**, **soixante et onze**
2. **Un** becomes **une** before a feminine noun: **trente et une filles**
3. **Quatre-vingts** becomes **quatre-vingt** before another number: **quatre-vingt-cinq**
4. **Cents** becomes **cent** before another number: **trois cent vingt**
5. **Mille** never adds an **-s:** **quatre mille**

B VOCABULAIRE ORDINAL NUMBERS

1er (ère)	**premier (première)**	5e	**cinquième**	9e	**neuvième**
2e	**deuxième**	6e	**sixième**	10e	**dixième**
3e	**troisième**	7e	**septième**	11e	**onzième**
4e	**quatrième**	8e	**huitième**	12e	**douzième**

Note: **Premier** becomes **première** before a feminine noun: **la première histoire**

C VOCABULAIRE METRIC EQUIVALENTS

1 gramme	= 0.035 ounces	**1 ounce**	= 28,349 grammes
1 kilogramme	= 2.205 pounds	**1 pound**	= 0,453 kilogrammes
1 litre	= 1.057 quarts	**1 quart**	= 0,946 litres
1 mètre	= 39.37 inches	**1 foot**	= 30,480 centimètres
1 kilomètre	= 0.62 miles	**1 mile**	= 1,609 kilomètres

APPENDIX 4 VERBS

A. REGULAR VERBS

Infinitive	*Present*		*Passé Composé*	
parler *(to talk, speak)*	je **parle** tu **parles** il **parle**	nous **parlons** vous **parlez** ils **parlent**	j'**ai parlé** tu **as parlé** il **a parlé**	nous **avons parlé** vous **avez parlé** ils **ont parlé**
	IMPERATIVE: **parle, parlons, parlez**			
finir *(to finish)*	je **finis** tu **finis** il **finit**	nous **finissons** vous **finissez** ils **finissent**	j'**ai fini** tu **as fini** il **a fini**	nous **avons fini** vous **avez fini** ils **ont fini**
	IMPERATIVE: **finis, finissons, finissez**			
vendre *(to sell)*	je **vends** tu **vends** il **vend**	nous **vendons** vous **vendez** ils **vendent**	j'**ai vendu** tu **as vendu** il **a vendu**	nous **avons vendu** vous **avez vendu** ils **ont vendu**
	IMPERATIVE: **vends, vendons, vendez**			

B. *-er* VERBS WITH SPELLING CHANGES

Infinitive	*Present*		*Passé Composé*
acheter *(to buy)*	j'**achète** tu **achètes** il **achète**	nous **achetons** vous **achetez** ils **achètent**	j'**ai acheté**
	Verb like **acheter:** amener *(to bring, take along)*		
espérer *(to hope)*	j'**espère** tu **espères** il **espère**	nous **espérons** vous **espérez** ils **espèrent**	j'**ai espéré**
	Verb like **espérer:** célébrer *(to celebrate)*, préférer *(to prefer)*		
commencer *(to begin, start)*	je **commence** tu **commences** il **commence**	nous **commençons** vous **commencez** ils **commencent**	j'**ai commencé**
manger *(to eat)*	je **mange** tu **manges** il **mange**	nous **mangeons** vous **mangez** ils **mangent**	j'**ai mangé**
	Verbs like **manger:** nager *(to swim)*, voyager *(to travel)*		
payer *(to pay, pay for)*	je **paie** tu **paies** il **paie**	nous **payons** vous **payez** ils **paient**	j'**ai payé**
	Verbs like **payer:** nettoyer *(to clean)*		

APPENDIX 4 VERBS *continued*

C. IRREGULAR VERBS

Infinitive	*Present*		*Passé Composé*
avoir *(to have, own)*	j' **ai** tu **as** il **a**	nous **avons** vous **avez** ils **ont**	j'**ai eu**
		IMPERATIVE: **aie, ayons, ayez**	
être *(to be)*	je **suis** tu **es** il **est**	nous **sommes** vous **êtes** ils **sont**	j'**ai été**
		IMPERATIVE: **sois, soyons, soyez**	
aller *(to go)*	je **vais** tu **vas** il **va**	nous **allons** vous **allez** ils **vont**	je **suis allé(e)**
		IMPERATIVE: **va, allons, allez**	
boire *(to drink)*	je **bois** tu **bois** il **boit**	nous **buvons** vous **buvez** ils **boivent**	j'**ai bu**
connaître *(to know)*	je **connais** tu **connais** il **connaît**	nous **connaissons** vous **connaissez** ils **connaissent**	j'**ai connu**
devoir *(to have to, should, must)*	je **dois** tu **dois** il **doit**	nous **devons** vous **devez** ils **doivent**	j'**ai dû**
dire *(to say, tell)*	je **dis** tu **dis** il **dit**	nous **disons** vous **dites** ils **disent**	j'**ai dit**
dormir *(to sleep)*	je **dors** tu **dors** il **dort**	nous **dormons** vous **dormez** ils **dorment**	j'**ai dormi**
écrire *(to write)*	j'**écris** tu **écris** il **écrit**	nous **écrivons** vous **écrivez** ils **écrivent**	j'**ai écrit**
		Verbs like **écrire**: décrire *(to describe)*	
faire *(to make, do)*	je **fais** tu **fais** il **fait**	nous **faisons** vous **faites** ils **font**	j'ai **fait**

Infinitive	*Present*		*Passé Composé*
lire *(to read)*	je **lis** tu **lis** il **lit**	nous **lisons** vous **lisez** ils **lisent**	j'**ai lu**
mettre *(to put, place)*	je **mets** tu **mets** il **met**	nous **mettons** vous **mettez** ils **mettent**	j'**ai mis**
Verb like **mettre:** promettre *(to promise)*			
ouvrir *(to open)*	j'**ouvre** tu **ouvres** il **ouvre**	nous **ouvrons** vous **ouvrez** ils **ouvrent**	j'**ai ouvert**
Verbs like **ouvrir:** découvrir *(to discover)*, offrir *(to offer)*			
partir *(to leave)*	je **pars** tu **pars** il **part**	nous **partons** vous **partez** ils **partent**	je **suis parti(e)**
pouvoir *(to be able, can)*	je **peux** tu **peux** il **peut**	nous **pouvons** vous **pouvez** ils **peuvent**	j'**ai pu**
prendre *(to take)*	je **prends** tu **prends** il **prend**	nous **prenons** vous **prenez** ils **prennent**	j'**ai pris**
Verbs like **prendre:** apprendre *(to learn)*, comprendre *(to understand)*			
savoir *(to know)*	je **sais** tu **sais** il **sait**	nous **savons** vous **savez** ils **savent**	j'**ai su**
sortir *(to go out, get out)*	je **sors** tu **sors** il **sort**	nous **sortons** vous **sortez** ils **sortent**	je **suis sorti(e)**
venir *(to come)*	je **viens** tu **viens** il **vient**	nous **venons** vous **venez** ils **viennent**	je **suis venu(e)**
Verb like **venir:** revenir *(to come back)*			
voir *(to see)*	je **vois** tu **vois** il **voit**	nous **voyons** vous **voyez** ils **voient**	j'**ai vu**

APPENDIX 4

C. IRREGULAR VERBS continued

Infinitive	*Present*		*Passé composé*
vouloir *(to want)*	je **veux** tu **veux** il **veut**	nous **voulons** vous **voulez** ils **veulent**	j'**ai voulu**

D. VERBS WITH ÊTRE IN THE PASSÉ COMPOSÉ

aller *(to go)*	je **suis allé(e)**	**passer** *(to go by, through)*	je **suis passé(e)**
arriver *(to arrive, come)*	je **suis arrivé(e)**	**rentrer** *(to go home)*	je **suis rentré(e)**
descendre *(to go down)*	je **suis descendu(e)**	**rester** *(to stay)*	je **suis resté(e)**
entrer *(to enter, go in)*	je **suis entré(e)**	**revenir** *(to come back)*	je **suis revenu(e)**
monter *(to go up)*	je **suis monté(e)**	**sortir** *(to go out, get out)*	je **suis sorti(e)**
mourir *(to die)*	il/elle **est mort(e)**	**tomber** *(to fall)*	je **suis tombé(e)**
naître *(to be born)*	je **suis né(e)**	**venir** *(to come)*	je **suis venu(e)**
partir *(to leave)*	je **suis parti(e)**		

FRENCH-ENGLISH VOCABULARY

The French-English vocabulary contains active and passive words from the text, as well as the important words of the illustrations used within the units. Obvious passive cognates have not been listed.

The numbers following an entry indicate the lesson in which the word or phrase is activated. (**I** stands for the list of classroom expressions at the end of the first **Images** section; **E** stands for **Entracte**.)

Nouns: If the article of a noun does not indicate gender, the noun is followed by *m. (masculine)* or *f. (feminine)*. If the plural *(pl.)* is irregular, it is given in parentheses.

Adjectives: Adjectives are listed in the masculine form. If the feminine form is irregular, it is given in parentheses. Irregular plural forms *(pl.)* are also given in parentheses.

Verbs: Verbs are listed in the infinitive form. An asterisk (*) in front of an active verb means that it is irregular. (For forms, see the verb charts in Appendix 4C.) Irregular present tense forms are listed when they are used before the verb has been activated. Irregular past participle *(p.p.)* forms are listed separately.

Words beginning with an **h** are preceded by a bullet (•) if the **h** is aspirate; that is, if the word is treated as if it begins with a consonant sound.

A

a: il y a there is, there are **9**
à at, in, to **6**
  à côté next door; next to
  à partir de as of, beginning
  à samedi! see you Saturday! **4B**
abolir to abolish
abondant plentiful, copious, large
un **abricot** apricot
absolument absolutely
un **accent** accent mark, stress
accepter to accept
un **accord** agreement
d' **accord** okay, all right **5**
  être d'accord to agree **6**
un **achat** purchase
un **acteur, une actrice** actor, actress
une **activité** activity
l' **addition** *f.* check
adorer to love
adroit skilled, skillful
un(e) **adulte** adult
aéronautique aeronautic, aeronautical
un **aéroport** airport
affectueusement affectionately *(at the end of a letter)*
une **affiche** poster **9**
affirmativement affirmatively
l' **Afrique** *f.* Africa
l' **âge** *m.* age
  quel âge a-t-il/elle? how old is he/she? **9**
  quel âge as-tu? how old are you? **2C**
  quel âge a ton père/ta mère? how old is your father/your mother? **2C**
âgé old
une **agence** agency
une **agence de tourisme** tourist office
une **agence de voyages** travel agency
agiter to shake
agité agitated
ah! ah!, oh!
  ah bon? oh? really? **8**
  ah non! ah, no!
ai *(see* **avoir***)*: **j'ai** I have **9**
  j'ai... ans I'm ... (years old) **2C**
une **aile** wing
aimer to like **7**
  est-ce que tu aimes...? do you like ...? **5**
  j'aime... I like ... **5**
  j'aimerais I would like
  je n'aime pas... I don't like ... **5**
ainsi thus
aîné older
  un frère aîné older brother
  une soeur aînée older sister
ajouter to add
l' **Algérie** *f.* Algeria *(country in North Africa)*
  algérien (algérienne) Algerian
l' **Allemagne** *f.* Germany
allemand German
* **aller** to go
  allez *(see* **aller***)*: **allez-vous en** go away!
  allez-y come on!, go ahead!, do it!
  comment allez-vous? how are you? **1C**
allô! hello! *(on the telephone)*
alors so, then **11**
une **alouette** lark
les **Alpes** *f.* (the) Alps
l' **alphabet** *m.* alphabet
l' **Alsace** *f.* Alsace *(province in eastern France)*
américain American **1B, 11**
  à l'américaine American-style
  un Américain, une Américaine American person
  l'Amérique *f.* America
un **ami, une amie** *(close)* friend **2A**
amicalement love *(at the end of a letter)*
l' **amitié** *f.* friendship
amitiés best regards *(at the end of a letter)*
amusant funny, amusing **11**
  amuser to amuse
  s'amuser to have fun
  on s'est bien amusé! we had a good time!
un **an** year
  avoir... ans to be ... (years old) **10**
  il/elle a... ans he/she is ... (years old) **2C**
  j'ai... ans I'm ... (years old) **2C**

l' **an dernier** last year
par an per year
un **ananas** pineapple
ancien (ancienne) former, old, ancient
un **âne** donkey
un **ange** angel
anglais English **1B, 11**
un Anglais, une Anglaise English person
un **animal** (*pl.* **animaux**) animal
une **animation** live entertainment
animé animated, lively
une **année** year **4B**
toute l'année all year long
un **anniversaire** birthday **4B**
joyeux anniversaire! happy birthday!
c'est quand, ton anniversaire? when is your birthday? **4B**
mon anniversaire est le (2 mars) my birthday is (March 2nd) 4B
un **annuaire** telephone directory
un **anorak** ski jacket
les **antiquités** *f.* antiquities, antiques
août *m.* August **4B**
un **appareil-photo** (*pl.* **appareils-photo**) *(still)* camera **9**
s' **appeller** to be named, called
comment s'appelle...? what's ...'s name? **2B**
comment s'appelle-t-il/elle? what's his/her name? **9**
comment t'appelles-tu? what's your name? **1A**
il/elle s'appelle... his/her name is ... **2B**
je m'appelle... my name is ... **1A**
apporter: apporte-moi (apportez-moi) bring me **I**
apprécier to appreciate
approprié appropriate
après after, afterwards
d'après according to
de l'après-midi in the afternoon, P.M. **4A**
l' **arabe** *m.* Arabic *(language)*
un **arbre** tree
un arbre généalogique family tree
l' **arche** *f.* **de Noé** Noah's Ark
l' **argent** *m.* money
l'argent de poche allowance, pocket money
arrêter to arrest; to stop
arriver to arrive, come
j' **arrive!** I'm coming!
une **arrivée** arrival
un **arrondissement** district
un **artifice: le feu d'artifice** fireworks
un **artiste, une artiste** artist
as (*see* **avoir**): **est-ce que tu as...?** do you have ...? **9**
un **ascenseur** elevator
un **aspirateur** vacuum cleaner
s' **asseoir: asseyez-vous!** sit down! **I**
assez rather **11; enough**
assieds-toi! sit down! **I**
associer to associate
l' **Atlantique** *m.* Atlantic Ocean
attention *f.*: **faire attention** to be careful, pay attention **8**
attentivement carefully
au (à + le) to (the), at (the), in (the) **6**
au revoir! good-bye! **1C**
une **auberge** inn
aucun: ne... aucun none, not any
aujourd'hui today **4B**
aujourd'hui, c'est... today is ... **4B**
aussi also, too **1B, 7**
une **auto (automobile)** car, automobile **9**
une **auto-école** driving school
un **autobus** bus
l' **automne** *m.* autumn, fall
en automne in (the) autumn, fall **4C**
autre other
d'autres others
un(e) autre another
avant before
avant hier the day before yesterday
en **avant** let's begin
avantageux (avantageuse) reasonable, advantageous
avec with **6**
avec moi, avec toi with me, with you **5**
avec qui? with who(m)? **8**
un **avis** opinion
avis de recherche missing person's bulletin
à votre avis in your opinion
* **avoir** to have **10**
avoir... ans to be ... (years old) **10**
avoir faim to be hungry **10**
avoir lieu to take place
avoir soif to be thirsty **10**
avril *m.* April **4B**

B

le **babyfoot** tabletop soccer game
le **babysitting: faire du babysitting** to baby-sit
les **bagages** *m.* bags, baggage
une **bande dessinée** comic strip
des **bandes dessinées** comics
la **Bannière étoilée** Star-Spangled Banner
une **banque** bank
une **barbe: quelle barbe!** what a pain! *(colloq.)*
le **bas** the bottom
au bas at the bottom
basé based
le **basket (basketball)** basketball
jouer au basket to play basketball **5**
un **bateau-mouche** sightseeing boat
battre to beat
bavard talkative
beau (bel, belle; *m.pl.* **beaux)** handsome, good-looking, beautiful **9, 12**
il est beau he is good-looking, handsome **9**
il fait beau it's beautiful (nice) out **4C**
un **beau-frère** stepbrother, brother-in-law
un **beau-père** stepfather, father-in-law
beaucoup (de) much, very much, many, a lot **7**
la **beauté** beauty
un **bec** beak
la **Belgique** Belgium
belle (*see* **beau**) beautiful **9, 12**
elle est belle she is beautiful **9**
une **belle-mère** stepmother, mother-in-law
une **belle-soeur** stepsister, sister-in-law
les **Bermudes** *f.* Bermuda

FRENCH-ENGLISH VOCABULARY *continued*

le besoin need
des besoins d'argent money needs
bête dumb, silly **11**
une bicyclette bicycle **9**
bien well, very well, carefully **7**
bien sûr of course **5**
ça va bien everything's fine (going well) **1C**
ça va très bien I'm (everything's) very well **1C**
c'est bien that's good (fine) **12**
je veux bien (…) I'd love to (…), I do, I want to **5**
oui, bien sûr… yes, of course … **5**
très bien very well **7**
bientôt: à bientôt! see you soon!
bienvenue welcome
le bifteck steak
un bifteck de tortue turtle steak
bilingue bilingual
la biologie biology
une biscotte dry toast
blaff de poisson *m.* fish stew
blanc (blanche) white **E1, 12**
Blanche-Neige Snow White
blanchir to blanch, turn white
bleu blue **E1, 12**
blond blonde **9**
il/elle est blond(e) he/she is blond **9**
une boisson drink, beverage **3B**
une boîte box
un bol deep bowl
bon (bonne) good **12**
ah bon? oh, really? **8**
de bonne humeur in a good mood
il fait bon the weather's good (pleasant) **4C**
le bonheur happiness
bonjour hello **1A, 1C**
une bouche mouth **E2**
une boucherie butcher shop
le boudin sausage
une boulangerie bakery
une boum party **5, 7**
boxe: un match de boxe boxing match
un bras arm **E2**
brésilien (brésilienne) Brazilian
la Bretagne Brittany *(province in northwestern France)*
bricoler to do things around the house
broche: à la broche on the spit
bronzé tan
un bruit noise
brun brown, dark-haired **9**
il/elle est brun(e) he/she has dark hair **9**
brunir to turn brown
Bruxelles Brussels
le bulletin de notes report card
un bureau desk **I, 9; office**
un bus bus
un but goal; end

C

ça that, it
ça fait combien? ça fait… how much is that (it)? that (it) is … **3C**
ça, là-bas that (one), over there **9**
ça va? how's everything? how are you? **1C**
ça va everything's fine, I'm OK **1C**
ça va (très) bien, ça va bien everything's going very well, everything's fine (going well) **1C**
ça va comme ci, comme ça everything's (going) so-so **1C**
ça va (très) mal things are going (very) badly **1C**
regarde ça look at that **9**
une cabine d'essayage fitting room
les cabinets *m.* toilet
un cadeau (*pl.* **cadeaux**) gift, present
cadet (cadette) younger
un frère cadet (a) younger brother
une soeur cadette (a) younger sister
le café coffee **3B**
un café au lait coffee with hot milk
un café café *(French coffee shop)* **6**
au café to (at) the café **6**
un cahier notebook **I, 9**
une calculatrice calculator **9**
un calendrier calendar
un camarade, une camarade classmate **9**
le Cambodge Cambodia *(country in Asia)*
un cambriolage burglary
un cambrioleur burglar
une caméra movie camera
la campagne countryside
une auberge de campagne country inn
le Canada Canada
canadien (canadienne) Canadian **1B, 11**
un Canadien, une Canadienne Canadian person
un canard duck
un car scolaire school bus
une carotte carrot
des carottes râpées grated carrots
un carré square
le Vieux Carré *the French Quarter in New Orleans*
une carte map **I**; card
une carte postale postcard
un cas case
en cas de in case of
le catch wrestling
une cathédrale cathedral
une cave cellar
un CD CD, compact disc **9**
ce (c') this, that, it
ce n'est pas that's/it's not **12**
ce que what
ce sont these are, those are, they are **12**
c'est it's, that's **2A, 9, 12**
c'est + *day of the week* it's … **4B**
c'est + *name or noun* it's … **2A**
c'est bien/mal that's good/bad **12**
c'est combien? how much is that/it? **3C**
c'est le (12 octobre) it's (October 12) **4B**
qu'est-ce que c'est? what is it? what's that? **9**
qui est-ce? who's that/this? **9**
ce n'est pas it's (that's) not **12**
un cédérom (un CD-ROM) CD-ROM
une cédille cedilla
cela that
célèbre famous
cent one hundred **2B**
une centaine about a hundred
un centime centime *(1/100 of a euro)*

un **centre** center
certain certain
certains some of them
c'est (*see* **ce**)
chacun each one, each person
une **chaise** chair **I, 9**
une **chaîne** (TV) channel
une **chaîne hi-fi** stereo set
une **mini-chaîne** compact stereo
la **chaleur** heat, warmth
une **chambre** bedroom **9**
un **champion, une championne** champion
la **chance** luck
une **chanson** song
chanter to sing **5, 7**
un **chanteur, une chanteuse** singer
chaque each, every
charmant charming
un **chat** cat **2C, E4**
un **château** (*pl.* **châteaux**) castle
chatter to chat (online)
chaud warm, hot
il fait chaud it's warm (hot) (*weather*) **4C**
chauffer to warm, heat up
un **chauffeur** driver
un **chef** boss; chef
un **cheval** (*pl.* **chevaux**) horse **E4**
les **cheveux** *m.* hair **E2**
chic *(inv.)* nice; elegant, in style
une chic fille a great girl
un **chien** dog **2C**
la **chimie** chemistry
chinois Chinese **11**
le **chinois** Chinese *(language)*
le **chocolat** hot chocolate, cocoa **3B**
une glace au chocolat chocolate ice cream
un **choix** choice
au choix choose one, your choice
une **chorale** choir
une **chose** thing **9**
chouette great, terrific **12**
le **cidre** cider
un **cinéaste, une cinéaste** film maker
le **cinéma** the movies
au cinéma to (at) the movies, movie theater **6**
cinq five **1A**
cinquante fifty **1C**
une **circonstance** circumstance
cité: la Cité Interdite Forbidden City

une **classe** class
en classe in class **6**
classique classical
un **client, une cliente** customer
un **clip** music video
un **cochon** pig
un **coiffeur, une coiffeuse** hairdresser
un **coin** spot
une **coïncidence** coincidence
le **Colisée** the Coliseum *(a large stadium built by the Romans)*
un **collège** junior high school
une **colonie** colony
une **colonne** column
combien how much
combien coûte...? how much does...cost? **3C**
combien de temps? how long?
combien d'heures? how many hours?
ça fait combien? how much is this (it)? **3C**
c'est combien? how much is this (it)? **3C**
commander to order
comme like, as, for
comme ci, comme ça so-so
ça va comme ci, comme ça everything's so-so **1C**
commencer to begin, start
comment? how? **8; what?**
comment allez-vous? how are you? **1C**
comment est-il/elle? what's he/she like? what does he/she look like? **9**
comment dit-on... en français? how do you say ... in French? **I**
comment lire reading hints
comment s'appelle...? what's...'s name? **2B**
comment s'appelle-t-il/elle? what's his/her name? **9**
comment t'appelles-tu? what's your name? **1A**
comment vas-tu? how are you? **1C**
un **commentaire** comment, commentary
le **commérage** gossip
communiquer to communicate
un **compact (disc), un CD** compact disc, CD **9**
complément object
compléter to complete

* **comprendre** to understand
je (ne) comprends (pas) I (don't) understand **I**
compter to count (on); to expect, intend
concerne: en ce qui concerne as for
un **concombre** cucumber
une **connaissance** acquaintance
faire connaissance (avec) to become acquainted (with)
* **connaître** to know, be acquainted with
tu connais...? do you know...? are you acquainted with...? **2B**
un **conseil** piece of advice, counsel
des conseils *m.* advice
un **conservatoire** conservatory
une **consonne** consonant
se **contenter** to limit oneself
le **contenu** contents
une **contradiction** disagreement
une **contravention** *(traffic)* ticket
cool cool, neat
un **copain, une copine** friend, pal **2A**
un petit copain, une petite copine boyfriend, girlfriend
copier to copy
une **copine** friend **2A**
coréen (coréenne) Korean
un **corps** body
correspondant corresponding
correspondre to correspond, agree
la **Corse** Corsica *(French island off the Italian coast)*
un **costume** man's suit
la **Côte d'Azur** Riviera *(southern coast of France on the Mediterranean)*
la **Côte d'Ivoire** Ivory Coast *(French-speaking country in West Africa)*
côté: à côté (de) next door; next to
une **côtelette de porc** pork chop
le **cou** neck **E2**
une **couleur** color **12**
de quelle couleur ...? what color ...? **12**
un **couloir** hall, corridor
coup: dans le coup with it
courageux (courageuse) courageous
le **courrier électronique** e-mail, electronic mail

une **course** race
un **cousin, une cousine** cousin **2C**
le **coût: le coût de la vie** cost of living
coûter to cost
combien coûte...? how much does...cost? **3C**
il (elle) coûte... it costs...**3C**
un **couturier, une couturière** fashion designer
un **crabe** crab
des matoutou crabes stewed crabs with rice
la **craie** chalk
un morceau de craie piece of chalk **I**
un **crayon** pencil **I, 9**
créer to create
un **crétin** idiot
une **crêpe** crepe *(pancake)* **3A**
une **crêperie** crepe restaurant
une **crevaison** flat tire
une **croisade** crusade
un **croissant** crescent *(roll)* **3A**
une **cuillère** spoon
une cuillère à soupe soup spoon
cuit cooked
culturel (culturelle) cultural
curieux (curieuse) curious, strange
la curiosité curiosity
le **cybercafé** internet café
un **cyclomoteur** moped

D

d'accord okay, all right
être d'accord to agree **6**
oui, d'accord yes, okay **5**
une **dame** lady, woman *(polite term)* **2A**
dangereux (dangereuse) dangerous
dans in **9**
danser to dance **5, 7**
la **date** date **4B**
quelle est la date? what's the date? **4B**
de (d') of, from, about **6**
de l'après-midi in the afternoon **4A**
de quelle couleur...? what color ...? **12**
de qui? of whom? **8**
de quoi? about what?
de temps en temps from time to time
pas de not any, no **10**
débarquer to land
décembre *m.* December **4B**
décider (de) to decide (to)
une **déclaration** statement
décoré decorated
* **découvrir** to discover
* **décrire** to describe
décrivez... describe...
un **défaut** shortcoming
un **défilé** parade
dehors outside
en dehors de outside of
déjà already; ever
demain tomorrow **4B**
à demain! see you tomorrow! **4B**
demain, c'est... (jeudi) tomorrow is ... (Thursday) **4B**
un **demi-frère** half-brother
une **demi-soeur** half-sister
demi: ... heures et demie half past ... **4A**
midi et demi half past noon **4A**
minuit et demi half past midnight **4A**
un **démon** devil
une **dent** tooth
un **départ** departure
se **dépêcher: dépêchez-vous!** hurry up!
dépend: ça dépend that depends
une **dépense** expense
derrière behind, in back of **9**
des some, any **10**
le **désert** desert
désirer to wish, want
vous désirez? what would you like? may I help you? **3B**
désolé sorry
le **dessin** art, drawing
un dessin animé cartoon
détester to hate, detest **1C**
deux two **1A**
le **deuxième étage** third floor
devant in front of **9**
développer to develop
deviner to guess
un **devoir** homework assignment **I**
les devoirs *m.* homework
d'habitude usually
différemment differently
différent different
difficile hard, difficult **12**
la **dignité** dignity
dimanche *m.* Sunday **4B**
dîner to have dinner **7**
dîner au restaurant to have dinner at a restaurant **5**
* **dire** to say, tell
que veut dire...? what does... mean? **I**
directement straight
un **directeur, une directrice** director, principal
dirigé directed, guided
dis! (*see* **dire**) say!, hey! **12**
dis donc! say there!, hey there! **12**
discuter to discuss
une dispute quarrel, dispute
dit (*p.p. of* **dire**) said
dit (*see* **dire**)**: comment dit-on... en français?** how do you say...in French? **I**
dites... (*see* **dire**) say..., tell...
dix ten **1A, 1B**
dix-huit eighteen **1B**
dix-neuf nineteen **1B**
dix-sept seventeen **1B**
un **dock** *docking station* **9**
un **docteur** doctor
dois (*see* **devoir**)**: je dois** I have to (must) **5**
domestique domestic
les **animaux** *m.* **domestiques** pets **2C**
dommage! too bad! **7**
donner to give
donne-moi... give me... **3A, I**
donnez-moi... give me **3B, I**
s'il te plaît, donne-moi... please, give me... **3B**
doré golden brown
* **dormir** to sleep
le **dos** back **E2**
douze twelve **1B**
drôle funny **12**
du *(partitive)* of the
du matin in the morning, A.M. **4A**
du soir in the evening, P.M. **4A**
dur hard
des oeufs *(m.)* **durs** hard-boiled eggs
durer to last
un **DVD** DVD **9**
dynamique dynamic

un **échange** exchange
les **échecs** *m.* chess
une **éclosion** hatching
économiser to save money
écouter to listen to **I, 7**
écouter la radio to listen to the radio **5**
l' **écran** *m.* screen *(computer)*
l' **éducation** *f.* education
l'éducation civique civics
l'éducation physique physical education
égyptien (égyptienne) Egyptian
électronique: une guitare électrique electric guitar
un **éléphant** elephant **E4**
un **élève, une élève** pupil, student **9**
élevé high
elle she, it **3C, 6, 10**
elle coûte... it costs ... **3C**
elle est (canadienne) she's (Canadian) **2B**
elle s'appelle... her name is ... **2B**
embrasser: je t'embrasse love and kisses *(at the end of a letter)*
un **emploi du temps** time-table *(of work)*
emprunter à to borrow from
en in, on, to, by
en ce qui concerne as for
en face opposite, across (the street)
en fait in fact
en famille at home
en plus in addition
en scène on stage
en solde on sale
un(e) **enfant** child
entier (entière) entire
l' **entracte** *m.* interlude
entre between
une entrée entry *(of a house)*
un **entretien** discussion
envers toward
l' **envie** *f.* envy; feeling
envoyer to send
envoyer un mail to send an e-mail
épicé hot (spicy)
une **épicerie** grocery store
les **épinards** *m.* spinach
une **équipe** team
une **erreur** error, mistake
es *(see* **être***)*
tu es + *nationality* you are ... **1B**
tu es + *nationality?* are you ...? **1B**
tu es de...? are you from ...? **1B**
un **escalier** staircase
un **escargot** snail
l' **Espagne** *f.* Spain
espagnol Spanish **11**
parler espagnol to speak Spanish **5**
un **esprit** spirit
essayer to try on, to try
l' **essentiel** *m.* the important thing
est *(see* **être***)*
est-ce que (qu')...? *phrase used to introduce a question* **6**
c'est... it's ..., that's ... **2A, 2C, 12**
c'est le + *date* it's ... **4B**
il/elle est + *nationality* he/she is ... **2B**
n'est-ce pas...? isn't it? **6**
où est...? where is ...? **6**
quel jour est-ce? what day is it? **4B**
qui est-ce? who's that (this)? **2A, 9**
l' **est** *m.* east
et and **1B, 6**
et demi(e), et quart half past, quarter past **4A**
et toi? and you? **1A**
établir to establish
un **étage** floor of a building, story
les **États-Unis** *m.* United States
l' **été** *m.* summer
en été in (the) summer **4C**
l'heure d'été daylight savings time
étendre to spread
une **étoile** star
étrange strange
étranger (étrangère) foreign
* **être** to be **6**
être à to belong to
être d'accord to agree **6**
une **étude** study
un **étudiant, une étudiant(e)** (college) student **9**
étudier to study **5, 7**
eu *(p.p. of* **avoir***)* **il y a eu** there was
euh... er ..., uh ...
euh non... well, no
un **euro** euro; monetary unit of Europe
européen (européenne) European
eux: eux-mêmes themselves
un **examen** exam, test
réussir à un examen to pass an exam, a test
un **exemple** example
par **exemple** for instance
un **exercice** exercise
faire des exercices to exercise
exiger to insist
expliquer to explain
expliquez... explain ...
exprimer to express
extérieur: à l'extérieur outside
extraordinaire extraordinary
il a fait un temps extraordinaire! the weather was great!

face: en face (de) opposite, across (the street) from
facile easy **12**
faible weak
la **faim** hunger
j'ai faim I'm hungry **3A**
tu as faim? are you hungry? **3A**
* **faire** to do, make **8**
faire attention to pay attention, be careful **8**
faire les magasins to go shopping (browsing from store to store)
faire partie de to be a member of
faire sauter to flip
faire un match to play a game (match) **8**
faire un voyage to take a trip **8**
faire une promenade to take a walk **8**
fait: en fait in fact
fait *(see* **faire***)*: **ça fait combien?** how much is that (it)? **3C**
ça fait... euros that's (it's) ... euros **3C**
il fait (beau, etc.) it's (beautiful, etc.) *(weather)* **4C**
quel temps fait-il? what (how)

is the weather? **4C**
familial with the family
une **famille** family **2C**
en **famille** at home
un **fana, une fana** fan
un **fantôme** ghost
la **farine** flour
fatigué tired
faux (fausse) false **12**
favori (favorite) favorite
les **félicitations** *f.* congratulations
une **femme** woman **9**
une **fenêtre** window **I, 9**
fermer to close **I**
une **fête** party, holiday
le **feu d'artifice** fireworks
une **feuille** sheet, leaf **I**
une feuille de papier sheet of paper **I**
un **feuilleton** series, serial story *(in newspaper)*
février *m.* February **4B**
la **fièvre** fever
une **fille** girl **2A**
un **film policier** detective movie
la **fin** end
flamand Flemish
un **flamant** flamingo
une **fleur** flower
un **fleuve** river
un **flic** cop *(colloq.)*
une **fois** time
à la fois at the same time
la **folie: à la folie** madly
folklorique: une chanson folklorique folksong
fonctionner to work, function
fondé founded
le **foot (football)** soccer
le football américain football
jouer au foot to play soccer **5**
une **forêt** forest
formidable great!
fort strong
plus fort louder **I**
un **fouet** whisk
la **fourrure** fur
un manteau de fourrure fur coat
frais: il fait frais it's cool *(weather)* **4C**
un **franc** franc *(former monetary unit of France)* **3C**
ça fait... francs that's (it's) ... francs **3C**
français French **1B, 11**
comment dit-on... en français? how do you say... in French? **I**
parler français to speak French **5**
le **français** French *(language)*
un **Français, une Française** French person
la **France** France **6**
en France in France **6**
francophone French-speaking
un **frère** brother **2C**
les **frites** *f.* French fries
un steak-frites steak and French fries **3A**
froid cold
il fait froid it's cold out *(weather)* **4C**
le **fromage** cheese
un sandwich au fromage cheese sandwich
furieux (furieuse) furious
une **fusée** rocket

un **garçon** boy **2A; waiter**
une **gare** train station
une **garniture** side dish
gauche left
une **gelée** jelly
généralement generally
généreux (généreuse) generous
la **générosité** generosity
génial brilliant: terrific **12**
des **gens** *m.* people **10**
gentil (gentille) nice, kind **11;** sweet
la **géographie** geography
une **girafe** giraffe **E4**
une **glace** ice cream **3A;** mirror, ice
glacé iced
un **goûter** afternoon snack
une **goyave** guava
grand tall **9;** big, large **12**
une grande surface big store, self-service store
grandir to get tall; to grow up
une grand-mère grandmother **2C**
un grand-père grandfather **2C**
grec (grecque) Greek
un **grenier** attic
une **grillade** grilled meat
une **grille** grid
grillé: le pain grillé toast
une tartine de pain grillé buttered toast
la **grippe** flu
gris gray **12**
gros (grosse) fat, big
la **Guadeloupe** Guadeloupe *(French island in the West Indies)*
une **guerre** war
une **guitare** guitar **9**
un **gymnase** gym

habillé dressed
habiter (à) to live (in + *city*) **7**
Haïti Haiti *(French- and Creole-speaking country in the West Indies)*
un • **hamburger** hamburger **3A**
la • **hâte** haste
en hâte quickly
• **haut** high
plus haut above
• **hélas!** too bad!
hésiter to hesitate
l' **heure** *f.* time, hour; o'clock **4A**
... heure(s) (dix) (ten) past ... **4A**
... heure(s) et demie half past ... **4A**
... heure(s) et quart quarter past ... **4A**
... heure(s) moins (dix) (ten) of ... **4A**
... heure(s) moins le quart quarter to ... **4A**
à... heures at ... o'clock **6**
à quelle heure...? at what time ...? **8**
à quelle heure est...? at what time is ...? **4A**
il est... heure(s) it's ... o'clock **4A**
par heure per hour, an hour
quelle heure est-il? what time is it? **4A**
heureux (heureuse) happy
avant-hier the day before yesterday
un **hippopotame** hippopotamus **E4**
une **histoire** story, history
l' **hiver** *m.* winter **4C**
en hiver in (the) winter **4C**

• **hollandais** Dutch
un **homme** man **9**
honnête honest
une **horreur** horror
quelle horreur! what a scandal! how awful!
un • **hot dog** hot dog **3A**
un **hôte, une hôtesse** host, hostess
un **hôtel de police** police department
l' **huile** *f.* oil
• **huit** eight **1A**
l' **humeur** *f.* mood
de bonne humeur in a good mood
un **hypermarché** shopping center

ici here **6**
une **idée** idea
ignorer to be unaware of
il he, it **3C, 6, 10**
il est it is **12**
il/elle est + *nationality* he/she is ... **2B**
il y a there is, there are **9**
il y a eu there was
il n'y a pas de... there is/are no ... **10**
est-ce qu'il y a...? is there, are there ...? **9**
qu'est-ce qu'il y a...? what is there ...? **9**
une **île** island
illustré illustrated
l' **impératif** *m.* imperative (command) mood
impoli impolite
l' **importance** *f.* importance
ça n'a pas d'importance it doesn't matter
importé imported
impressionnant impressive
l' **imprimante** *f.* printer
inactif (inactive) inactive
inclure to include
l' **indicatif** *m.* area code
indiquer to indicate, show
indiquez... indicate ...
les **informations** *f.* news
l' **informatique** *f.* computer science
s' **informer (de)** to find out about
un **ingénieur** engineer
un **inspecteur, une inspectrice** police detective
intelligent intelligent **11**
intéressant interesting **11**
l' **intérieur** *m.* interior, inside
l' **Internet** *m.* the Internet
surfer sur l'Internet (sur le Net) to surf the Internet
interroger to question
interviewer to interview
inutilement uselessly
un **inventaire** inventory
un **invité, une invitée** guest
inviter to invite **7**
israélien (israélienne) Israeli
italien (italienne) Italian **11**
un **Italien, une Italienne** Italian person

j' (*see* **je**)
jamais ever; never
jamais le dimanche! never on Sunday!
la **Jamaïque** Jamaica
une **jambe** leg **E2**
janvier *m.* January **4B**
japonais Japanese **11**
jaune yellow **E1, 12**
jaunir to turn yellow
je I **6**
un **jeu** (*pl.* **jeux**) game
les jeux d'ordinateur computer games
les jeux télévisés TV game shows
les jeux vidéo video games
jeudi *m.* Thursday **4B**
jeune young **9**
les **jeunes** *m.* young people
un **job** (part-time) job
jouer to play **7**
jouer aux jeux vidéo to play video games **5**
jouer au tennis (volley, basket, foot) to play tennis (volleyball, basketball, soccer) **5**
un **jour** day **4B**
le Jour de l'An New Year's Day
par jour per week, a week
quel jour est-ce? what day is it? **8**
un **journal** (*pl.* **journaux**) newspaper
une **journée** day, whole day
bonne journée! have a nice day!
joyeux (joyeuse) happy
juillet *m.* July **8**
le quatorze juillet Bastille Day *(French national holiday)*
juin *m.* June **4B**
un **jumeau** (*pl.* **jumeaux**), **une jumelle** twin
le **jus** juice
le jus d'orange orange juice **3B**
le jus de pomme apple juice **3B**
le jus de raisin grape juice **3B**
le jus de tomate tomato juice **3B**
jusqu'à until
juste right, fair
le mot juste the right word

un **kangourou** kangaroo **E4**
un **kilo** kilogram

l' (*see* **le, la**)
la the **2B, 10**
là here, there **6**
là-bas over there **6**
ça, là-bas that (one), over there **9**
oh là là! uh, oh!; oh, dear!; wow!; oh, yes!
laid ugly
laisser (un message) to leave (a message)
une **lampe** lamp **9**
une **langue** language
large wide
se **laver** to wash (oneself), wash up
le the **2B, 10**
le + *number* + *month* the ... **4B**
le (lundi) on (Mondays) **10**
une **leçon** lesson
un **lecteur MP3** MP3 player **9**
lent slow
les the **10**
une **lettre** letter
se **lever: lève-toi!** stand up! **I**
levez-vous! stand up! **I**
un **lézard** lizard **E4**
le **Liban** Lebanon *(country in the*

FRENCH-ENGLISH VOCABULARY *continued*

Middle East)
libanais Lebanese
libéré liberated
une **librairie** bookstore
libre free
un **lieu** place, area
avoir lieu to take place
une **ligne** line
limité limited
la **limonade** lemon soda **3B**
un **lion** lion **E4**
* **lire** to read
comment lire reading hints
lisez… (*see* **lire**) read … **I**
une **liste** list
une liste des courses shopping list
un **lit** bed **9**
un **living** living room *(informal)*
un **livre** book **I, 9**
local (*m.pl.* **locaux**) local
une **location** rental
logique logical
logiquement logically
loin d'ici far (from here)
le **loisir** leisure, free time
un **loisir** leisure-time activity
Londres London
longtemps (for) a long time
moins longtemps que for a shorter time
le **loto** lotto, lottery, bingo
un **loup** wolf **E4**
lui-même: en lui-même to himself
lundi *m.* Monday **4B**
le **Luxembourg** Luxembourg
un **lycée** high school

M

m' (*see* **me**)
M. (monsieur) Mr. (Mister) **1C**
ma my **2C**
et voici ma mère and this is my mother **2C**
ma chambre my bedroom **9**
une **machine** machine
une **machine à coudre** sewing machine
Madagascar Madagascar *(French-speaking island off of East Africa)*
Madame (Mme) Mrs., ma'am **1C**
Mademoiselle (Mlle) Miss **1C**
un **magasin** (department) store
faire les magasins to go shopping (browsing from store to store)
magnétique magnetic
un **magnétophone** tape recorder
magnifique magnificent
mai *m.* May **4B**
maigre thin, skinny
un **mail** e-mail
une **main** hand **E2**
maintenant now **7**
mais but **6**
j'aime…, mais je préfère… I like …, but I prefer … **5**
je regrette, mais je ne peux pas… I'm sorry, but I can't … **5**
mais oui! sure! **6**
mais non! of course not! **6**
une **maison** house
à la maison at home **6**
mal badly, poorly **1C, 7**
ça va mal things are going badly **1C**
ça va très mal things are going very badly **1C**
c'est mal that's bad **12**
malade sick
malheureusement unfortunately
malin clever
manger to eat **7**
j'aime manger I like to eat **5**
un **manteau de fourrure** fur coat
un **marchand, une marchande** merchant, shopkeeper, dealer
un **marché** open-air market
un **marché aux puces** flea market
marcher to work, to run *(for objects)* **9; to walk** *(for people)* **9**
il/elle (ne) marche (pas) bien it (doesn't) work(s) well **9**
est-ce que la radio marche? does the radio work? **9**
mardi *m.* **Tuesday 4B**
le **Mardi gras** Shrove Tuesday
le **mariage** wedding, marriage
marié married
une **marmite** covered stew pot
le **Maroc** Morocco *(country in North Africa)*
une **marque** brand (name)
une **marraine** godmother
marrant fun
marron *(inv.)* brown **12**
mars *m.* March **4B**
martiniquais from Martinique
la **Martinique** Martinique *(French island in the West Indies)*
un **match** game, (sports) match
faire un match to play a game, (sports) match **8**
les **maths** *f.* math
le **matin** in the morning
du matin in the morning, A.M. **4A**
des **matoutou crabes** *m.* stewed crabs with rice
mauvais bad **12**
c'est une mauvaise idée that's a bad idea
il fait mauvais it's bad *(weather)* **4C**
méchant mean, nasty **11**
un **médecin** doctor
un médecin de nuit doctor on night duty
la **Méditerranée** Mediterranean Sea
mélanger to mix, stir
même same; even
eux-mêmes themselves
les mêmes choses the same things
une **mémoire** memory
mentionner to mention
merci thank you **1C**
oui, merci yes, thank you **5**
mercredi *m.* Wednesday **4B**
une **mère** mother **2C**
mériter to deserve
la **messagerie vocale** voice mail
le **métro** subway
mexicain Mexican **11**
midi *m.* noon **4A**
mieux better
mignon (mignonne) cute **11**
militaire military
mille one thousand **2B**
une **mini-chaîne** compact stereo **9**
minuit *m.* midnight **4A**
mixte mixed
Mlle Miss **1C**
Mme Mrs. **1C**
une **mob (mobylette)** motorbike, moped **9**
la **mode** fashion
moi me **1A**
moi, je m'appelle (Marc) me, my name is (Marc) **1A**
avec moi with me **5**

donne-moi give me **3A**
donnez-moi give me **3B**
excusez-moi… excuse me … **13**
prête-moi… lend me … **3C**
s'il te plaît, donne-moi… please give me … **3B**
un **moine** monk
moins less
moins de less than
… heure(s) moins (dix) (ten) of … **4A**
… heure(s) moins le quart quarter of … **4A**
un **mois** month **4B**
par mois per month, a month
mon (ma; mes) my **2C**
mon anniversaire est le… my birthday is the … **4B**
voici mon père this is my father **2C**
le **monde** world
du monde in the world
tout le monde everyone
la **monnaie** money; change
Monsieur (M.) Mr., sir **1C**
un monsieur (*pl.* **messieurs**) gentleman, man *(polite term)* **2A**
une **montre** watch **9**
montre-moi (montrez-moi) show me **I**
un **morceau** piece
un morceau de craie piece of chalk **I**
un **mot** word
une **moto** motorcycle **9**
la **moutarde** mustard
un **mouton** sheep
moyen (moyenne) average, medium
en moyenne on the average
un **moyen** means
muet (muette) silent
un **MP3** MP3 player **9**
le **multimédia** multimedia

n' (*see* **ne**)
nager to swim **7**
j'aime nager I like to swim **5**
une **nationalité** nationality **1B**
ne (n')
ne… aucun none, not any
ne… pas not **6**
ne… plus no longer
n'est-ce pas? right?, no?, isn't it (so)?, don't you?, aren't you? **6**
né born
nécessaire necessary
négatif (négative) negative
négativement negatively
la **neige** snow
neiger to snow
il neige it's snowing **4C**
le **Net** the Internet
neuf nine **1A**
un **neveu** (*pl.* **neveux**) nephew
un **nez** nose **E2**
une **nièce** niece
un **niveau** (*pl.* **niveaux**) level
Noël *m.* Christmas
noir black **E1, 12**
un **nom** name; noun
un **nombre** number
nombreux (nombreuses) numerous
nommé named
non no **1B, 6**
non plus neither
mais non! of course not! **6**
le **nord** north
le nord-est northeast
normalement normally
une **note** grade
nous we **6**
la **Nouvelle-Angleterre** New England
la **Nouvelle-Calédonie** New Caledonia *(French island in the South Pacific)*
novembre *m.* November **4B**
le onze novembre Armistice Day
la **nuit** night
un **numéro** number

O

objectif (objective) objective
un **objet** object **9**
une **occasion** occasion; opportunity
occupé occupied
un **océan** ocean
octobre *m.* October **4B**
une **odeur** odor
un **oeil** (*pl.* **yeux**) eye **E2**
officiel (officielle) official
offert (*p.p. of* **offrir**) offered
* **offrir** to offer, to give
oh là là! uh,oh!, oh, dear!, wow!, oh, yes!
un **oiseau** (*pl.* **oiseaux**) bird
une **omelette** omelet **3A**
on one, they, you
on est… today is …
on va dans un café? shall we go to a café?
on y va let's go
comment dit-on… en français? how do you say… in French? **I**
un **oncle** uncle **2C**
onze eleven **1B**
opérer to operate
l' **or** m. gold
orange *(inv.)* orange *(color)* **E1, 12**
une **orange** orange *(fruit)*
le jus d'orange orange juice **3B**
un **ordinateur** computer **9**
un **ordinateur portable** laptop computer
une **oreille** ear **E2**
organiser to organize **7**
originairement originally
l' **origine** *f.* origin, beginning
d'origine bretonne from Brittany
orthographiques: les signes *m.* **orthographiques** spelling marks
ou or **1B, 6**
où where **6, 8**
où est…? where is …? **6**
oublier to forget
l' **ouest** *m.* west
oui yes **1B, 6**
oui, bien sûr… yes, of course … **5**
oui, d'accord… yes, okay … **5**
oui, j'ai… yes, I have … **9**
oui, merci… yes, thank you … **5**
mais oui! sure! **6**
un **ouragan** hurricane
un **ours** bear **E4**
ouvert open
* **ouvrir** to open
ouvre… (ouvrez…) open … **I**

pâle pale
une **panne** breakdown
une panne d'électricité power failure
une **panthère** panther
une **papaye** papaya
le **papier** paper
une feuille de papier a sheet (piece) of paper **I**
par per
par exemple for example
par jour per day
un **parc** park
un parc public city park
parce que (parce qu') because **8**
paresseux (paresseuse) lazy
parfait perfect
rien n'est parfait nothing is perfect
parfois sometimes
parisien (parisienne) Parisian
parler to speak, talk **I, 7**
parler (français, anglais, espagnol) to speak (French, English, Spanish) **5**
un **parrain** godfather
une **partie** part
* **partir** to leave
à **partir de** as of, beginning
partitif (partitive) partitive
pas not
ne... pas not **6**
pas de not a, no, not any **10**
pas possible not possible
pas toujours not always **5**
pas très bien not very well
le **passé composé** compound past tense
passionnément passionately
une **pâte** dough
patient patient
le **patinage** ice skating, roller skating
une **patinoire** skating rink
une **pâtisserie** pastry, pastry shop
une **patte** foot, paw *(of bird or animal)*
un **pays** country
un **PC portable** laptop computer
la **peau** skin, hide
* **peindre** to paint
peint painted
une **pellicule** film (camera)
pénétrer to enter
pénible bothersome, a pain **12**
une **pension** inn, boarding house
Pentecôte *f.* Pentecost
perdu *(p.p. of* **perdre***)* lost
un **père** father **2C**
* **permettre** to permit
un **perroquet** parrot
une **personne** person **2A**
personnel (personnelle) personal
personnellement personally
péruvien (péruvienne) Peruvian
petit small, short **9, 12**
il/elle est petit(e) he/she is short **9**
un petit copain, une petite copine boyfriend, girlfriend
plus petit(e) smaller
le petit-fils, la petite-fille grandson, granddaughter
peu little, not much
un peu a little, a little bit **7**
un peu de a few
peut *(see* **pouvoir***)*
peut-être perhaps, maybe **6**
peux *(see* **pouvoir***)*
est-ce que tu peux...? can you ...? **5**
je regrette, mais je ne peux pas... I'm sorry, but I can't ... **5**
la **photo** photography
une **phrase** sentence **I**
la **physique** physics
une **pie** magpie **E4**
un **pied** foot **E2**
piloter to pilot (a plane)
une **pincée** pinch
une **pizza** pizza **3A**
un **placard** closet
plaît: s'il te plaît please *(informal)* **3A;** excuse me (please)
s'il te plaît, donne-moi... please, give me ... **3B**
s'il vous plaît please *(formal)* **3B;** excuse me (please)
un **plan** map
une **plante** plant
le **plat principal** main course
un **plateau** tray
pleut: il pleut it's raining **4C**
plier to fold
plumer to pluck
plus more
plus de more than
plus joli que prettier than
en plus in addition
le plus the most
ne... plus no longer, no more
non plus neither
plusieurs several
une **poche** pocket
l'argent *m.* **de poche** allowance, pocket money
une **poêle** frying pan
un **point de vue** point of view
un **poisson** fish **E4**
un poisson rouge goldfish
blaff de poisson fish stew
poli polite
un **politicien, une politicienne** politician
une **pomme** apple
le jus de pomme apple juice **3B**
une purée de pommes de terre mashed potatoes
le **porc: une côtelette de porc** pork chop
un **portable** cell phone **9**
une **porte** door **I, 9**
un **porte-monnaie** change purse, wallet
portugais Portuguese
poser: poser une question to ask a question
une **possibilité** possibility
la **poste** post office
poster un message post a message **9**
pouah! yuck! yech!
une **poule** hen **E4**
pour for **6**
pour que so that
pour qui? for whom? **8**
le **pourcentage** percentage
pourquoi why **8**
pratique practical
pratiquer to participate in
des **précisions** *f.* details
préféré favorite
préférer to prefer, to like (in general)
je préfère I prefer **5**
tu préférerais? would you prefer?
un **premier (première)** first
le premier de l'an New Year's Day

le premier étage second floor
le premier mai Labor Day *(in France)*
c'est le premier juin it's June first **4B**
un **prénom** first name
près near
près d'ici nearby, near here
tout près very close
une **présentation** appearance
la présentation extérieure outward appearance
des **présentations** *f.* introductions
pressé in a hurry
prêt ready
un **prêt** loan
prêter à to lend to, to loan
prête-moi... lend me... **3C**
principalement mainly
le **printemps** spring **4C**
au printemps in the spring **4C**
un **prix** price
un **problème** problem
un **produit** product
un **prof, une prof** teacher *(informal)* **2A, 9**
un **professeur** teacher **9**
professionnel (professionnelle) professional
un **programme** program
un **projet** plan
une **romenade** walk
faire une promenade à pied to go for a walk **8**
* **promettre** to promise
une **promo** special sale
proposer to suggest
propre own
un **propriétaire, une propriétaire** landlord/landlady, owner
la **Provence** Provence *(province in southern France)*
pu: n'a pas pu was not able to
public: un parc public city park
un jardin public public garden
la **publicité** commercials, advertising, publicity
une **puce** flea
un marché aux puces flea market
puis then, also
puisque since
les **Pyrénées** (the) Pyrenees *(mountains between France and Spain)*

qu' *(see* **que***)*
une **qualité** quality
quand when **8**
c'est quand, ton anniversaire? when is your birthday? **4B**
quarante forty **1C**
un **quart** one quarter
... heure(s) et quart quarter past ... **4A**
... heure(s) moins le quart quarter of ... **4A**
quatorze fourteen **1B**
quatre four **1A**
quatre-vingt-dix ninety **2B**
quatre-vingts eighty **2B**
que that, which
que veut dire...? what does ... mean? **I**
qu'est-ce que (qu') what *(phrase used to introduce a question)* **8**
qu'est-ce que c'est? what is it? what's that? **9**
qu'est-ce que tu veux? what do you want? **3A**
qu'est-ce qu'il y a? what is there? **9;** what's the matter?
qu'est-ce qui ne va pas? what's wrong?
un **Québécois, une Québécoise** person from Quebec
québécois from Quebec
quel (quelle)...! what a...!
quel âge a ta mère/ton père? how old is your mother/your father? **2C**
quel âge a-t-il/elle? how old is he/she? **9**
quel âge as-tu? how old are you? **2C**
quel jour est-ce? what day is it? **4B**
quel temps fait-il? what's (how's) the weather? **4C**
quelle est la date? what's the date? **4B**
quelle heure est-il? what time is it? **4A**
à quelle heure? at what time? **4A**
à quelle heure est...? at what time is ...? **4A**
de quelle couleur...? what color is ...? **12**
quelques some, a few **9**
une **question** question
une **queue** tail
qui who, whom **8**
qui est-ce? who's that (this)? **2A, 9**
qui se ressemble... birds of a feather ...
à qui? to whom? **8**
avec qui? with who(m)? **8**
c'est qui? who's that? *(casual speech)*
de qui? about who(m)? **8**
pour qui? for who(m)? **8**
quinze fifteen **1B**
quoi? what? **9**
quotidien (quotidienne) daily
la vie quotidienne daily life

raconter to tell about
une **radio** radio **9**
écouter la radio to listen to the radio **5**
raisin: le jus de raisin grape juice **3B**
une **raison** reason
rapidement rapidly
un **rapport** relationship
une **raquette** racket **9**
rarement rarely, seldom **7**
un **rayon** department *(in a store)*
réalisé made, directed
récemment recently
une **recette** recipe
recherche: un avis de recherche missing person's bulletin
un **récital** (*pl.* **récitals**) *(musical)* recital
reconstituer to reconstruct
un **réfrigérateur** refrigerator
refuser to refuse
regarder to look at, watch **I, 7**
regarde ça look at that **9**
regarder la télé to watch TV **5**
un **régime** diet
être au régime to be on a diet
régional (*m.pl.* **régionaux**) regional

regretter to be sorry
je regrette, mais… I'm sorry, but … **5**
régulier (régulière) regular
une **reine** queen
rencontrer to meet
une **rencontre** meeting, encounter
un **rendez-vous** date, appointment
j'ai un rendez-vous à… I have a date, appointment at … **4A**
la **rentrée** first day back at school in fall
rentrer to go back, come back; to return
réparer to fix, repair
un **repas** meal
* **repeindre** to repaint
répéter to repeat **I**
répondre (à) to answer, respond (to) **I**
répondez-lui (moi) answer him (me)
répondre que oui to answer yes
une **réponse** answer
un **reportage** documentary
représenter to represent
réservé reserved
une **résolution** resolution
un **restaurant** restaurant
au restaurant to (at) the restaurant **6**
dîner au restaurant to have dinner at a restaurant **5**
un restaurant trois étoiles three star restaurant
rester to stay
retard: un jour de retard one day behind
en **retard** late
retourner to return; to turn over
réussir to succeed
réussir à un examen to pass an exam
* **revenir** to come back
revoir: au revoir! good-bye! **1C**
le **rez-de-chaussée** ground floor
un **rhinocéros** rhinoceros **E4**
riche rich
rien (de) nothing
rien n'est parfait nothing is perfect
ne… rien nothing
une **rive** (river) bank
une **rivière** river, stream
le **riz** rice
une **robe** dress
le **roller** in-line skating
romain Roman
le **rosbif** roast beef
rose pink **12**
rosse nasty *(colloq.)*
une **rôtie** toast *(Canadian)*
rôtir to roast
une **roue** wheel
rouge red **E1, 12**
rougir to turn red
rouler to roll
roux (rousse) red-head
une **rue** street
dans la rue (Victor Hugo) on (Victor Hugo) street
russe Russian

S

sa his, her
un **sac** book bag, bag **I**; bag, handbag **9**
sais (*see* **savoir**)
je sais I know **I, 9**
je ne sais pas I don't know **I, 9**
tu sais you know
une **saison** season **4C**
toute saison all year round (any season)
une **salade** salad **3A**; lettuce
un **salaire** salary
une **salle** hall, large room
une salle à manger dining room
une salle de bains bathroom
une salle de séjour informal living room
un salon formal living room
salut hi!; good-bye! **1C**
une **salutation** greeting
samedi Saturday **4B**
samedi soir Saturday night
à samedi! see you Saturday! **4B**
le samedi on Saturdays **10**
une **sandale** sandal
un **sandwich** sandwich **3A**
sans without
des **saucisses** *f.* sausages
le **saucisson** salami
* **savoir** to know *(information)*
je sais I know **I, 9**
je ne sais pas I don't know **I, 9**
tu sais you know
un **saxo (saxophone)** saxophone
une **scène** scene, stage
les **sciences** *f.* **économiques** economics
les **sciences** *f.* **naturelles** natural science
un **scooter** motor scooter **9**
second second
seize sixteen **1B**
un **séjour** stay; informal living room
le **sel** salt
selon according to
selon toi in your opinion
une **semaine** week **4B**
cette semaine this week
la semaine dernière last week
la semaine prochaine next week
par semaine per week, a week
semblable similar
le **Sénégal** Senegal *(French-speaking country in Africa)*
sensationnel (sensationnelle) sensational
séparer to separate
sept seven **1A**
septembre *m.* September **4B**
une **série** series
sérieux (sérieuse) serious
un **serveur, une serveuse** waiter, waitress
servi served
une **serviette** napkin
ses his, her
seul alone, only; by oneself
seulement only, just
un **short** shorts
si if, whether
si! so, yes! *(to a negative question)* **10**
un **signal** (*pl.* **signaux**) signal
un **signe** sign
un signe orthographique spelling mark
un **singe** monkey **E4**
situé situated
six six **1A**
le **skate** skateboarding
faire du skate to go skateboarding
un **skate** skateboard
le **ski** skiing
le **ski nautique** waterskiing

faire du ski to ski
faire du ski nautique to go water-skiing
skier to ski
snob snobbish
le **snowboard** snowboarding
faire du snowboard to go snowboarding
un **snowboard** snowboard
la **Société Nationale des Chemins de Fer (SNCF)** *French railroad system*
une **société** society
un **soda** soda **3B**
une **soeur** sister **2C**
la **soie** silk
la **soif** thirst
avoir soif to be thirsty
j'ai soif I'm thirsty **3B**
tu as soif? are you thirsty? **3B**
un **soir** evening
ce soir this evening, tonight
demain soir tomorrow night (evening)
du soir in the evening, P.M. **4A**
hier soir last night
le soir in the evening
une **soirée** (whole) evening; (evening) party
soixante sixty **1C, 2A**
soixante-dix seventy **2A**
un **soldat** soldier
un **solde** *(clearance)* sale
en solde on sale
la **sole** sole *(fish)*
le **soleil** sun
les lunettes *f.* **de soleil** sunglasses
sommes (*see* **être**)
nous sommes... it is, today is ... *(date)*
son (sa; ses) his, her
un **sondage** poll
une **sorte** sort, type, kind
* **sortir** to leave, come out
un **souhait** wish
la **soupe** soup
une **souris** mouse (computer)
sous under **9**
le **sous-sol** basement
souvent often **7**
soyez (*see* **être**): soyez
les **spaghetti** *m.* spaghetti
spécialement especially
spécialisé specialized
une **spécialité** specialty
le **sport** sports
faire du sport to play sports
des vêtements *m.* **de sport** sports clothing
une voiture de sport sports car
sportif (sportive) athletic **11**
un **stade** stadium
un **stage** sports training camp; internship
une **station-service** gas station
un **steak** steak **3A**
un steak-frites steak and French fries **3A**
un **stylo** pen **I, 9**
le **sucre** sugar
le **sud** south
suggérer to suggest
suis (*see* **être**)
je suis + *nationality* I'm ... **1B**
je suis de... I'm from... **1B**
suisse Swiss **11**
la **Suisse** Switzerland
suivant following
suivi followed
un **sujet** subject, topic
super terrific **7;** great **12**
un **supermarché** supermarket
supersonique supersonic
supérieur superior
supplémentaire supplementary, extra
sur on **9;** about
sûr sure, certain
bien sûr! of course! **6**
oui, bien sûr... yes, of course ...! **5**
tu es sûr(e)? are you sure?
sûrement surely
la **surface: une grande surface** big store, self-service store
surfer to go snowboarding
surfer sur l'Internet (sur le Net) to surf the Internet
surtout especially
un **survêtement** jogging or track suit
un **sweat** sweatshirt
une **sweaterie** shop specializing in sweatshirts and sportswear
sympa nice, pleasant *(colloq.)*
sympathique nice, pleasant **11**
une **synagogue** Jewish temple or synagogue
un **synthétiseur** electronic keyboard, synthesizer

T

t' (*see* **te**)
ta your **2C**
une **table** table **I, 9**
une **tablette** *tablet computer* **9**
mettre la table to set the table
un **tableau** (*pl.* **tableaux**) chalkboard **I**
Tahiti Tahiti *(French island in the South Pacific)*
une **taille** size
de taille moyenne of medium height or size
un **tailleur** woman's suit
se **taire: tais-toi!** be quiet!
une **tante** aunt **2C**
la **tarte** pie
une **tasse** cup
un **taxi** taxi
en taxi by taxi
te (to) you
un **tee-shirt** T-shirt
la **télé** TV **9**
à la télé on TV
regarder la télé TV **5**
télécharger to download
un **téléphone** telephone **9**
téléphoner (à) to call, phone **5, 7**
télévisé: des jeux *m.* **télévisés** TV game shows
un **temple** Protestant church
le **temps** time; weather
combien de temps? how long?
de temps en temps from time to time
quel temps fait-il? what's (how's) the weather? **4C**
tout le temps all the time
le **tennis** tennis
jouer au tennis to play tennis **5**
des tennis *m.* tennis shoes, sneakers
un **terrain de sport** *(playing)* field
une **terrasse** outdoor section of a café, terrace
la **terre** earth
une pomme de terre potato
terrifiant terrifying
tes your
la **tête** head **E2**

FRENCH-ENGLISH VOCABULARY *continued*

le **thé** tea **3B**
un thé glacé iced tea
un **théâtre** theater
le **thon** tuna
tiens! look!, hey! **2A, 10**
un **tigre** tiger **E4**
timide timid, shy **11**
le **tissu** fabric
un **titre** title
toi you
avec toi with you **5**
et toi? and you? **1A**
les **toilettes** *f.* bathroom, toilet
un **toit** roof
une **tomate** tomato
le jus de tomate tomato juice **3B**
un **tombeau** tomb
ton (ta; tes) your **2C**
c'est quand, ton anniversaire? when's your birthday? **4B**
tort: avoir tort to be wrong
une **tortue** turtle **E4**
un bifteck de tortue turtle steak
toujours always **7**
je n'aime pas toujours... I don't always like ... **5**
un **tour** turn
à votre tour it's your turn
la **Touraine** Touraine *(province in central France)*
tourner to turn
la **Toussaint** All Saints' Day *(November 1)*
tout (toute; tous, toutes) all, every, the whole
tous les jours every day
tout ça all that
tout le monde everyone
tout le temps all the time
toutes sortes all sorts, kinds
tout completely, very
tout droit straight
tout de suite right away
tout près very close
tout all, everything
pas du tout not at all
un **train** train
tranquille quiet
laisse-moi tranquille! leave me alone!
un **travail** (*pl.* **travaux**) job
travailler to work **5, 7**
une **traversée** crossing
treize thirteen **1B**
trente thirty **1C**
un **tréma** diaeresis
très very **11**
très bien very well **7**
ça va très bien things are going very well **1C**
ça va très mal things are going very badly **1C**
trois three **1A**
troisième third
en troisième ninth grade *(in France)*
trop too, too much
trouver to find, to think of
comment trouves-tu...? what do you think of ...?; how do you find ...?
s'y trouve is there
tu you **6**
la **Tunisie** Tunisia *(country in North Africa)*

un, une one **1A**; a, an **2A, 10**
unique only
uniquement only
une **université** university, college
l' **usage** *m.* use
un **ustensile** utensil
utile useful
utiliser to use
en utilisant (by) using
utilisez... use ...

va (*see* **aller**)
va-t'en! go away!
ça va? how are you? how's everything? **1C**
ça va! everything's fine (going well); fine, I'm OK **1C**
on va dans un café? shall we go to a café?
on y va let's go
les **vacances** *f.* vacation
bonnes vacances! have a nice vacation!
en vacances on vacation **6**
les grandes vacances summer vacation
une **vache** cow
vais (*see* **aller**): **je vais** I'm going
la **vaisselle** dishes
faire la vaisselle to do the dishes
valable valid
une **valise** suitcase
vanille: une glace à la vanille vanilla ice cream
varié varied
les **variétés** *f.* variety show
vas (see **aller**)
comment vas-tu? how are you? **1C**
vas-y! come on!, go ahead!, do it!
le **veau** veal
une **vedette** star
un **vélo** bicycle **9**
à vélo by bicycle
faire une promenade à vélo to go for a bicycle ride
un vélo tout terrain (un VTT) mountain bike
un **vendeur, une vendeuse** salesperson
vendre to sell
vendredi *m.* Friday **4B**
vendu (*p.p. of* **vendre**) sold
* **venir** to come
le **vent** wind
une **vente** sale
le **ventre** stomach **E2**
venu (*p.p. of* **venir**) came, come
vérifier to check
la **vérité** truth
un **verre** glass
verser to pour
vert green **E1, 12**
les haricots *m.* **verts** green beans
une **veste** jacket
des **vêtements** *m.* clothing
des vêtements de sport sports clothing
veut (*see* **vouloir**): **que veut dire...?** what does ... mean? **I**
veux (*see* **vouloir**)
est-ce que tu veux...? do you want ...? **5**
je ne veux pas... I don't want ... **5**
je veux... I want ... **5**
je veux bien... I'd love to,

I do, I want to ... **5**
qu'est-ce que tu veux? what do you want? **3A**
tu veux...? do you want ...? **3A**
la **viande** meat
la **vie** life
la **vie quotidienne** daily life
viens (*see* **venir**)
viens... come ... **oui, je viens** yes, I'm coming along with you
vieux (vieil, vieille; *m.pl.***vieux)** old
le **Vieux Carré** *the French Quarter in New Orleans*
le **Viêt-nam** Vietnam *(country in Southeast Asia)*
vietnamien (vietnamienne) Vietnamese
une **vigne** vineyard
un **village** town, village
un petit village small town
une **ville** city
en ville in town, **6**
une grande ville big city, town
le **vin** wine
vingt twenty **1B, 1C**
violet (violette) purple, violet **E1**
un **violon** violin
une **visite** visit
rendre visite à to visit *(a person)*
visiter to visit *(places)*
vite! fast!, quick!
vive: vive les vacances! three cheers for vacation!
* **vivre** to live
le **vocabulaire** vocabulary
voici... here is, this is..., here come(s) ... **2A**
voici + du, de la *(partitive)* here's some
voici mon père/ma mère here's my father/my mother **2C**
voilà... there is ..., there come(s) ... **2A**
voilà + du, de la *(partitive)* there's some
la **voile** sailing
faire de la voile to sail
la planche à voile windsurfing
* **voir** to see
voir un film to see a movie
un **voisin, une voisine** neighbor **9**
une **voiture** car **9**
une voiture de sport sports car
en voiture by car
faire une promenade en voiture to go for a drive by car
une **voix** voice
le **volley (volleyball)** volleyball
un **volontaire, une volontaire** volunteer
comme volontaire as a volunteer
vos your
votre (*pl.* **vos**) your
voudrais (*see* **vouloir**)**: je voudrais** I'd like **3A, 3B, 5**
* **vouloir** to want
vouloir + du, de la *(partitive)* to want some (of something)
vouloir dire to mean
voulu (*p.p. of* **vouloir**) wanted
vous you **6;** (to) you
vous désirez? what would you like? may I help you? **3B**
s'il vous plaît please **3B**
un **voyage** trip
bon voyage! have a nice trip!
faire un voyage to take a trip **8**
voyager to travel **5, 7**
vrai true, right, real **12**
vraiment really
le **VTT** mountain biking
faire du VTT to go mountain biking
un VTT mountain bike
vu (*p.p. of* **voir**) saw, seen
une **vue** view
un point de vue point of view

les **WC** *m.* toilet
un **week-end** weekend
bon week-end! have a nice weekend!
ce week-end this weekend
le week-end on weekends
le week-end dernier last weekend
le week-end prochain next weekend

y there
il y a there is, there are **9**
est-ce qu'il y a...? is there ...?, are there ...? **9**
qu'est-ce qu'il y a? what is there? **9**
allons-y! let's go!
vas-y! come on!, go ahead!, do it!
le **yaourt** yogurt
des **yeux** *m.* (*sg.* **oeil**) eyes **E3**

un **zèbre** zebra
zéro zero **1A**
zut! darn! **1C**

ENGLISH-FRENCH VOCABULARY

The English-French vocabulary contains only active vocabulary.

The numbers following an entry indicate the lesson in which the word or phrase is activated. (**I** stands for the list of classroom expressions at the end of the first **Images** section; **E** stands for **Entracte.**)

Nouns: If the article of a noun does not indicate gender, the noun is followed by *m. (masculine)* or *f. (feminine)*. If the plural *(pl.)* is irregular, it is given in parentheses.

Verbs: Verbs are listed in the infinitive form. An asterisk (*) in front of an active verb means that it is irregular. (For forms, see the verb charts in Appendix 4C.)

Words beginning with an **h** are preceded by a bullet (•) if the **h** is aspirate; that is, if the word is treated as if it begins with a consonant sound.

A

a
- **a, an** un, une **2A, 10**
- **a few** quelques **9**
- **a little (bit)** un peu **7**
- **a lot** beaucoup **7**

about whom? de qui? **8**
- **are you acquainted with ...?** tu connais...? **2B**

afternoon: in the afternoon de l'après-midi **4A**

to agree *être d'accord **6**

all right d'accord **5**

also aussi **1B, 7**

always toujours **7**
- **not always** pas toujours **5**

A.M. du matin **4A**

am (*see* **to be**)
- **I am ...** je suis + *nationality* **1B**

American américain **2**
- **I'm American** je suis américain(e) **1B, 11**

amusing amusant **11**

an un, une **2A, 10**

and et **1B, 6**
- **and you?** et toi? **1A**

annoying pénible **12**

any des, du, de, la, de l', de
- **not any** pas de **10**

apple juice le jus de pomme **3B**

appointment un rendez-vous
- **I have an appointment at...** j'ai un rendez-vous à... **4A**

April avril *m.* **4B**

are (*see* **to be**)
- **are there?** est-ce qu'il y a? **9**
- **are you...?** tu es + *nationality?* **1B**
- **there are** il y a **9**
- **these/those/they are** ce sont **12**

arm un bras E2

at à **6**
- **at ... o'clock** à ... heure(s) **6**
- **at home** à la maison **6**
- **at the restaurant** au restaurant **6**
- **at what time?** à quelle heure? **4A, 8**
- **at what time is ...?** à quelle heure est ...? **4A**

athletic sportif (sportive) **11**

attention: to pay attention *faire attention **8**

August août *m.* **4B**

aunt une tante **2C**

automobile une auto, une voiture **9**

autumn l'automne *m.*
- **in (the) autumn** en automne **4C**

B

back le dos E2
- **back: in back of** derrière **9**

bad mauvais **12**
- **I'm/everything's (very) bad** ça va (très) mal **1C**
- **it's bad (weather)** il fait mauvais **4C**
- **that's bad** c'est mal **12**
- **too bad!** dommage! **7**

badly mal **1C**
- **things are going (very) badly** ça va (très) mal **1C**

bag un sac **I, 9**

to be *être **6**
- **to be ... (years old)** *avoir... ans **10**
- **to be careful** *faire attention **8**
- **to be cold** (*weather*) il fait froid **4C**
- **to be hot** (*weather*) il fait chaud **4C**
- **to be hungry** *avoir faim **10**
- **to be thirsty** *avoir soif **10**

beautiful beau (bel, belle; *m.pl.* beaux) **9**
- **it's beautiful (nice) weather** il fait beau **4C**

because parce que (qu') **8**

bed un lit **9**

bedroom une chambre **9**

behind derrière **9**

beverage une boisson **3B**

bicycle un vélo, une bicyclette **9**

big grand **9, 12**

birthday un anniversaire **4B**
- **my birthday is (March 2)** mon anniversaire est le (2 mars) **4B**
- **when is your birthday?** c'est quand, ton anniversaire? **4B**

bit: a little bit un peu **7**

black noir **E1, 12**

blond blond **9**

blue bleu **E1, 12**

book un livre **I, 9**

bothersome pénible **12**

boy le garçon **2A, 2B**

brother un frère **2C,**

brown brun **9;** marron *(inv.)* **12**

but mais **5**

café un café **6**
at (to) the café au café **6**
calculator une calculatrice **9**
to **call** téléphoner **7**
camera un appareil-photo (*pl.* appareils-photo) **9**
can you ...? est-ce que tu peux...? **5**
I can't je ne peux pas **5**
Canadian canadien (canadienne) **1B, 11**
he's/she's (Canadian) il/elle est (canadien/canadienne) **2B**
cannot: I cannot je ne peux pas **5**
I'm sorry, but I cannot je regrette, mais je ne peux pas **5**
car une auto, une voiture **9**
careful: to be careful *faire attention **8**
cat un chat **2C**
CD-ROM un cédérom (un CD-ROM)
chair une chaise **I, 9**
chalk la craie **I**
piece of chalk un morceau de craie **I**
chalkboard un tableau (*pl.* tableaux) I
Chinese chinois **11**
chocolate: hot chocolate un chocolat **3B**
cinema le cinéma **6**
to the cinema au cinéma **6**
city: in the city en ville **6**
class une classe **6**
in class en classe **6**
classmate un (une) camarade **9**
coffee le café **3B**
cold le froid
it's cold (*weather*) il fait froid **4C**
college student un étudiant, une étudiante **9**
color une couleur **12**
what color? de quelle couleur? **12**
come: here comes ... voici... **2A**
compact disc un compact (disc), un CD **9**
computer un ordinateur, un PC **9**
cool: it's cool (*weather*) il fait frais **4C**
to **cost** coûter
how much does ... cost? combien coûte...? **3C**
it costs ... il/elle coûte... **3C**
course: of course! bien sûr! **5;** mais oui! **6**
of course not! mais non! **6**
cousin un cousin, une cousine **2C**
crepe une crêpe **3A**
croissant un croissant **3A**
cute mignon (mignonne) **11**

to **dance** danser **5, 7**
dark-haired brun **9**
darn! zut! **1C**
date la date **4B**
I have a date at ... j'ai un rendez-vous à... **4A**
what's the date? quelle est la date? **4B**
day un jour **4B**
what day is it? quel jour est-ce? **4B**
December décembre *m.* **4B**
desk un bureau **I, 9**
difficult difficile **12**
to have (eat) dinner dîner **7**
to have dinner at a restaurant dîner au restaurant **5**
to **do** *faire **8**
docking station un dock **9**
dog un chien **2C**
door une porte **I, 9**
downtown en ville **6**
drink une boisson **3B**
dumb bête **11**
DVD un DVD **9**

ear une oreille **E2**
easy facile **12**
to **eat** manger **7**
I like to eat j'aime manger **5**
to eat dinner dîner **7**
eight huit **1A**
eighteen dix-huit **1B**
eighty quatre-vingts **2B**
elephant un éléphant **E4**
eleven onze **1B, 3C**
English anglais(e) **1B, 11**
evening: in the evening du soir **4A**
everything tout
everything's going (very) well ça va (très) bien **1C**
everything's (going) so-so ça va comme ci, comme ça **1C**
how's everything? ça va? **1C**
eye un oeil (*pl.* yeux) **E2**

fall l'automne **4C**
in (the) fall en automne **4C**
false faux (fausse) **12**
family une famille **2C**
father: this is my father voici mon père **2C**
February février *m.* **4B**
few: a few quelques **9**
fifteen quinze **1B**
fifty cinquante **1C**
fine ça va **1C**
fine! d'accord **5**
everything's fine ça va bien **1C**
it's (June) first c'est le premier (juin) **4B**
five cinq **1A**
foot un pied **E2**
for pour **6**
for whom? pour qui? **8**
forty quarante **1C**
four quatre **1A**
fourteen quatorze **1B**
franc (former monetary unit of France) un franc **3C**
that's (it's) ... francs ça fait... francs **3C**
France la France **6**
in France en France **6**
French français(e) **1B, 11**
how do you say ... in French? comment dit-on... en français? **I**
French fries des frites *f.*
steak and French fries un steak-frites **3A**

Friday vendredi *m.* **4B**
friend un ami, une amie **2A**; un copain, une copine **2A**
  boyfriend, girlfriend un petit copain, une petite copine
  school friend un (une) camarade **9**
from de **6**
  are you from ...? tu es de...? **1B**
  I'm from ... je suis de... **1B**
front: in front of devant **9**
funny amusant **11**; drôle **12**

G

game un match
  to play a game (match) *faire un match **8**
gentleman un monsieur (*pl.* messieurs) **2A**
girl une fille **2A**
to **give** donner
  give me donne-moi, donnez-moi **3A, 3B**
  please give me s'il te plaît donne-moi **3B**
good bon (bonne) **12**
  good morning (afternoon) bonjour **1A**
  that's good c'est bien **12**
  the weather's good (pleasant) il fait bon **4C**
  good-bye! au revoir!, salut! **1C**
  good-looking beau (bel, belle; *m.pl.* beaux) **9, 12**
grandfather un grand-père **2C**
grandmother une grand-mère **2C**
grape juice le jus de raisin **3B**
gray gris **12**
great super **12**
green vert **E1, 12**
guitar une guitare **9**

hair les cheveux *m.* **E2**
  he/she has dark hair il/elle est brun(e) **9**
half: half past ... ... heure(s) et demie **4A**
  half past midnight minuit et demi **4A**
  half past noon midi et demi **4A**
hamburger un hamburger **3A**
hand une main **E2**
handbag un sac **9**
handsome beau (bel, belle; *m.pl.* beaux) **9, 12**
hard difficile **12**
to **have** *avoir **10**
  do you have ...? est-ce que tu as...? **9**
  I have j'ai **9**
  I have to (must) je dois **5**
  to have dinner at a restaurant dîner au restaurant **5**
he il **3C, 6, 10**
he/she is ... il/elle est + *nationality* **2B**
head la tête **E2**
hello bonjour **1A, 1C**
help: may I help you? vous désirez? **3B**
her: her name is ... elle s'appelle... **2B**
  what's her name? comment s'appelle-t-elle? **9**
here ici **6**
  here comes, here is voici **2A**
  here's my mother/father voici ma mère/mon père **2C**
hey! dis! **12**; tiens! 2A, 10
  hey there! dis donc! **12**
hi! salut! **1C**
high school student un (une) élève **9**
his: his name is ... il s'appelle... **2B**
  what's his name? comment s'appelle-t-il? **9**
home, at home à la maison **6**; chez (moi, toi...) **15**
homework assignment un devoir **I**
horse un cheval (*pl.* chevaux) **E4**
hot chaud **4C**
  hot chocolate un chocolat **3B**
  hot dog un •hot dog **3A**
  it's hot (*weather*) il fait chaud **4C**
how? comment? **8**
  how are you? comment allez-vous?, comment vas-tu?, ça va? **1C**
  how do you say ... in French? comment dit-on... en français? **I**
  how much does ... cost? combien coûte...? **3C**
  how much is that/this/it? c'est combien?, ça fait combien? **3C**
  how old are you? quel âge as-tu? **2C**
  how old is he/she? quel âge a-t-il/elle? **9**
  how old is your father/mother? quel âge a ton père/ta mère? **2C**
  how's everything? ça va? **1C**
  how's the weather? quel temps fait-il? **4C**
hundred cent **2B**
hungry avoir faim **3A**
  are you hungry? tu as faim? **3A**
  I'm hungry j'ai faim **3A**
  to be hungry avoir faim **10**

I je **6**
  I don't know je ne sais pas **I, 9**
  I have a date/appointment at ... j'ai un rendez-vous à... **4A**
  I know je sais **I, 9**
  I'm fine/okay ça va **1C**
  I'm (very) well/so-so/(very) bad ça va (très) bien/comme ci, comme ça/(très) mal **1C**
ice la glace **3A**
ice cream une glace **3A**
in à **6**; dans **9**
  in (Boston) à (Boston) **6**
  in class en classe **6**
  in front of devant **9**
  in the afternoon de l'après-midi **4A**
  in the morning/evening du matin/soir **4A**
  in town en ville **6**
to **indicate** indiquer
interesting intéressant **11**
to **invite** inviter **7**
is (*see* **to be**)
  is there? est-ce qu'il y a? **9**

isn't it (so)? n'est-ce pas? **6**
there is il y a **9**
it il, elle **6, 10**
it's ... c'est... **2A**
it's ... (o'clock) il est... heure(s) **4A**
it's ... euros ça fait... euros **3C**
it's fine/nice/hot/cool/ cold/ bad (*weather*) il fait beau/ bon/chaud/frais/ froid/mauvais **4C**
it's (June) first c'est le premier (juin) **4B**
it's not ce n'est pas **12**
it's raining il pleut **4C**
it's snowing il neige **4C**
what time is it? quelle heure est-il? **4A**
who is it? qui est-ce? **2A, 9**
Italian italien, italienne **11**

January janvier *m.* **4B**
Japanese japonais(e) **11**
juice le jus
apple juice le jus de pomme **3B**
grape juice le jus de raisin **3B**
orange juice le jus d'orange **3B**
tomato juice le jus de tomate **3B**
July juillet *m.* **4B**
June juin *m.* **4B**

kind gentil (gentille) **11**
know connaître *(people);* savoir *(facts)*
do you know ...? tu connais...? **2B**
I (don't) know je (ne) sais (pas) I, **9**

lady une dame **2A**
lamp une lampe **9**
large grand **9, 12**
left gauche
on (to) the left à gauche **13**
leg une jambe **E2**
lemon soda la limonade **3B**
lend me prête-moi **3C**
like: what does he/she look like? comment est-il/elle? **9**
what's he/she like? comment est-il/elle? **9**
to like aimer **7**
do you like? est-ce que tu aimes? **5**
I also like j'aime aussi **5**
I don't always like je n'aime pas toujours **5**
I don't like je n'aime pas **5**
I like j'aime **5**
I like ..., but I prefer ... j'aime..., mais je préfère... **5**
I'd like je voudrais **3A, 3B, 5**
what would you like? vous désirez? **3B**
to listen écouter **7**
to listen to the radio écouter la radio **5**
little petit **9, 12**
a little (bit) un peu **7**
to live habiter **7**
to look (at) regarder **7**
look! tiens! **2A, 10**
look at that regarde ça **9**
what does he/she look like? comment est-il/elle? **9**
lot: a lot beaucoup **7**
to love: I'd love to je veux bien **5**

to make *faire **8**
man un homme **9;** un monsieur (polite term) **2A**
many beaucoup (de) **7**
map une carte **I**
March mars m. **4B**
match un match **8**
to play a match *faire un match **8**
May mai *m.* **4B**
maybe peut-être **6**
me moi **1A**
mean méchant **11**
what does ... mean? que veut dire...? I
Mexican mexicain(e) **11**
midnight minuit *m.* **4A**
Miss Mademoiselle (Mlle) **1C**
Monday lundi *m.* **4B**
month un mois **4B**
moped une mob (mobylette) **9**
morning: good morning bonjour **1A**
in the morning du matin **4A**
mother une mère **2C**
this is my mother voici ma mère **2C**
motorbike une mob (mobylette) **9**
motorcycle une moto **9**
motorscooter un scooter **9**
mouth une bouche **E2**
movie theater un cinéma **6**
at (to) the movies au cinéma **6**
MP3 player un (lecteur) MP3 **9**
Mr. Monsieur (M.) **1C**
Mrs. Madame (Mme) **1C**
much, very much beaucoup **7**
how much does ... cost? combien coûte...? **3C**
how much is it? ça fait combien?, c'est combien? **3C**
must: I must je dois **5**
my mon, ma; mes **2C**
my birthday is (March 2) mon anniversaire est le **(2 mars) 4B**
my name is ... je m'appelle... **1A**

name: his/her name is ... il/elle s'appelle... **2B**
my name is ... je m'appelle... **1A**
what's...'s name? comment s'appelle...? **2B**
what's his/her name? comment s'appelle-t-il/elle? **9**
what's your name? comment t'appelles-tu? **1A**
nasty méchant **11**
nationality la nationalité **1B**
neat chouette **12**
neck le cou **E2**
neighbor un voisin, une voisine **9**
nice gentil (gentille), sympathique **11**

it's nice (beautiful) weather il fait beau **4C**
night: tomorrow night demain soir **4A**
nine neuf **1A**
nineteen dix-neuf **1B**
ninety quatre-vingt-dix **2B**
no non **1B, 6**
  no ... pas de **10**
  no? n'est-ce pas? **6**
noon midi *m.* **4A**
nose le nez **E2**
not ne... pas **6**
  not a, not any pas de **10**
  not always pas toujours **5**
  it's (that's) not ce n'est pas **12**
  of course not! mais non! **6**
notebook un cahier **I, 9**
November novembre *m.* **4B**
now maintenant **7**

o'clock heure(s)
  at ... o'clock à... heures **4A**
  it's ... o'clock il est... heure(s) **4A**
object un objet **9**
October octobre *m.* **4B**
of de **6**
  of course not! mais non! **6**
  of course! bien sûr **5**
  of whom de qui **8**
often souvent **7**
oh: oh, really? ah, bon? **8**
okay d'accord **5**
  I'm okay ça va **1C**
old: he/she is ... (years old) il/elle a... ans **2C**
  how old are you? quel âge as-tu? **2C**
  how old is he/she? quel âge a-t-il/elle? **9**
  how old is your father/mother? quel âge a ton père/ta mère? **2C**
  I'm ... (years old) j'ai... ans **2C**
  to be ... (years old) *avoir ... ans **10**
omelet une omelette **3A**
on sur **9**
  on Monday lundi **10**
  on Mondays le lundi **10**
  on vacation en vacances **6**
one un, une **1**
open *ouvrir
  open ... ouvre... (ouvrez...) **I**
or ou **1B, 6**
orange (*color*) orange (*inv.*) **E1, 12**
  orange juice le jus d'orange **3B**
to **organize** organiser **7**
over there là-bas **6**
  that (one), over there ça, là-bas **9**
to **own** *avoir **10**

P.M. du soir **4A**
pain: a pain pénible **12**
paper le papier **I**
  sheet of paper une feuille de papier **I**
past: half past ... ... heure(s) et demie **4A**
  quarter past ... ... heure(s) et quart **4A**
to **pay: to pay attention** *faire attention **8**
pen un stylo **I, 9**
pencil un crayon **I, 9**
people des gens *m.* **10**
perhaps peut-être **6**
person une personne **2A, 9**
pet un animal (*pl.* animaux) domestique **2C**
to **phone** téléphoner **7**
piece: piece of chalk un morceau de craie **I**
pink rose **12**
pizza une pizza **3A**
to **play** jouer **7**
  to play a game (match) *faire un match **8**
  to play basketball (soccer, tennis, volleyball) jouer au basket (au foot, au tennis, au volley) **5**
pleasant sympathique **11**
  it's pleasant (good) weather il fait bon **4C**
please s'il vous plaît (*formal*) **3B**; s'il te plaît (informal) **3A**
  please give me ... s'il te plaît, donne-moi... **3B**
poorly mal **1C**
post (a message) poster un message **9**
poster une affiche **9**
to **prefer: I prefer** je préfère + *inf.* **5**
  I like ..., but I prefer ... j'aime..., mais je préfère... **5**
pretty joli **9**
pupil un (une) élève **9**
purple violet (violette) **E1**

quarter un quart
  quarter of ... ... heure(s) moins le quart **4A**
  quarter past ... ... heure(s) et quart **4A**

racket une raquette **9**
radio une radio **9**
  to listen to the radio écouter la radio **5**
rain: it's raining il pleut **4C**
rarely rarement **7**
rather assez **11**
really: oh, really? ah, bon? **8**
red rouge **E1, 12**
  at (to) the restaurant au restaurant **6**
  have dinner at a restaurant dîner au restaurant **5**
right vrai **12; droite**
  right? n'est-ce pas? **6**
  all right d'accord **5**
room une chambre **9; une salle**
to **run** (*referring to objects*) marcher **9**

salad une salade **3A**
same: the same things les mêmes choses
sandwich un sandwich **3A**
Saturday samedi *m.* **4B, 23**
  see you Saturday! à samedi! **4B**
say ... dites...
  say! dis (donc)! **12**

how do you say ... in French? comment dit-on... en français? **I**
school friend un (une) camarade **9**
season une saison **4C**
see you tomorrow! à demain! **4B**
seldom rarement **7**
September septembre *m.* **4B**
seven sept **1A**
seventeen dix-sept **1B**
seventy soixante-dix **2A**
she elle **6, 10, 15**
sheet of paper une feuille de papier **I**
short court; petit **9, 12**
he/she is short il/elle est petit(e) **9**
to **shut** fermer **I**
shy timide **11**
silly bête **11**
to **sing** chanter **5, 7**
sir Monsieur (M.) **1C**
sister une soeur **2C**
six six **1A**
sixteen seize **1B**
sixty soixante **1C, 2A**
small petit **9, 12**
snow: it's snowing il neige **4C**
so alors **7**
so-so comme ci, comme ça **1C**
everything's (going) so-so ça va comme ci, comme ça **1C**
soda un soda **3B**
lemon soda une limonade **3B**
some des **10;** quelques **9;** du, de la, de l'
sorry: to be sorry regretter
I'm sorry, but (I cannot) je regrette, mais (je ne peux pas) **5**
Spanish espagnol(e) **11**
to **speak** parler **7**
to speak (French, English, Spanish) parler (français, anglais, espagnol) **5**
spring le printemps **4C**
in the spring au printemps **4C**
steak un steak **3A**
steak and French fries un steak-frites **3A**
stereo set une chaîne stéréo **9**
stomach le ventre **E2**
student (*high school*) un (une) élève **9;** (*college*) un étudiant, une étudiante **9**
to **study** étudier **5, 7**
stupid bête **11**
summer l'été *m.* **4C**
in the summer en été **4C**
Sunday dimanche *m.* **4B**
supper: to have (eat) supper dîner **7**
sure bien sûr **5**
sure! mais oui! **6**
to **swim** nager **7**
I like to swim j'aime nager **5**
Swiss suisse **11**

tablet (computer) une tablette **9**
table une table I, **9**
to **take** *prendre **I**
to take a trip *faire un voyage **8**
to **talk** parler **7**
tall grand **9, 12**
tea le thé **3B**
teacher un (une) prof **2A, 9;** un professeur **9**
telephone un téléphone **9**
to telephone téléphoner **7**
television la télé **9**
to watch television regarder la télé **5**
ten dix **1A, 1B**
to play tennis jouer au tennis **5**
terrific génial **12;** super **12**
text message un texto **9**
thank you merci **1C**
that is ... c'est... **9, 12**
that (one), over there ça, là-bas **9**
that's ... c'est... **2A, 9, 12;** voilà **2A**
that's ... euros ça fait... euros **3C**
that's bad c'est mal **12**
that's good (fine) c'est bien **12**
that's not ... ce n'est pas... **12**
what's that? qu'est-ce que c'est? **9**
the le, la, l' **2B, 10; les 10**
then alors **11;** ensuite
there là **6**
there is (are) il y a **9**
there is (here comes someone) voilà **2A**
over there là-bas **6**
that (one), over there ça, là-bas **9;** ce...-là
what is there? qu'est-ce qu'il y a? **9**
these ces
these are ce sont **12**
they ils, elles **6; eux; on**
they are ce sont **12**
thing une chose
things are going (very) badly ça va (très) mal **1C**
thirsty: to be thirsty *avoir soif
are you thirsty? tu as soif? **3B**
I'm thirsty j'ai soif **3B**
thirteen treize **1B**
thirty trente **1C**
3:30 trois heures et demie **4A**
this ce, cet, cette
this is ... voici... **2A**
those ces
those are ce sont **12**
thousand mille **2B**
three trois **1A**
Thursday jeudi *m.* **4B**
time: at what time is ...? à quelle heure est...? **4A**
at what time? à quelle heure? **4A**
what time is it? quelle heure est-il? **4A**
to à **6;** chez
to (the) au, à la, à l', aux
in order to pour
to class en classe **6**
to whom à qui **8**
today aujourd'hui **4B**
today is (Wednesday) aujourd'hui, c'est (mercredi) **4B**
tomato une tomate
tomato juice le jus de tomate **3B**
tomorrow demain **4B**
tomorrow is (Thursday) demain, c'est (jeudi) **4B**
see you tomorrow! à demain! **4B**
too aussi **1B, 7; trop**
too bad! dommage! **7**
town un village
in town en ville **6**

to travel voyager **5, 7**
trip: to take a trip *faire un voyage **8**
true vrai **12**
Tuesday mardi *m.* **4B**
TV la télé **9**
to watch TV regarder la télé **5**
twelve douze **1B**
twenty vingt **1B, 1C**
two deux **1A**

uncle un oncle **2C**
under sous **9**
to understand *comprendre
I (don't) understand je (ne) comprends (pas) I
unfashionable démodé
United States les États-Unis *m.*
upstairs en • haut
us nous
(to) us nous
to use utiliser

vacation les vacances *f.*
on vacation en vacances **6**
very très **11**
very well très bien **7**
very much beaucoup **7**
to visit (*place*) visiter **7**

walk une promenade
to take (go for) a walk *faire une promenade à pied **8**
to walk *aller à pied; marcher **9**
to want *avoir envie de; *vouloir
do you want ...? tu veux...? **3A**
do you want to ...? est-ce que tu veux...? **5**
I don't want ... je ne veux pas... **5**
I want ... je veux... **5**
I want to je veux bien
what do you want? qu'est-ce que tu veux? **3A;** vous désirez? 3B
warm chaud **4C**
it's warm (*weather*) il fait chaud **4C**
watch une montre **9**
to watch regarder **7**
to watch TV regarder la télé **5**
water l'eau *f.*
we nous **6**
to wear *mettre; porter
weather: how's (what's) the weather? quel temps fait-il? **4C**
it's ... weather il fait... **4C**
Wednesday mercredi *m.* **4B**
week une semaine **4B**
well bien **7**
well! eh bien!
well then alors **11**
everything's going (very) well ça va (très) bien **1C**
what comment? quoi?; qu'est-ce que **8**
what color? de quelle couleur? **12**
what day is it? quel jour est-ce? **4B**
what do you want? qu'est-ce que tu veux? **3A;** vous désirez? 3B
what does ... mean? que veut dire...? I
what does he/she look like? comment est-il/elle? **9**
what is it? qu'est-ce que c'est? **9**
what is there? qu'est-ce qu'il y a? **9**
what time is it? quelle heure est-il? **4A**
what would you like? vous désirez? **3B**
what's ...'s name? comment s'appelle...? **2B**
what's he/she like? comment est-il/elle? **9**
what's his/her name? comment s'appelle-t-il/elle? **9**
what's that? qu'est-ce que c'est? **9**
what's the date? quelle est la date? **4B**
what's the price? quel est le prix?
what's the weather? quel temps fait-il? **4C**
what's your address? quelle est ton adresse?
what's your name? comment t'appelles-tu? **1A**
at what time is ...? à quelle heure est...? **4A**
at what time? à quelle heure? **4A, 8**
when quand **8**
when is your birthday? c'est quand, ton anniversaire? **4B**
where où **6, 8**
where is ...? où est...? **6**
white blanc (blanche) **12**
who qui **8**
who's that/this? qui est-ce? **2A, 9**
about whom? de qui? **8**
for whom? pour qui? **8**
of whom? de qui? **8**
to whom? à qui? **8**
with whom? avec qui? **8**
why pourquoi **8**
wife une femme
window une fenêtre **I, 9**
winter l'hiver *m.* **4C**
in the winter en hiver **4C**
with avec **6**
with me avec moi **5**
with you avec toi **5**
with whom? avec qui? **8**
woman une dame (*polite term*) **2A; une femme 9**
to work travailler **5, 7;** (*referring to objects*) marcher **9**
does the radio work? est-ce que la radio marche? **9**
it (doesn't) work(s) well il/elle (ne) marche (pas) bien **9**
would: I'd like je voudrais **3A, 3B, 5**
wrong faux (fausse) **12**

year un an, une année **4B**
he/she is ... (years old) il/elle a... ans **2C**
I'm ... (years old) j'ai... ans **2C**
to be ... (years old) *avoir... ans **10**

yellow jaune E**1, 12**
yes oui **1B, 6;** (*to a negative question*) si! 10
yes, of course oui, bien sûr **5**
yes, okay (all right) oui, d'accord **5**
yes, thank you oui, merci **5**
you tu, vous **6;** on
you are ... tu es + *nationality* **1B**
and you? et toi? **1A**
(to) you te, vous
your ton, ta; tes **2C**
what's your name? comment t'appelles-tu? **1A**
young jeune **9**

zero zéro **1A**

INDEX

A

B

C

D

E

F

G

L

M

CREDITS

Front Cover
©David Noble/Travel Pictures

Back Cover
Level 1a: ©David Noble/Travel Pictures
Level 1b: ©Patrice Coppee/Workbook Stock/Getty Images
Level 1: ©Travelpix Ltd/Stone/Getty Images
Level 2: ©David Sanger/The Image Bank/ Getty Images
Level 3: ©Shaen Adey/Gallo Images/Getty Images

Photography
All photos by Lawrence Migdale/PIX except the following: 1 (bg) ©Stockbyte/ Getty Images; 1 ©Rebecca and Jean-Paul Valette; 5 (bl) ©Fotolia; 5 (tr) ©pbpgalleries/ Alamy; 5 (br) ©Marka/Alamy; 31 (b) ©Vibe Images/Alamy; 40 (tl) ©Stockbyte/ Getty Images; 40 (c) ©Stockbyte/ Getty Images; 40 (tr) ©Stockbyte/ Getty Images; 40 (bl) ©Stockbyte/ Getty Images; 40 (br) ©Stockbyte/ Getty Images; 41 (tl) ©Stockbyte/ Getty Images; 41 (tc) ©Stockbyte/Getty Images; 41 (tr) ©Stockbyte/Getty Images; 41 (bl) ©Stockbyte/Getty Images; 41 (bc) ©Stockbyte/Getty Images; 41 (br) ©Stockbyte/Getty Images; 53 ©Ocean/ Corbis; 53 ©Dieter Heinemann/Westend61/ Corbis; 72 (l) ©Tetra Images/Alamy; 89 (t) ©Fotolia; 95 (r) ©Tetra Images/ Alamy; 105 (cl) ©Lebrecht Music and Arts Photo Library/Alamy; 121 ©Regine Mahaux/Cultura/Getty Images; 121 ©Britt Erlanson/Cultura/Getty Images; 121 ©Vincent Besnault/Digital Vision/ Getty Images; 123 (b) ©Chinatown/ Alamy; 123 (c) ©Bloomberg/Getty Images; 126 (t) ©The Art Gallery Collection/ Alamy; 126 (cl) ©Francis G. Mayer/ Corbis; 128 (t) ©Eric Nguyen/Alamy; 129 (tl) ©Stockbyte/Getty Images; 129 (cl) ©Stockbyte/Getty Images; 129 (b) ©Geoff Manasse/Digital Vision/Getty Images; 147 (tl) ©Siede Preis/Photodisc/Getty Images; 147 (tr) PhotoDisc/Getty Images; 147 (br) ©Dynamic Graphics Group/ Jupiterimages/Getty Images; 147 (tr) ©Ryan McVay/PhotoDisc/gettyimages; 151 (t) ©Andre Jenny/Alamy; 151 (cl) ©culture-images/Lebrecht Photo Library; 158 (c) ©Rubberball/Mike Kemp/Alamy; 173 (tr) ©Getty Images; 177 (cr) ©Trinity Mirror/Mirrorpix/Alamy; 189 (tl) ©Oleksiy Maksymenko/Alamy; 189 (tr) ©Pablo Scapinachis Armstrong/Alamy; PA2 (cr) ©Geoff Manasse/Digital Vision/Getty Images